DISCIPLES AND DISSIDENTS

DISCIPLES & DISSIDENTS

PRISON WRITINGS OF THE

PRINCE OF PEACE PLOWSHARES

THEY SHALL BEAT THEIR SWORDS INTO PLOWSHARES AND THEIR SPEARS INTO PRUNING HOOKS..."

STEVEN BAGGARLY
PHILIP BERRIGAN
MARK COLVILLE
SUSAN CRANE
STEVEN KELLY, S. J.
TOM LEWIS-BORBELY

Edited By
FRED WILCOX

With A Foreword By
HOWARD ZINN

Haley's
Athol, Massachusetts

Haley's
Post Office Box 248
Athol, Massachusetts 01331
1.800.215.8805

Compiled and edited by Fred Wilcox.
Cover design by Elizabeth McAlister
    in cooperation with Linda James of Cotter Communications.
Book design by Marcia Gagliardi.
Copy edited by Dorothy Hayden with assistance from Ann Gagliardi.
Photographs from the collections of the authors.
Illustrations by Tom Lewis-Borbely.
Printed by the Highland Press.

Special thanks to Greg Boertje-Obed, Herb Mackey, Hattie Nestel, and
    Dade Singapuri.

Library of Congress Cataloging-in-Publication Data

God shall judge between the nations,
and impose terms on many peoples.
They shall beat their swords into plowshares
and their spears into pruning hooks;
One nation shall not raise the sword against another,
nor shall they train for war again.

Isaiah 2:4

Contents

A Noble Tradition

a foreword by Howard Zinn

The six men and women who called themselves "The Prince of Peace Plowshares" and boarded a properly named "destroyer" in Bath, Maine, to protest nuclear terrorism, are part of a long and honorable history of disobedience to authority in the name of peace and justice. So long as those in power have brandished weapons, supported slavery, stolen the wealth of the earth for the benefit of a few—human beings of courage have found it necessary to break the law and challenge that power.

The philosophical base for such disobedience rests on the words of the Declaration of Independence, written at the high point of revolutionary idealism, before the practical needs of the colonial elite manifested themselves in the Constitutional Convention. The Declaration insisted that government itself is an artificial creation, not divinely ordained but established by the people for certain ends, those ends being the equal right of all to life, liberty, and the pursuit of happiness. And when the government itself failed in its duties, when it became destructive of those ends, then it was the right of the people to "alter or abolish" it.

Even before those words were written, the colonists put that philosophy into practice. For when their British rulers tried to enlist them in the imperial wars with France, they surrounded the house of the governor, locked up a deputy sheriff, and stormed the town house where the General Court sat. They were condemned by a merchants' group as a "Riotous Tumultuous Assembly of Foreign Seaman, Servants, Negroes, and Other Persons of Mean and vile Condition."

The events leading up to the American Revolution were filled with actions of civil disobedience, which guardians of "law and order" in our time would like to forget: the protests against the Stamp Tax which went as far as destroying some of the property of a tax collector, and the famous Boston Tea Party, in which bales of tea were dumped into Boston harbor.

When, after the Revolution, farmers in western Massachusetts rebelled against the oppressive measures enacted by the rich men who controlled the state government, and some of the Founding Fathers became fearful, Thomas Jefferson wrote from Paris to Abigail Adams: "The spirit of resistance to government is so valuable on certain occasions that I wish it to be always kept alive."

The reluctance to participate in war was strong enough so that in the War of 1812 Congress was not able to pass a law for compulsory military service. The spirit of resistance to war and militarism was kept alive all through the nineteenth century, by people like Adam Ballou, a member of a New England pacifist society, who declared that it was impermissible to "kill, maim, or otherwise absolutely injure any other human being."

Henry David Thoreau, jailed for protesting against the Mexican War by refusal to pay his taxes, wrote in 1849 in his essay "Resistance to Civil Government": "Must the citizen ever for a moment, or in the least degree, resign his conscience to the legislator? . . . It is not desirable to cultivate a respect for the law, so much as for the right." Soldiers in the Mexican War, without benefit of philosophy, but repelled by the carnage all around them, went farther than Thoreau and deserted by the thousands.

Civil disobedience became widespread in the 1850s, as blacks and whites in the anti-slavery movement, defying the Fugitive Slave law, joined to rescue escaped slaves, in Christiana, Pennsylvania; in Syracuse, in Boston, in Oberlin, Ohio. When they were apprehended and brought before juries, in a number of instances the juries refused to convict them, recognizing that the moral law against slavery superseded human law.

For instance, in Boston in 1851, a fugitive slave named Shadrack was seized by authorities and brought to court. Fifty black people went into the courtroom and rescued him. Eight blacks and whites were indicted for obstructing the Fugitive Slave Act. A jury refused to convict.

The formal structure of the American government, whatever its claims to democracy, has never been adequate to remedy deep-rooted injustice. Working people all through the nineteenth and twentieth centuries have had to go on strike, to defy laws of trespass and private property, in order to achieve an eight-hour day, raise wages, improve conditions of the workplace. In his book *The Wise Minority*, Leon Friedman writes: "There is hardly a reform movement in the history of the United States that did not feel it necessary or desirable to violate established laws as part of the campaign for justice."

The sit-ins of young black people in 1960 were not just a violation of local segregation laws but of federal law as expressed in Supreme Court decisions that exempted private enterprises from the equal rights provisions of the Fourteenth Amendment. And civil disobedience in a dozen different forms became the central tactic of the Southern movement against racial segregation. Without that, it is doubtful that the Civil Rights Act of 1964 and the Voting Rights Act of 1965 would have passed.

Civil disobedience has always been the recourse of people of conscience, of people facing overwhelming power and needing to awaken their fellow citizens to action. That was the situation as the United States went to war in Vietnam. Stopping the American juggernaut seemed hopeless until people began defying the law in larger and larger numbers; defying the draft, trespassing on the property of draft boards, blocking buses and trains, occupying public buildings.

When the Catonsville Nine were arrested for entering a draft board in Catonsville, Maryland, removing draft records, and setting them afire in a public "ceremony," one of their number, Father Daniel Berrigan, delivered a meditation:

> Our apologies, good friends, for the fracture of good order, the burning of paper instead of children. . . . We could not, so help us God, do otherwise. . . . We say: killing is disorder, life and gentleness and community and unselfishness is the only order we recognize. For the sake of that order we risk our liberty, our good name. The time is past when good men can remain silent, when obedience can segregate men from public risk, when the poor can die without defense.

That spirit, of defying the law on behalf of the children of the world—the most helpless victims of war and militarism—has been carried on in the decades since the end of the Vietnam War by the men and women of the various Plowshares actions, beginning with the action of eight men and women against a General Electric plant in Pennsylvania where nose cones for nuclear weapons were manufactured.

The defiance became international, and in October of 1999, in Scotland, when three women did symbolic damage to a Trident submarine, the Sheriff of the Greenock Court instructed the jury to acquit them, which the jury did. The Sheriff pointed to the dangers of nuclear war and concluded that the women had the obligation in terms of international law "to do whatever they could to stop the deployment and use of nuclear weapons. . . ."

The men and women of the Prince of Peace Plowshares have carried on in the historic tradition of violating the law in order to protest against the war machine. They speak, in the following pages, for all of us who want a world at peace.

Creating Hope in the Emperor's Apocalyptic World

an introduction by Fred A. Wilcox

At dawn on September 9, 1980, six men and two women walk across a nearly empty parking lot, climb a short set of stairs, and quickly enter General Electric's plant at King of Prussia, Pennsylvania. For more than a year, they have met to talk about this action, praying on some occasions, debating on others, sharing and sometimes laughing at their fears. All of the eight have spent time in jail or prison for their opposition to war, and they are fully aware of the possible consequences of this action. They are also aware that the United States and Soviet Union have accumulated enough nuclear warheads to destroy the planet several times over, yet the designing, testing, and deployment of weapons of mass destruction continues unabated.

Once inside, they pound on the Mark 12A nose cones with hammers, rip apart blueprints marked "Top Secret," and pour vials of their own blood over the nose cones and prints. The eight do not attempt to evade arrest, choosing instead to pray and chant until the police arrive to arrest them. Bail is set at $250,000 per defendant, except for Daniel and Philip Berrigan, who are held without bail. They cannot, but more importantly, say the Plowshare Eight, *they will not* pay the bondsman. To post bail, they explain, would be to admit guilt. To cooperate would be to concede that their action is somehow illegal. This, they insist, is simply not the case. Their intention at King of Prussia had not been to break the law but to "beat swords into plowshares" and to expose "the criminality of nuclear weaponry and corporate piracy . . . "

The action at King of Prussia is the beginning of the Plowshares movement which, over the next two decades, will become a worldwide effort to disarm atomic weapons and bring an end to militarism. Inspired by the words of Isaiah,

> . . . *and they shall beat their swords into plowshares and their spears into pruning hooks; nation shall not lift up sword against nation, neither shall they learn war any more*

activists in the United States, Germany, Sweden, Australia, and England will risk long prison terms, serious injury, and even death in order to express their opposition to nuclearism and their love for the world.

Dismissed by some as lunatics or worse, sometimes ostracized and ridiculed, the Berrigans and friends are prophets in the truest sense, trying to warn us that, even if atomic missiles are never used against our enemies, we are poisoning our planet with plutonium and radioactive isotopes, thus contributing to the painful death of millions of human beings from a variety of cancers; that we are draining money that could be used to build schools and day care centers, to house the homeless and pay teachers' salaries, to build mass transit systems and clean up toxic waste sites, to care for the poor and elderly.

What is perhaps most remarkable about the Plowshares movement is that so many men and women continue to take extraordinary risks in order to speak truth to power and in order to disarm weapons so deadly that, by comparison, they make the atomic bomb dropped on Hiroshima seem like a firecracker.

Government reaction to Plowshares actions has been harsh, even brutal in some cases.

In sentencing Plowshares activists, many judges have demonstrated their ignorance of, indeed even their contempt for, international law. In many respects, federal trials are the kind of scenario one would expect to find in South Africa under apartheid or in the courtrooms of dictatorial governments. During the trials of Plowshares activists, defendants are legally muzzled, held in contempt if they attempt to articulate what motivated them to pour blood over or pound upon a plane, ship, or missile site. Armed federal marshals stand by, prepared whenever it pleases the judge, to drag defendants from the courtroom. Judges order juries to ignore testimony from historians, scientists, and experts in international law, thus forcing jurors to limit their deliberations to prescribed definitions of guilt and innocence.

In spite of all this, the movement continues, men and women go to jail, and guardians of the American empire prepare to fight wars on two fronts, to build an antiballistic missile system, to destroy the world in order to save it.

On Ash Wednesday, February 12, 1997, Philip Berrigan and five friends board the USS *The Sullivans,* a nuclear-capable Aegis destroyer built at Bath Iron Works in Bath, Maine. They pound on the ship with hammers, douse it with vials of their own blood, and are arrested by sailors armed with shotguns and pistols.

Calling Berrigan "a moral giant" and the "conscience of a generation," a state judge refuses to jail the activists. Nevertheless, the federal government dispatches marshals to arrest the six and to haul them into court where, on May 7, 1997, a jury convicts the defendants—Steven Baggarly, Susan Crane, Steve Kelly, S. J., Tom Lewis-Borbely, Mark Colville, and Philip Berrigan—of conspiracy and of damaging government property. Serious charges, they carry a maximum penalty of fifteen years in prison and five hundred thousand dollars in fines.

At their trial, Federal District Judge Gene Carter refuses to allow the Prince of Peace Plowshares activists to explain why they risked a long prison term and quite possibly their lives to pound upon and pour blood over the USS *The Sullivans.* They are not allowed to tell the jury that international law is binding on the United States and that nuclear weapons violate international treaties that forbid preparations for wars of mass destruction. Thus, to use or even to threaten to use nuclear weapons is a war crime or an attempted war crime. They are not permitted to speak about their religious convictions that forbid the taking of human life.

When the defendants do attempt to explain their motives, Judge Carter threatens them with contempt of court and instructs the jury to ignore principles of international law, the Nuremberg Principles, the United Nations Charter, Provisions of the Geneva Convention, and rulings of the International Court at The Hague.

That Judge Carter was recommended to the bench by former Maine Senator William Cohen—at the time of the trial, Mr. Cohen is the United States Secretary of Defense—is not germane to the case. Nor does Judge Carter's personal relationship with Buzz Fitzgerald, recently retired as CEO of Bath Iron Works, constitute a conflict of interest. All that matters in this case, Judge Carter informs the jury, "are the facts."

The trial, says Philip Berrigan,

> was a big joke. A total farce. Judge Carter denied us every oppor-
> tunity to mount a defense. So in the end, we turned our backs
> on him. We read aloud from John's Gospel and the Sermon on
> the Mount, and then the marshals took us out in handcuffs. We
> had to watch the rest of *our* trial on closed circuit TV in a base-
> ment holding cell.
>
> We aren't interested in just talking about ourselves. We want
> to tell people what's going on in this country. We want people
> to know that the government has entered into a new phase of
> the arms race—we are racing with ourselves. Arms manufactur-
> ing is the number one American business, and all the major
> transnational corporations are implicated, with lots of help from
> politicians in Washington. The American people are paying taxes
> so that transnationals can get rich arming *both* sides in the forty
> wars raging across our planet.
>
> The government is beating plowshares into swords, creating
> an entirely new arsenal of nuclear weapons. And the court's role
> is to defend the empire's criminal behavior. In order to do that,
> judges are willing to gag defendants like ourselves. The court
> condemned us. But keep in mind that the murder of Jesus Christ
> was legal, and preparations to end all life on earth are also legal.
> We break the state's law because we are compelled by our faith
> to follow a higher law. That is, the teachings that tell us to love,
> not kill, our enemies; to forgive, not murder, those who trespass
> against us; to love and nurture, and not to destroy, mother earth.

On October 27, 1997, Judge Carter sentences Philip Berrigan, who has served more than eight years behind bars for acts of conscience, to twenty-four months in prison. The prosecutor, Assistant United States Attorney Helene Kazanjian, calls Berrigan and friends terrorists for waking the crew of the USS *The Sullivans* and for splashing blood on the ship. She demands they be incarcerated longer than the eight months they have already served in Cumberland County Jail; she insists they must pay restitution, and she remains unmoved by the defen- dants' appeal to international law and to the laws of God.

Philip Berrigan responds by telling the court that

> God did not provide one law for those in power and another for
> others; if it is criminal for me to kill, it is criminal for my gov-
> ernment to kill. The United States has spent fourteen trillion
> dollars on arms since 1946. Our government has intervened in
> the affairs of fifty nations and has violated the laws of God and

humanity by designing, deploying, using, and threatening to use atomic weapons.

If this court knew international law as it should be,

for example, the World Court decision of 1996, the United Nations Charter, Nuremberg Statutes, and the Geneva Conventions,

it would accept it as the law of the United States and would not have suppressed it as a defense during our trial in May. Brilliant scholars like Ramsey Clark, Peter Weiss, Richard Falk, and Francis Boyle argue that atomic weapons are not only a threat to world peace but that designing, building, and deploying them violates international law.

Ramsey Clark, who helped send Daniel and Philip Berrigan to prison when he was acting as United States Attorney General in Lyndon Johnson's administration, tells the court that Judge Carter does not have to follow federal guidelines in determining the sentences for the Prince of Peace Plowshares. The defendants, says Clark, are not ordinary criminals acting out of selfishness, greed, or lust. They are honorable people, motivated by the desire to prevent nuclear war. Judge Carter can allow them to go free, and he will still be obeying his pledge to uphold the Constitution.

Mark Colville tells the court about his brother-in-law, a Vietnam veteran and Agent Orange victim who died after a painful battle with cancer. At the time of his death, the veteran had received $853.37 in compensation from the Department of Veterans Affairs. Colville reminds the judge that Aegis destroyers built in Maine cost one billion dollars, "while nearly half of Maine's children experience hunger on a regular basis." These children are going hungry while the government has become a "runaway armament factory," selling weapons to 162 out of 182 countries. Colville reiterates Ramsey Clark's argument that Judge Carter does not have to follow sentencing guidelines, and he urges him to exercise a just and moral judgment by changing his allegiance from death to life.

"I invite you," he concludes, "to refuse to punish me, to give me your blessing . . ."

Judge Carter refuses to accept the invitation. Instead, he sentences Philip Berrigan to twenty-four months; Mark

Colville, thirteen months; Susan Crane, twenty-seven months; Steven Baggarly, thirteen months; Steve Kelly, S. J., twenty-one months; Tom Lewis, six months. Supporters sing "We Shall Overcome" and later hold a vigil at Bath Iron Works dry dock. Nine people chain and handcuff themselves to the gate. All are arrested.

In Cumberland County Jail, Berrigan and friends spend much of their time confined to their cells, reading scripture, jotting notes for essays. Early on, when they are still allowed to meet together, *Disciples and Dissidents* begins to take shape. Some of the Prince of Peace Plowshares activists are relatively new to prison while others have spent years behind bars. A few have just gone through the crucible of the federal courts for the first time, while others are seasoned veterans of the judicial system. All are committed to speaking truth to power; all are willing to accept the consequences of working for peace in an empire that is addicted to violence and war.

The Prince of Peace Plowshare activists serve their time, but upon their release from jail they are informed by government officials that they are no longer allowed to live with friends and family. Steven Baggarly is ordered not to return to the Catholic Worker community in Norfolk, Virginia, where his wife and child are waiting for him. Philip Berrigan is warned that he might be "violated" if he returns to Jonah House, a community of nonviolent resistance he helped found, and where he and his family have been living for more than twenty-five years.

On December 19, 1999, Philip Berrigan, Steve Kelly, Susan Crane, and Liz Walz enter the Warfield Air National Guard facility in Essex, Maryland. They hammer upon and pour blood over two A-10 Warthogs, aircraft that carry 30 millimeter, seven-barrel Gatling guns capable of spewing 3,900 rounds per minute. During the Gulf massacre, and later the massive bombing of Yugoslavia, A-10 Warthogs saturated the landscape with hundreds of tons of depleted uranium, a dense radioactive waste used in munitions because it can pierce four inches of armor. On impact, depleted uranium ignites, burning "enemy" soldiers to death inside tanks and armored personnel carriers. It also aerosolizes, spreading fine radioactive dust particles into the air, water, and food supplies of civilian populations.

Hanging their banner *Plowshares vs. Depleted Uranium* at the site and placing a large rosary over one gatling gun, the four activists stop to pray for the millions of victims who have been and the millions who will be poisoned by the empire's quest for world dominance. They are arrested by Federal Air Police, who spray Steve Kelly with pepper spray and tackle Susan Crane when she refuses to stop her disarmament efforts. Three weeks after their arrest, the four are indicted on five charges: sabotage, carrying a ten-year sentence; conspiracy to commit sabotage (ten years); malicious destruction of property (three years); conspiracy to maliciously destroy property (three years); trespass (ninety days).

Writing from a jail cell, Philip Berrigan expresses the love and passion that inspires Plowshare activists to continue their struggle to bring light into the heart of the emperor's dark world:

> I cannot forget the dying children of Iraq and the two million dead of our war, sanctions, and depleted uranium. I cannot forget my shame and sorrow over the second American nuclear war in Iraq and the third nuclear war in Yugoslavia. Despite the spin doctors who control damage, DU shells and bombs are nuclear weapons. I cannot forget my country's war psychosis— its obsession with better tools for killing, its mammoth war chest, its think tanks and war labs, its sick ambition 'to own the weather' as a 'force multiplier.' I cannot forget that historical moment when Washington abandoned the American people to become the marionette of billionaires, transnational corporations, banks, and deluded lobbyists with deep pockets. Above all, I cannot forget our Savior turning his face resolutely toward Jerusalem and the Cross. "Whoever wants to come after me must deny self, pick up the cross, and follow me."

The American empire is determined to silence dissent, but intimidation, threats, and gratuitous cruelty will only strengthen the witness of those who are determined to create hope in the emperor's apocalyptic world. This is the profound message of the gospels—that even in the darkest world, hope springs from people who are willing to challenge the empire's power to exploit its subjects, despoil the environment, wage war against peace and justice.

The following essays were written in the belly of the beast, that place, those places where the empire's contradictions are most violently apparent—jail cells where the poor are beaten, humiliated, and tortured; state and federal prisons where victims of racism, police brutality, sexual assault, and parental violence are insulted, raped, and beaten in order to teach them the true meaning of justice.

Many comparisons have been made, some accurate, some not, between the American and Roman empires. Citizens of Rome were extremely fond of sport, some of it quite cruel and some, like the gladiatorial games, even deadly. Legions of Roman men marched off to war, killing and dying to expand or maintain the empire's borders. Emperors came and went. Caligula, clearly insane, committed unspeakable crimes. Claudius managed to annex the southern half of Britain before he was poisoned by Agrippina, the mother of his adopted son Nero. Nero murdered his own mother and wife. Romans grew increasingly fond of money, running up debt, speculating, practicing usury, scheming to corner markets, investing in what they hoped would be lucrative businesses. The rich lived lavishly, indulging themselves with luxury, engaging in orgiastic bouts of eating and drinking, ignoring the contradictions that would eventually lead to the demise of their empire.

As we enter the millennium, the American empire continues to expand its financial and military borders throughout the world. Legions of American soldiers await orders to launch attacks on our "enemies." Emperors—Richard Nixon, Gerald Ford, Jimmy Carter, Ronald Reagan, George Bush, William Jefferson Clinton—come and go, threatening to use atomic weapons against our adversaries, supporting dictators in El Salvador and Guatemala, assassinating popular leaders in Chile, committing mass murder in Vietnam, killing hundreds of thousands of Iraqi children, continuing three centuries of genocide against native peoples.

In the United States of America the gap between rich and poor is greater and is growing faster than in any other country in the western world. As citizens of the empire we pay our taxes to build weapons that, if used, will destroy not only ourselves but all life on earth. Television provides our bread and circuses. We can attend the coliseum, watch our gladiators bomb Iraq, decide who will live and die—all from the comfort of our own living rooms. "Make money," intones the blue eye of the television. "Make more money. Scheme, speculate, practice usury." The Roman Empire lasted five hundred years; the American empire is going to last forever." Or perhaps destroy itself and the rest of the world in a hail of contradictions.

All empires have had their prophets, voices in the wilderness trying to convince the Caesars to practice humility rather than hubris. The Berrigans and friends have witnessed, firsthand, the terrible truth behind the emperor's gilded rhetoric. They have paid a heavy price for their commitment to peace and justice, but like the early Christians who challenged the might of Rome, their spirits have not been broken, their vision remains steadfast, and they are an inspiration to people in this country and throughout the world who are determined to keep on creating hope in the emperor's apocalyptic world.

It is an honor and privilege to know and to have worked on *Disciples and Dissidents* with Steven Baggarly, Philip Berrigan, Mark Colville, Susan Crane, Steve Kelly, S. J., and Tom Lewis-Borbely. They inspire me and countless others to summon the strength to work harder for peace and social justice. I thank them for their courage and for speaking truth to power.

Writings in this book were created from 1997 to 1999 when Steven Baggarly, Philip Berrigan, Mark Colville, Susan Crane, Steven Kelly, and Tom Lewis-Borbely were in prison after their Ash Wednesday, 1997, Prince of Peace Plowshares action on the USS *The Sulllivans* while it was docked at Bath Iron Works in Bath, Maine. Writings have been edited and updated to take into account events since they were written. The usual scriptural basis is the Saint Joseph Edition of *The New American Bible*, published by Catholic Book Publishing Co., New York. Scriptural citations have been modified to honor the Plowshares participants' preferences for "kindom" instead of "kingdom" and for gender neutral language.

Chapter 1

Valley of Lies: Reflections on the Empire's New World Order

The Good Shepherd

by Susan Crane

I am the good shepherd . . . The good shepherd lays down life for the sheep. A hired worker, who is not a shepherd and who does not own the sheep, sees the wolf coming and leaves the sheep and runs away, and the wolf catches and scatters them. This is because the hired worker works for pay and has no concern for the sheep.

John 10:11-13

The antagonists: the hired man, the thief, and the wolf. The hired man is just doing his job. He works only for pay and, therefore, is the most dangerous. His passion is for expediency, time management, and economics. He is not concerned with mercy or compassion. The hired man is a false shepherd.

In the Hebrew scripture, Ezekiel cuts through appearances. Priests, politicians, and judges alike are excoriated. The indictment comes down against them as they are rich and comfortable while the sheep are starving:

> *Woe to the shepherds of Israel who have been*
>   *pasturing themselves!*
>   *Should not shepherds, rather, pasture sheep?*
> *You have fed off their milk,*
> *worn their wool,*
> *and slaughtered the fatlings,*
> *but the sheep you have not pastured.*
>   *You did not strengthen the weak, nor heal*
> *the sick, nor bind up the injured.*
>   *You did not bring back the strayed nor seek*
>   *the lost, but lorded it over them harshly*
> *and brutally.*
>   *So they were scattered for lack of a shepherd*
> *and became good for the wild beasts.*

Ezekiel 34

False shepherds fail the people, feeding them lies instead of truth. We yearn for a shift in perspective, to see things clearly, to have our blindness lifted. But false shepherds benefit from our confusion. Why the silence from our priests, those representatives of Christ in the world to whom we listen, whom we love, respect, and rely on for spiritual direction and even for models for our lives? "Thou shall not kill." "Love your enemies," the message from the Gospel is always a message of nonviolence. We hear the command not to kill if it has to do with woman's bodies and abortion. After all, seen in that light, the command doesn't threaten the empire's economic structures. But when the command not to kill has to do with men, their war toys, and the entire United States war-directed economy, the topic is always negotiable, always open for discussion. A "command" suddenly turns into little more than a "suggestion." Perhaps we should be asking whether the priests speak truth to power or only what they think people—the empire's leaders—wish to hear? Did the church speak out against Hitler, the Vietnam War, the testing of atomic weapons, the building and deployment of thousands of atomic warheads?

Sadly, the empire and the shepherds get along all too well. The religious institutions enjoy property tax exemptions and possible draft exemptions, freedom to hold services and publish, and in return, they bless the warships and troops, continuing the belief that God is on our side while we make war.

Politicians, also known as public servants, are secular shepherds. They are supposed to act as children's advocates, making policies that reflect compassion for our sons and daughters, our elders, and those with mental difficulties. Yet even a cursory glance around our nation shows it isn't the case. In the South Bronx and other poverty-stricken neighborhoods, children go to bed hungry in rat-infested tenements. In East Saint Louis, Missouri, children attend dilapidated schools that reek of sewage and despair. Meanwhile, Boeing paid no federal taxes in 1995 while reaping thirty-three million dollars. Chief executive officers of major corporations make more than one hundred times the average worker's yearly wages, and in Maine, when the Prince of Peace Plowshares activists were in jail, Bath Iron Works received a $194 million tax write-off.

Excessive profits, tax write-offs, bloated salaries: all are taken from the fleece of the sheep, with the consent, indeed the collusion, of those who are supposed to be good shepherds. One can see the fraud, racism, and corporate greed at work in our nation's capital. Just blocks from the president's mansion, American citizens live in poverty and slumlord-perpetuated squalor. Just a short drive from the House of Representatives, children are killing other children with automatic weapons. Far from being an anomaly, the city of Washington, D.C., is metaphor for the growing gap between the rich and the poor in the United States.

The Hebrew word for justice is *misphat*, which is not a neutral word. Rather, it has everything to do with actively doing justice for the poor. Therefore, the vocation of a judge should be to protect the poor, the orphan, and the widow. But like so many of their counterparts in business and politics, the empire's judges are indifferent to, even hostile toward, justice. Their main concern is keeping their positions, which means they are willing to wear sheep's robes but act more like wolves than good shepherds.

There are true shepherds who teach us how to be human. Brother Juventyn at the Franciscan monastery remembered how Father Maximilian Kolbe was preparing the brothers for difficult days ahead when the German army would invade Poland:

> Father Kolbe, like a loving father, had for some time been preparing us for those trying days. On August 28, he spoke to us about the three stages of life. The first stage is the preparation for acuity; the second, acuity itself; the third, suffering. He said,
>
>> The third state of life, the one of suffering, I think will be my lot shortly. But by whom, where, how, and in what form the suffering will come is still unknown. However, I'd like to suffer and die in a knightly manner, even to the shedding of the last drop of my blood in order to hasten the day of gaining the whole world for God through the Immaculate Mother. I wish the same for you as for me. What nobler thing can I wish you, my dear sons? If I knew something better, I'd wish it for you, but I don't. According to John 15:13, Christ himself said, "Greater love than this no one has, than to lay down one's life for one's friends."
>
> Father was a Catholic priest who founded a friary in Poland and published a religious newspaper with a wide circulation. When the Germans invaded Poland, the Franciscans were arrested or dispersed. Father Kolbe was eventually taken to Auschwitz.[1]

At great risk to himself, Father Kolbe continued to hear confessions, lead prayers, and offer comfort and hope. He urged the other prisoners to pray for the Nazis. "No one's conversion is impossible," he told a friend. Kolbe's prayer was "to love without limits."

When a prisoner escaped, the SS commander selected ten men to die in the starvation bunker. Sobbing with despair, one of the condemned lamented leaving his wife and children alone in a war-torn world. Father Kolbe stepped up to the commander and volunteered to take the distraught man's place. Surprisingly, the commander agreed, and the ten were locked naked, without food or water, into the bunker. Before this, prisoners in the bunker had screamed with terror, begging to be released from the sadistic dungeon. But Father Kolbe managed to calm the starving men, who spent their dying days singing and praying. After two weeks, Father Kolbe was still alive, so the Nazis gave him a lethal injection.

Father Kolbe teaches that our life progression can be like God's. When Jesus was young, he obeyed his parents, learned a trade, and studied the Torah. But as an adult, he became a shepherd, and then the Lamb of God. We are called to move beyond being sheep and to become shepherds in our work and vocations. We are called to have compassion and love for those entrusted to our care.

As a community school teacher in Ukiah, California, I found consolation in teaching local youth who were school phobic, truant, or had been expelled from district schools. School administrators and teachers worked together to create a warm, safe atmosphere where students learned academic, social, and work skills. The staff was a team, and the students benefited from our concern for each other and the students.

Also in Ukiah, religious and social change organizations worked together to organize a community dining room, shadow paintings on August 6, war tax redirection giveaways, and environmental and peace and justice demonstrations. At Concord Naval Weapons Station, a group of us—calling ourselves the Global Peace Farmers—climbed over fences into the deadly force zone to plant seeds and to publicize the nuclear weapons that were stored there. Father Bill O'Donnell and the Bay Area Religious Peace Activists frequently demonstrated at the weapons station or at Lawrence Livermore Laboratories, speaking the nonviolent Gospel in word and deed.

All such actions brought personal consolation and peace; still, I felt too compliant with the empire. I wanted to give my entire life to Jesus, even if this meant relinquishing my will and personal liberty. Where I lived hardly mattered, whether I was rich or poor wasn't important, if I were in jail or out of jail didn't concern me. I just wanted to do God's will.

Meanwhile, I was living in a country that participates in collective sin. How can we even ask forgiveness for our sin when we have no intention of even stopping? We neglect the poor of the world, grinding them into the dirt. We build weapons and use them to threaten the poor, designating the poor as enemies. All of this is considered legal. The only way I could respond to collective sin is to stand outside the law that already makes it legal.

Converting a Trident missile at Lockheed Martin with Father Steve Kelly of the Society of Jesus on August 7, 1995, was my attempt to obey God and to unmask the evil that builds, deploys, and plans to use nuclear weapons. It was a nonviolent action to convert the Trident and to disarm my heart. After serving ten months in jail, I returned to Ukiah. The school administrators kindly hired me to teach summer school despite my having been convicted on two felony counts, but I couldn't make a longer commitment to the classroom. I know that the poverty of my students, the violence that enveloped their lives, and their utter indifference to their future were and are rooted in our national addiction to violence and to idolatry of all things military. I began to realize that the discernment process that led me to Lockheed Martin was, more profoundly, a summons to commit my life to the deepest obedience to God. Moreover, I understood that it would mean disobedience to every aspect of the everyday culture that threatens life, love, and wholeness.

I didn't think the federal government had any moral standing to supervise my life. The government, of course, disagreed, and when I refused to cooperate with the federal probation officer, a judge sentenced me to another month in prison. He told me to self-surrender at the end of summer school, but I didn't consider myself a criminal accountable as such to a government that regards the bombing of Hiroshima and Nagasaki legal, that prides itself on its flying incinerators, that can drop bombs anywhere in the world in fifteen minutes, that sacrifices the lives of children to the idols of war. I hadn't done anything wrong. On the contrary, through our Plowshares witness, we had made a statement reminding people that these weapons have no right to exist and must be converted.

By not reporting to the marshals, I felt a deeper solidarity with the poor and with early Christians who were outlaws. I needed to come into full communion with the church, to talk to women who had been in prison, to process what had happened to me, and to live in a resistance community. That's why I traveled east to Jonah House, where I was fortunate to join the Prince of Peace Plowshares community in scripture study and reflection. To be a parent, teacher, and responsible thinking adult, it seemed to me that I had to speak out in the clearest way possible about violence in our society.

> The taproot of violence in our society today is our intent to use nuclear weapons,

says Father Richard McSorley of the Society of Jesus.

> Once we have agreed to do that, all other evil is mild in comparison. Until we squarely face the question of our intent to use nuclear weapons, any hope of large-scale improvements of public morality is doomed to failure.

In the face of systemic violence, what would a shepherd do? Chase down the wolves. Expose the beasts. Disarm the weapons.

by Steven Baggarly

No one can serve two masters. They will either hate one and love the other, or be devoted to one and despise the other. You cannot serve both God and Mammon.

Matthew 6:24

Mammon is an Aramaic term for wealth or property. The Gospels are unequivocal about the right use of property:

Whoever has two cloaks should share with the person who has none. And whoever has food should do likewise.

Luke 3:11

Give to everyone who asks of you, and from the one who takes what is yours; do not demand it back . . . lend expecting nothing in return.

Luke 6:30,35

Do not store up for yourselves treasures on earth.

Matthew 6:19

Hoarded mammon poses obstacles to discipleship:

Every one of you who does not renounce all their possessions cannot be my disciple.

Luke 14:33

Go, sell what you have, and give to the poor . . . then come, follow me.

Mark 10:21

It can hinder access to God's kindom in our midst:

How hard it is for those who have wealth to enter the kindom of God . . . It is easier for a camel to pass through the eye of a needle than for one who is rich to enter the kindom of God.

Mark 10:23,25

Woe to you who are rich.

Luke 6:24

Yet, when we use mammon to look out for each other, everyone is cared for:

Do not worry about . . . what you will eat or drink . . . or what you will wear . . . but seek first the kindom of God and God's righteousness and all these things will be given you besides.

Matthew 6:25,33).

Give and gifts will be given to you.

Luke 6:38

Blessed are you who are poor.

Luke 6:20

Our society views property, wealth, and money as sources of security and survival. In actuality, God is the only security and the facilitator of survival:

Yours are the heavens, yours the earth; you founded the world and everything in it.

Psalm 89:12

When people hoard rather than share, the law of God's ownership of everything is broken, and widespread suffering results. Claiming more than one's share robs the poor, and the United States consumes between seven and eight times its share of what the world provides. The government even uses surplus food as a weapon, withholding it from hungry nations whose politics don't line up. We can't both hoard and serve God. Faith in God requires that our day-to-day economic life be based on sharing.

At the Catholic Worker and at Jonah House, we attempt to live the Gospels' communitarian economics. We try to hold all things in common, holding each other accountable as stewards of money that isn't really ours. This helps everyone to keep from undue attachment to material possessions and helps to check extravagance. There are no salaries, no saving for children's education, no retirement accounts, no taxable income.

Catholic Worker houses traditionally survive from what we are able to beg. Donations are used to keep our hospitality houses open to impoverished friends, to supply food for sharing on the streets and with neighbors, to meet individual needs of people living on the street, and to keep vehicles running. In-kind donations of food, clothing, and toiletries are shared by homeless guests, soup line patrons, and community members. Jonah House supports itself by painting houses, finding jobs through word of mouth. Money earned goes into a common purse that sustains peace work, the community house, painting equipment, travel, and personal expenses like toiletries, thrift store shopping, and books. Our communities live with only the necessities and a few simple comforts as we try to be responsible to the poor, our donors, and each other.

Community and plain living are the first acts of resistance to our culture of domination that esteems rugged individualism and accumulation. They are also vital to sustained resistance against the state: when a whole community maintains a single, simple household, some of its members are freed up to go to jail. The burdens of breadwinning in isolated nuclear families work against such freedom.

Gospel morality applies not only to individuals and communities but to entire societies and globally as well. In this light, United States

9

corporate capitalism is exposed as institutionalized mammon worship, all of its mechanisms working toward centralizing capital, maximizing profits, and compounding wealth. At the root of capitalism lies usury (loaning money at interest), which transforms money from a means of exchange into a wealth-producing commodity. The Hebrew scriptures circumscribe usury—its inherent upward redistribution of wealth, its perpetual plying of the rich with free money while relentlessly extracting extra fees from people with scant means—at Exodus 22:25, Leviticus 24:35-38, and Deuteronomy 23:19-20 and then forbid usury at Psalms 15:5 and Ezekiel 18:8-17, 22:12. Jesus teaches his followers to

lend expecting nothing back,

Luke 6:34

leaving no room for the economics of personal gain.

Usury and its offspring, investment, lead to a staggering maldistribution of wealth both domestically and worldwide. Today, the wealthiest half percent of families in the United States own more than forty percent of the national wealth.[1] The net worth of the top one percent of United States citizens is greater than that of the bottom ninety percent.[2] The world's richest 225 people (sixty of them from the United States) are worth the income of forty-seven percent of the world population, or 2.5 billion people. Globally, the wealthiest twenty percent of the world's population consumes eighty-seven percent of what the world produces, while the poorest twenty percent can afford 1.1 percent.[3] In addition, the net transfer of resources from poorer countries to the wealthy, through debt repayments and inequalities in global trade, is massive. The human suffering behind these numbers is incomprehensible. Approximately 1.3 billion people still don't have the food, water, and simple medicines they need to survive.[4] Forty million people will die hunger-related deaths this year, including 250,000 children each week.[5] Eric Gill, the English artist and writer, accurately understood war and usury as the two great problems of modern times.

The biblical Letter of James reveals the close relationship between mammon and war.

Where do the wars and where do the conflicts among you come from? Is it not from your desires that make war within your members? You covet but do not possess. You kill and envy but you cannot obtain; you fight and wage war . . . Do you not know that to be a lover of the world [domination] means enmity to God?

James 4:1-2, 4

United States corporate capitalism wages war against the poor everywhere, and thus against God. Not only does its superpower status allow for United States capitalism's offensive war of pillage and plunder, but the huge United States military is then needed to defend the status quo all over the world. In 1965, President Johnson gave a landmark speech that laid out the vast holdings of the American empire, the disproportionate amounts of finance, technology, resources, heavy equipment, and consumer goods that it hoards. Then he detailed the lethal weaponry at his command and connected the two. "Other people want what we have," he said, "and we ain't gonna give it to them."

Serving mammon ends in the taking up of arms and total rejection of God. Just below mammon's surface lurks not only the specter of poverty, but of war.

Saint Francis: "If we own nothing, we have nothing to defend."

John Woolman: "May we look upon our treasures, the furniture of our houses and our garments and try [to see?] whether the seeds of war have nourishment in these, our possessions."

Bishop Raymond Hunthausen: "We have to begin by recognizing that our country's overwhelming array of nuclear arms has a very precise purpose; it is meant to protect our wealth. The United States is not illogical in amassing the most destructive weapons in history. We need them. We are the richest people in history."

The Widow's Mite

by Steven Baggarly

> [Jesus] sat down opposite the treasury and observed how the crowd put money into the treasury. Many rich people put in large sums. A poor widow came and put in two small coins worth a few cents. Calling his disciples to himself, he said to them, "Amen, I say to you, this poor widow put in more than all the other contributors to the treasury. For they have all contributed from their surplus wealth, but she, from her poverty, has contributed all she had, her whole livelihood."
>
> Mark 12:41-44

Jesus makes his way out of the temple after offering insight about the widow's gift. When the disciples gawk at the temple's architectural grandeur, Jesus warns them,

> Do you see these great buildings? There will not be one stone left upon another that will not be thrown down.
>
> Mark 13:2

He sits opposite the temple to continue teaching them. By sitting opposite the treasury and then opposite the temple, Jesus sits in judgment. The religious authorities have remade Yahweh from God who lives in a tent, leads people out of slavery, and defends "the widow and the orphan" into the one who resides in a palatial temple and ceremoniously enlarges the holdings of the wealthy while shaking down impoverished widows for every last penny. Jesus does not merely praise the widow's piety. His words and actions denounce the structures of domination that crush her.

Before Jesus's observations about the treasury, he talks about the scribes,

> who like to go around in long robes and accept greetings in the marketplaces, seats of honor in synagogues and places of honor at banquets. They devour the houses of widows and, as a pretext, recite lengthy prayers. They will receive a very severe condemnation.

Mark 12:38-40

Caretakers and beneficiaries of a corrupt and violent system, the scribes have succumbed to the temptation of religious domination. Like economic and political power, institutional religious power exacts a cost from poor and victimized people. Every building block of the temple system will therefore be cast down. In Mark's thirteenth chapter, Jesus sits opposite the temple and uses apocalyptic language to describe the passing of the temple and the emergence of a new time.

The condition of women continues to illustrate the prevailing order. In a patriarchal world, the domination of women is basic. Today, of the 1.3 billion hungry and desperately poor people on the planet, seventy percent are women.[1] Women do two-thirds of the world's work, receive one-tenth of the world's income, and own less than one percent of its property.[2] An estimated 2.15 billion women are anemic and twice as many women as men lack sufficient protein for normal growth. Nearly all of the 595,000 deaths during childbirth last year could have been prevented by minimal health care facilities. Two-thirds of illiterate adults are women. Everywhere, fewer girls than boys are in school at all levels.[3] At least two million girls are forced into prostitution each year, while another two million undergo ritual genital mutilation[4]. Mass rape is an integral part of warfare, women considered among war's "spoils." Domestic violence is a global epidemic. The poverty, abuse, illness, and death of women are intrinsic to patriarchy, which values power above all else.

In the men's cell block of Cumberland County Jail, Maine, where the Prince of Peace Plowshares men are kept, we have minimal contact with women. We are not, however, separated from the devastating effects of living in a male-dominated society. Degrading references to women permeate the atmosphere. Some men refer to women only in terms used to describe animals, evil, or filth, or only in terms of body parts.

A number of inmates are brimming with anger towards women. They boast of using or manipulating women, and some are in prison for assaulting, threatening, or stalking their girlfriends, lovers, co-workers, or wives. Commonly, a beating or other violence against a woman is perceived as "her fault." Patriarchy educates everyone to believe women are inferior and subordinate to men, resulting in serious psychological, spiritual, and physical damage to both women and men.

Violence against women is a cornerstone of American culture. Fifty-four percent of women are battered by their male partners, seventy-eight percent are sexually harassed in their workplace or classroom, and forty-two percent of United States women are victims of attempted or completed sexual assault.[5] Thirteen percent of women in the United States have been raped over the past twenty years, one a minute, twelve million in all. Television, movies, music, and the print media promote violence against women as entertainment—one in eight American movies contains a rape scene. The United States is the leading exporter of pornography and pro-rape propaganda in the world. Domestically, the pornography industry brings in more money than the movie and music industries combined.[6] Every five years, domestic violence kills as many women as the total number of United States soldiers killed during eight years of all-out war in Vietnam.

Violence against women, the violence of war, and preparations for nuclear holocaust are all part of the same program. Patriarchy is inherently violent, from the most intimate relations to the global. Any struggle for peace and justice must also be a struggle against patriarchy and a clarion call for women's rightful place in the human family. The more women are listened to, heard, and heeded, the more egalitarianism and partnership can supplant domination, and the more human we can all become.

One simple way we try to resist patriarchy in the Cumberland County Jail cell block is by using feminine pronouns to refer to God the Parent and also the Holy Spirit, during our nightly Bible study group. In this book, the publisher decided not to use pronouns in referring to God; therefore, God is "gender-neutral" in this text. While this choice does not tie God into the male-dominating mind set, it fails to have the same impact as referring to God as "she" or "her."

Likewise, we drop the "g" when talking about the kin(g)dom of God, to make it plain that God's reign will not be just another incarnation of patriarchy but, instead, an egalitarian realm. Inclusive language is a simple act of justice after thousands of years of inaccuracy and the idolatry of God's portrayal as exclusively male.

Like all structures that relegate women to second-class citizenship and suppress their voices, the temple system is doomed to fail. Jesus condemns the entire patriarchal ethos as he sits opposite its systems that bleed poor widows dry.

The Suffering Woman Becomes the Daughter of God

by Susan Crane

When Jesus had crossed over again in the boat to the other side, a large crowd gathered around him; and so he stayed by the seashore.

One of the synagogue officials named Jairus came up, and on seeing him, fell at his feet and implored him earnestly, saying, "My little daughter is at the point of death; please come and lay your hands on her, so that she will get well and live." And he went off with him; and a large crowd was following him and pressing in on him.

A woman who had had a hemorrhage for twelve years, and had endured much at the hands of many physicians, and had spent all that she had and was not helped at all, but rather had grown worse—after hearing about Jesus, she came up in the crowd behind him and touched his cloak. For she said, "If I just touch his garments, I will get well."

Immediately the flow of her blood was dried up; and she felt in her body that she was healed of her affliction.

Immediately Jesus, perceiving in himself that the power proceeding from him had gone forth, turned to the crowd and said, "Who touched my garments?"

And his disciples said to him, "You see the crowd pressing in on you, and you say, 'Who touched me?'"

And he looked around to see the woman who had done this. But the woman, fearing and trembling, aware of what had happened to her, came and fell down before him and told him the whole truth. And he said to her, "Daughter, your faith has made you well; go in peace and be healed of your affliction."

Mark 5:21-34

As one part of five sets of sandwiched-together stories, Mark tells of a woman who suffers from hemorrhages. In the beginning of the story, Jairus, a synagogue official, asks Jesus to heal his daughter. On their way to Jairus's house, a woman who has hemorrhaged for twelve years touches Jesus's cloak, and he asks who touched him. The woman comes forward and tells her story. Jesus informs the woman that her faith has healed her. Meanwhile, Jairus hears that his daughter has died, but they walk to Jairus's house anyway and chase the mourners away. Then, Jesus heals the daughter.

Immediately, we see contrasts between the suffering woman and Jairus. The suffering woman is unnamed, impure, a pariah, an outcast. She has no money, she talks to herself, and she approaches Jesus secretly from behind. Jairus is a well-established synagogue official, highly respected in his community. Walking directly up to him to talk, he earnestly approaches Jesus. The suffering woman and Jairus exemplify two different approaches to Jesus that we might imitate in our prayer life. According to temperament, desire, or our life situation, we may approach Jesus like the suffering woman or like Jairus.

The purity code in Leviticus 15:19 and following verses helps us understand what life was like for the woman who had been bleeding for twelve years. Any place she sat became unclean until evening, anyone who touched her became unclean, required to wash their clothes and their body, nevertheless remaining ritually unclean until evening. Only a dead body would be more unclean than the woman.

Both of the healings in the story happen as a result of faith. The suffering woman believes that if she can just touch Jesus's clothes, she will be healed. Her belief is an important instruction to disciples, even though Jesus can heal without the faith of others. In order to heal the child, he chases the mourners out of the room and goes in with only his disciples and the parents. In this environment, he can heal the child.

Likewise today, God needs people with faith to heal the results of the injustice around us. If we really believed and had faith in what Jesus says about nonviolence, we would not believe that weapons bring us safety. But we live in a culture that has put its trust in weapons, and so it seems preposterous to even talk about unilateral disarmament. If we had the faith of the suffering woman, we would be willing to disarm. Sometimes it's easy to think that we can continue our regular lives and God will take care of everything, but this story makes clear that God needs us to be faithful and reach out so that we can be healed of our violent and unjust ways. Then, we can live in harmony and peace.

In preparation for boarding the USS *The Sullivans* at Bath Iron Works in Maine, we found many scripture passages that juxtaposed faith and fear as opposites. The stories of the suffering woman and of Jairus continue the theme. By having faith, the suffering woman aligns her will with God's will, and healing happens. She controls her fear in order to walk through the crowd, touch Jesus's clothes, and then tell him the whole truth. Similarly, Jairus has to control his fear that his daughter is dead and allow Jesus to take charge of his house. We want to control our fear in the same way when it keeps us from acting as our conscience prompts. Our fear is one reason we continue to build nuclear weapons; at least, that is the reason most people give to justify having the world's most powerful military. We fear our nation will be invaded by another. Our collective sin is great because our collective faith is weak. When we fail to take charge of our fears and undertake the work of disarmament, we allow the militaristic status quo to continue.

The stories of the suffering woman and of Jairus also show a theme of gift versus exchange. The woman has spent all her savings going to doctors. The doctors, then as well as now, see healing as a commodity to be bought and sold. In contrast, Jesus stands outside the commodity society and offers healing as a gift.

Jesus feels the power go out of him when the suffering woman touches his cloak from behind, and he asks, "Who touched my clothes?" He feels energy leave him—he has done work that expends energy—as he heals her. Healing is work. The episode demonstrates that, wherever we are in our ability to heal others—from a kind word, a kind act, or a laying on of hands, we can recognize healing as work that takes our energy. In the give and take of daily relationships, if we realize we are called to heal, our attitude changes. We expect it to be hard work that drains our energy, and so we are not surprised when we feel the effect. We can be more patient in the recognition that healing is hard work.

Like women we meet every day in jail, the nameless suffering woman in Mark's story is fearful. She has used all her money on doctors who effected no cure, and she bears the results of twelve years of being considered unclean. But this woman, on the bottom of the social scale, becomes the daughter of God: comforting words to those of us in jail.

Prisoners, mentally ill people, and poor immigrants are treated as unclean, surplus people. In jail, during scripture reflection, we ask what God requires of us. The answers we voice: to stand next to those with the AIDS virus or hepatitis and with those who are different because of race or religion or physical problems like tracheotomies, body weight, or lack of teeth. The spirit invites us to walk alongside and share with such people. And so we walk alongside of each other—all dressed in felonious orange.

Jairus, like other political leaders then and now, is named by the Gospel writer. The woman, unnamed, represents all of us ordinary unnamed people who are ignored by historians and news writers. Social change movements for abolition, worker rights, and civil rights were composed of ordinary and faithful people like the suffering woman. She controlled her fear enough to seek healing, and so do those in social change movements.

God grant us the faith, like the suffering woman, to walk through crowds of people even if we are seen as criminals and felons. Help us to listen to God's prompting and to act on our faith.

Going Alone to the Well

by Susan Crane

There came a woman of Samaria to draw water. Jesus said to her, "Give me a drink." For his disciples had gone away into the city to buy food.

Therefore the Samaritan woman said to him, "How is it that you, being a Jew, ask me for a drink, since I am a Samaritan woman?" (For Jews have no dealings with Samaritans.)

Jesus answered and said to her, "If you knew the gift of God, and who it is who says to you, 'Give me a drink,' you would have asked him, and he would have given you living water."

She said to him, "Sir, you have nothing to draw with and the well is deep; where then do you get that living water? You are not greater than our father Jacob, are you, who gave us the well, and drank of it himself and his sons and his cattle?"

Jesus answered and said to her, "Everyone who drinks of this water will thirst again; but whoever drinks of the water that I will give shall never thirst; but the water that I will give will become in that person a well of water springing up to eternal life."

The woman said to Him, "Sir, give me this water, so I will not be thirsty nor come all the way here to draw."

He said to her, "Go, call your husband and come here."

The woman answered and said, "I have no husband." Jesus said to her, "You have correctly said, 'I have no husband'; for you have had five husbands, and the one whom you now have is not your husband; this you have said truly."

The woman said to him, "Sir, I perceive that you are a prophet. Our ancestors worshiped in this mountain, and you people say that in Jerusalem is the place where people ought to worship."

Jesus said to her, "Woman, believe me, an hour is coming when neither in this mountain nor in Jerusalem will you worship the Creator. You worship what you do not know; we worship what we know, for salvation is from the Jews. But an hour is coming, and now is, when the true worshipers will worship the Creator in spirit and truth; for such people the Creator seeks to be worshipers. God is spirit, and those who worship God must worship in spirit and truth."

The woman said to him, "I know that Messiah is coming (the one who is called Christ); when that one comes that one will declare all things to us."

Jesus said to her, "I am he, the one who is speaking to you."

At this point his disciples came, and they were amazed that he had been speaking with a woman, yet no one said, "What do you seek?" or, "Why do you speak with her?"

So the woman left her water pot, and went into the city and said to the people, "Come, see a man who told me all the things that I have done; this is not the Christ, is it?" They went out of the city and came to him.

John 4:7-27

There was so much enmity between the Jews and Samaritans that they might kill each other on sight. Nevertheless, Jesus and his disciples walk through Samaria without fear.

When Jesus arrives in the Samaritan town, he doesn't go to the political, religious, or social leaders. Instead, he approaches a woman, one who is excluded even from the usual women's social interactions and must go to the well alone.

To those of us in jail, this story is good news. We are the outcast, the throwaway people, seen as animals, beyond help or rehabilitation—scapegoats to be punished and kept separate from the good people on the outside. The Samaritan woman—enemy and outcast—is one of us. Yet Jesus chooses to talk to her, to reveal himself truly to her, and to thrust her into a leadership role. She goes back to town and tells the people about Jesus. Many believe because of her words.

As I look around me in the jail, I see immigrants, women of color, the poor, mentally-ill, and addicted. I see women with blackened eyes, bruises, and head wounds, women whose children are left behind without their mothers. I hear similar stories from battered women here. A man uses fists and feet, cops are called, women get arrested. Did she pick up a fork in self defense? Did she have a beer in violation of probation? Maybe. But conventional thought blames a woman for a man's violence: "She provoked the violence." "She could have avoided it if she had just done what her man wanted." It sounds, not so surprisingly, like reasons we as a nation use to batter other countries in drive-by wars.

Violence permeates our culture. The patriarchal paradigm dominates our nation, our institutions, and our thought processes. Violence is at all levels, and the worst falls on those at the bottom, often women and children.

Women at the bottom are the people Jesus insists on speaking with: he talks to us Samaritans. "I am he, the one who is speaking to you." Jesus offers dignity and encouragement, validating you as you listen and act. Jesus identifies himself with the God of Moses in the burning bush: "I . . . am." The God of liberation, Jesus tells the woman he is the Messiah and thereby calls us all to liberation and acts of justice.

The Samaritan woman risked disapproval and scorn when she carried on a conversation with Jesus, a stranger, a foreigner, an enemy. As Jesus remains with the Samaritans, he becomes one with them and consequently is later himself identified as a Samaritan:

Are we not right in saying that you are a Samaritan?"

John 8:48

Both the woman and Jesus demonstrate how we should act toward those labeled as enemy. We must give hospitality even to our enemies, visit even our enemies in jail, and live even with our enemies. Sister Anne Montgomery with the Christian Peacemakers Team has been living in Hebron, Israel, with Palestinian people. She has accompanied Palestinians to their olive groves or farmlands that are being taken over by the Israelis for resettlement housing. She has joined in their protests against demolition of their homes by Israeli soldiers: more than twenty-five hundred Palestinian homes have been destroyed by the Israeli government since 1967. Like Sister Anne, we become one with the outcasts of society when we go to jail.

"I am he, the one who is speaking to you." How does God speak to us today? Through Creation, the church, and our brothers and sisters, through others' witness, through music, through scripture. And through the quiet whisper we hear when we listen in solitude.

Gaudium et Spes, a papal encyclical and, thus, Roman Catholic teaching, describes the whisper of our conscience as follows:

Deep within their consciences, men and women discover a law which they have not laid upon themselves and which they must obey. Its voice, ever calling them to love and to do what is good and to avoid evil, tells them inwardly at the right moment: do this; shun that. For they have in their hearts a law inscribed by God. Their dignity rests in observing this law, and by it they will be judged. Their conscience is people's most secret core, and their sanctuary. There they are alone with God whose voice echoes in their depths.

The Samaritan woman had the sense to listen to Jesus and to act. Listening to Jesus had been ordained by God, Jesus's father:

"This is my beloved son, listen to him"

Mark 9:7

Jesus's mother, too, has sanctioned Jesus's actions:

"Whatever he says to you, do it,"

John 2:5

she tells the servants at the Cana wedding. Like the disciples and the servants, we are to listen and act. When we meditate on scripture, when we take time in prayer, when we listen to our conscience, we can hear God speaking. We are prompted, then, to do what is good, to love our brothers and sisters, to avoid evil, to forgive, to defend justice, to beat swords into plowshares. We are prompted "to love without limits," as Father Maximilian Kolbe says.

We need to act on the prompting to listen to God's voice and to believe we can witness and be disciples.

Cleansing the Temple: Divorcing Church from State

by Mark Colville

with consideration of John 2

To suggest that God might be in complicity in exploitation is blasphemous, intolerable, and worthy of our outrage. It is also a commonly accepted practice in the United States, due in large part to the sins of omission of the vast majority of North American Christians. When believers fail to resist injustice, they accept the notion that God approves of injustice.

A case in point: In the summer of 1998 in Groton, Connecticut, another Seawolf fast-attack submarine was christened—yes, "Christened"—and then added to the ever-growing fleet of nuclear hell ships threatening the future of the planet. Seawolfs, each costing taxpayers several billion dollars and carrying enough nuclear warheads to destroy a continent, are a slightly smaller and more versatile version of the Trident (also built by General Dynamics in Groton), which is the most destructive weapon ever known to humanity. The $2.5 billion price tag represents the cost of immunizing and providing essential nutrients to all children in the world. The name Seawolf refers to the sailor who gets the most women into bed while his ship is in port. Thus, the obscene weapon and its ceremonial launching bring forth a symbolic and real convergence of violence, misogyny, exploitation, and blasphemy. Yet, the churches remain virtually silent about the state-sponsored moral contradictions.

In his day, Jesus went to Jerusalem in order to lay down his life in a struggle against corrupt, collusive powers of religion and state. His first public act upon entering the city was a bold and shocking one of civil resistance at John 2:13-22, performed at Jerusalem's cultural and symbolic center. The cleansing of the temple, as the act is called, is one of few episodes recorded in all four Gospels, and it is central in the life of faith of the early church.

To situate the story properly, we need to understand that God resists the very concept of "temple" as a distraction from true worship—namely, doing justice to the poor and welcoming the stranger (as described in Second Samuel and First Kings in the Hebrew scripture). God prefers to dwell in a tent because God's proper place was not sedentary, and the tent with God moves among the people. When Solomon finally built the first temple, it had all the trappings of wealth and power and was, predictably, located next to the king's palace. It signified the original union of church and state, but it did not manifest the preference of the God of the Israelites.

The temple authorities of Jesus's day were a privileged class who consolidated economic and religious power through administering the system of sacrifice, manipulating the law of Moses, and colluding with the Roman government. The animals used in rituals were commonly bought and sold in the vast temple precincts. When he cleansed the temple, Jesus did not object to the fact that animals were made available there. He objected to the fact that people were being swindled there by the animal merchants. The buyers were captive, because the system required Jews to perform ritual sacrifice at Passover, and a worshiper needed to pay for animals to sacrifice. Thus, the temple's construction and the comfortable life-style of its authorities were all financed by the oppression of common folk seeking God's favor. When Jesus burst onto the scene, he overturned tables and chased out animals. His intention was to subvert and deconstruct the oppressive system.

The episode is not about Jesus losing his temper. It was a symbolic, prophetic, revolutionary action, undertaken purposely at the cultural power center.

In our own day, the churches' tax exempt status solidifies and perpetuates the collusion of church and state, rendering virtually nonexistent prophetic action by the institutional church. By tax exemption, the government purchases the silence of the institutional church or at least ensures no more than token opposition to its crimes. The prophetic voice of the church, too, so sorely needed, cannot be found because the church is married to the state instead of to God. Beholden to the state for assets and property, our religious institutions have become imprisoned in their own temples.

Still, the church has its scripture, and in the word of God there always dwells the possibility of freedom and conversion. Jesus identifies himself as the new temple at John 2:19, thereby announcing God's noncooperation with injustice—God's refusal to be in complicity with the state. Jesus endorses nonviolent civil resistance with his nonviolent direct action against the temple system of sacrifice.

Jesus's action makes it clear that civil resistance is a legitimate and necessary means of achieving justice and right relationship to God.

Today, the United States confronts us with its presence as the most violent nation in the history of human civilization. Nuclearism is the religion of this state, and nuclear weapons are its idols. Breaking this nation's laws by smashing its idols is consistent with the practice of Christianity and even essential to it. We pray daily for the conversion of the institutional church, that it might come to terms with its scripture. At the same time, we realize that the church's silence and paralysis can never excuse us from acting in fidelity to God's word.

Following Jesus must involve taking up the cross and tangling with the killing machine, our nation's unbridled, legalized commitment to death and ultimate violence. Our action will be political, illegal, and nonviolent, just like Jesus's action in the temple. Hammering swords into plowshares is, at its root, an act of defending the poor, just like Jesus's action in the temple. Just as Jesus abhorred the affluence of the temple officials, we abhor the affluence of the weapons manufacturer CEO's. Just as Jesus abhorred that the temple poor were required to pay obeisance in the temple, we abhor the military's theft of funds from social welfare, education, and health care.

Hammering swords into plowshares is the kind of action that builds a solid foundation for a life of true discipleship by following Jesus into his civil resistance and action on behalf of God's word.

Shalom

by Steven Baggarly

Peace I leave with you; my peace I give to you; not as the world gives do I give to you. Do not let your heart be troubled, nor let it be fearful.

John 14:27

John's account of Jesus's crucifixion and resurrection is framed by Jesus's conferring peace to his disciples. During the Last Supper discourse, Jesus gives his peace, "not as the world gives . . ." just before he is arrested. In two post-resurrection appearances described in John, Jesus penetrates locked rooms and greets them with peace at John 20:19-20 and 20:26-27. Each time, he refers to the profound Hebrew concept of *shalom*, the totality of peace when God, humanity, and Creation dwell once again in harmonious relationship.

In his call for shalom, Jesus shares the vision of Hebrew prophets:

> By the river on its bank, upon one side and on the other, will grow all kinds of trees for food. Their leaves will not wither and their fruit will not fail. They will bear every month because their water flows from the sanctuary, and their fruit will be for food and their leaves for healing.
>
> Ezekiel 47:12

> And the wolf will dwell with the lamb, and the leopard will lie down with the young goat, and the calf and the young lion and the fatling together; and a little child will lead them. . . . The nursing child will play by the hole of the cobra, and the weaned child will put its hand on the viper's den. They will not hurt or destroy in all my holy mountain, for the earth will be full of the knowledge of the God as the waters cover the sea.
>
> Isaiah 11:6,8-9

> Behold, days are coming . . . when I will make a new covenant with the house of Israel and with the house of Judah . . . But this is the covenant which I will make with the house of Israel after those days . . . I will put my law within them and on their heart I will write it; and I will be their God, and they shall be my people. They will not teach again, . . . saying "Know God," for they will all know me, from the least of them to the greatest of them . . .
>
> Jeremiah 31:31, 33-34

> Then they will hammer their swords into plowshares and their spears into pruning hooks; nation will not lift up sword against nation, and never again will they train for war. Each of them will sit under their vine and under their fig tree, with no one to make them afraid . . .
>
> Micah 4:3-4

The hope continues among early Christians:

> Behold, the tabernacle of God is among people, and God will dwell among them, and they shall be God's people, and God will be among them, and God will wipe away every tear from their eyes; and there will no longer be any death; there will no longer be any mourning, or crying, or pain; the first things have passed away.
>
> Revelations 21:3-4

A share in the vision of shalom is the peace that Jesus leaves to his disciples. He not only announces the kindom of shalom but inaugurates its advent, calling people everywhere to join God in helping to bring it about fully. It means working for justice through loving neighbor as self. Wherever people act nonviolently for justice and the reconciliation of enemies, the old order begins to pass away.

Shalom contradicts the worldly notion of peace. According to the United States government, the atomic bombings of Hiroshima and Nagasaki were necessary in order to bring peace at the end of World War II. The ensuing Cold War meant a huge military buildup and United States involvement in wars, revolutions, police actions, and coups throughout the world. Decades of intermediary killing fields and threats of nuclear annihilation were deemed necessary in order to win the "peace." With the fall of the Soviet Union in 1989, reverence for "peace through strength" ran deeper than ever and so continues. In recent "humanitarian" and "peacekeeping" missions to Somalia, Bosnia, Kosovo, and Serbia, United States forces killed ten thousand Somalis, according to the state department, and several thousand Yugoslavians as it tried to bomb the Serbian army into submission. Official bases for peace now are the maintenance of Cold War levels of military power, the ability to fight two major wars simultaneously, and continued readiness for first-strike nuclear war. The world's so-called peace rests on violence and exploitation. It is not the peace of shalom; it is the peace of cemeteries, morgues, and mass graves.

For fifty years, Pax Americana has been enforced at gunpoint. The cornerstone of every empire in history is and has been military hardware, and although it already owns history's most lethal arsenal, the United States government relentlessly pursues new weapons systems in an attempt to secure its false peace. In 1995, it spent fifty-five billion dollars to procure weapons and thirty-seven billion dollars on weapons development, both leading the world.[1] The Pentagon continues to reserve another thirty billion dollars per year in a "black budget" for research and development of weapons so secret that even Congress is denied access to the programs.

Between 1997 and 1999, the department of war will have finished building three submarine classes—Trident, Los Angeles, and Seawolf—each among the most powerful weapons in the world. Nevertheless, scientists and weapons experts are already working on a new generation of attack submarines. There are 440 F-22 fighters, three thousand joint strike fighter-bombers, and 548 upgraded F-18s slated to replace what are already the most advanced air force, navy, and marine aircraft in the world. Twenty B-2 stealth bombers and fifty-seven Aegis guided missile destroyers are in mid-production, both players in nuclear war scenarios. Laser weapons and six-inch mini planes for urban battlefields are among many special warfare items under development.

Even international commitments have not slowed Washington's frantic efforts to arm heaven and earth. While the war department denies that it is continuing nuclear weapons production, it has unveiled an earth-penetrating hydrogen bomb that can burrow fifty feet deep and explode downward to take out underground installations.[2] In 1999, the defense department began officially to purchase tritium from civilian nuclear reactors in order to enhance the explosive power of its warheads.[3] The Pentagon is also testing missiles for an antiballistic missile shield and developing HAARP, a weather-control system with antiballistic missile applications. Both would violate previous agreements with the Russians and could lead to a new arms race.[4] The Comprehensive Test Ban Treaty, touted by United States officials as a major step toward reducing the likelihood of nuclear war, hasn't prevented the United States from conducting computerized "subcritical" atomic tests to ensure the reliability of its nuclear stockpile and to pave the way for a new generation of small hydrogen bombs.[5]

For the peace of Jesus—shalom—to take place in the United States, all murderous weapons must be beaten into plowshares. We must change our attitudes toward violence and nonviolence, our obsession with wealth and power, our indifference to the fate of Mother Earth, our fear of taking a strong stand for peace and justice and love—even if it means ridicule, loss of friends and jobs, and jail. The nonviolent revolution needed to bring about peace and social justice is the work of the discipleship community.

To prepare his fearful disciples for the work of change, Jesus appeared to them in their locked room in order to show them his hands and his side after the crucifixion and resurrection.

"As God sent me, so I send you,"

John 20:21

says Jesus, displaying his wounds from the cross, clearly showing them the price of peace. The cross will be the lot of any who dare struggle for the kindom of shalom, Jesus seems to say.

"Peace be with you,"

John 20:19, 26

Jesus greets them. And so, shalom is not only the end but also the means. Jesus's peace enables us to continue despite vast odds, official threats, jail, and a bulwark of public despair, indifference, and unbelief.

"Do not let your hearts be troubled or afraid,"

John 14:27

Jesus says. His peace, the only real security, is the antidote to fear and inaction, allowing us to cooperate as we can with God's work of bringing shalom to a thoroughly armed and frightened world.

Inside a Locked Room?

by Steven Kelly, S. J.

On the evening of that first day of the week, when the doors were locked, where the disciples were, for fear of the Jews, Jesus came and stood in their midst and said to them, "Peace be with you." When he had said this, he showed them his hands and his side. The disciples rejoiced when they saw Jesus. Jesus said to them again, "Peace be with you. Shalom aleichem. As God has sent me, so I send you." And when he had said this, he breathed on them and said to them, "Receive the holy spirit. Whose sins you forgive are forgiven them, and whose sins you retain are retained."

John 20:19-23

Where does John's account of Jesus appearing to the disciples in the locked room find the church of today? Does contemporary religion, like the disciples who feared the Judeans and their Roman collaborators, remain inside its locked room? If complicity between the temple and imperial authorities manipulated capital punishment when the Judeans handed Jesus over, wouldn't today's disciples anticipate suffering the same fate? Overwhelmed by the power and violence of the empire outside, the disciples are paralyzed. Does the paralysis of the disciples inside the locked room resonate with us today?

The pattern of shrinking from imperial threat holds true today. Religion in the United States sits in a locked room located in the heart of the superpower, afraid to confront the death process and idolatry outside the locked doors. Beyond United States borders, thousands of Jerusalems are within dominion of the interests of the United States. The iron heel of United States retaliation around the world is only quietly, if ever, questioned. The United States has six percent of the world's population and uses almost half of the globe's resources. We secure inequality through our position as the world's leading armaments manufacturer and weapons exporter. The United States spends seventy-five million dollars a day on nuclear weapons as the centerpiece of a four hundred billion Pentagon budget. Where is the Gospel today? Most believers, if not actually co-opted, are complicit in denying the theft from the world's poor.

As in the disciples' time, the prevailing structural, systemic, and social sin is the empire threatening on the other side of our locked room. Why have believers, who dwell in the heart of the empire, remained paralyzed in the locked room? Are we clinging to methods and benefits of the empire's powers?

Like our predecessors, how do we go forth from our fear-filled inside location to respond to the call of the spirit? Unarmed and diagnosing our fear of loss of affluence and influence, Jesus comes to the locked doors of religious institutions. Jesus stands within the fortress of our fears of being harmed and humiliated to show that he has already been there and that death has lost its power.

Shalom aleichem is a peace given that, unlike what the world provides, quells the fear of losing our lives. The poet Esquivel echoes: "If they threaten us, they threaten us with the resurrection." Diagnosis goes below the paralysis symptoms: we lack faith in Christ's peacemaking. Our faith finds real security in the gift of Christ's peace—a match of ends and means. Breathing Christ's peace, we can emerge from our locked room and engage the militarism and larceny of the empire as did the community of disciples at Acts 4 by witnessing the power of the resurrection.

Christ's Temptations—and Ours

by Philip Berrigan

Then Jesus was led up by the spirit into the wilderness to be tempted by the devil. And after he had fasted forty days and forty nights, he then became hungry. And the tempter came and said to him, "If you are the son of God, command that these stones become bread."

But he answered and said, "It is written, 'One shall not live on bread alone, but on every word that proceeds out of the mouth of God.'"

Then the devil took him into the holy city and had him stand on the pinnacle of the temple, and said to him, "If you are the son of God, throw yourself down, for it is written, 'God will command God's angels concerning you'; and 'On their hands they will bear you up, so that you will not strike your foot against a stone.'"

Jesus said to the devil, "Oh the other hand, it is written, 'You shall not put God to the test.'"

Again the devil took him to a very high mountain and showed him all the kingdoms of the world and their glory; and he said to him, "All these things I will give you, if you fall down and worship me."

Then Jesus said to the devil, "Go, Satan! For it is written, 'You shall worship God and serve God only.'"

Then the devil left him; and behold, angels came and began to minister to him.

Matthew 4:1-11

Jesus, full of the Holy Spirit, returned from the Jordan and was led around by the spirit in the wilderness for forty days, being tempted by the devil. And he ate nothing during those days, and when they had ended, he became hungry. And the devil said to him, "If you are the son of God, tell this stone to become bread."

And Jesus answered the devil, "It is written, 'One shall not live on bread alone.'"

And the devil led him up and showed him all the kingdoms of the world in a moment of time. And the devil said to him, "I will give you all this domain and its glory; for it has been handed over to me, and I give it to whomever I wish. Therefore if you worship before me, it shall be yours."

Jesus answered the devil, "It is written, 'You shall worship God and serve God only.'"

And the devil led him to Jerusalem and had him stand on the pinnacle of the temple, and said to him, "If you are the son of God, throw yourself down from here, for it is written, 'God will command God's angels concerning you to guard you,' and, 'On their hands they will bear you up, so that you will not strike your foot against a stone.'"

And Jesus answered and said to the devil, "it is said, 'You shall not put God to the test.'"

And when the devil had finished every temptation, the devil left him until an opportune time.

Luke 4:1-13

Like us, Jesus was tempted by power and by the temptation to dominate others. Like us, Jesus was tempted to divide human beings into some hierarchical scheme—those who count and those who do not count, those who have power and those who do not have power, those who can benefit us in some way and those who do not serve our self interest. Jesus's temptations, like our own, were fundamentally social, corporate, and political. The question raised is, how does the word of God regard power?

All power on heaven and earth has been given me.

Matthew 28:8

God's power is final and absolute, and it will be realized in God's time. God's power is nonviolent, truthful, loving, always constructive, never destructive.

For God makes God's sun rise on the bad and the good, and causes rain to fall on the just and the unjust.

Matthew 5:46

God's power is never over people, never dominating, never coercive. It is always loving and just, for or with people.

In contrast, the American empire undermines relationships, insults God, alienates neighbors, and buys and sells the world's natural resources. The American empire pollutes and destroys Mother Earth so that only a few can live in luxury while the rest struggle to survive. The empire practices coercion instead of legitimate power; domination, exploitation, and repression instead of the liberation of God's people through love and compassion.

Satan urges Jesus to embrace the false power of violence in the episode of three temptations narrated by Matthew and Luke. In the first temptation to economic exploitation, Satan entices Jesus to control bread—jobs—in order to wield power over people. In the same way, the defense department (which may as well be called the war department) controls jobs, thus assuring control over votes. Not votes for Democrats or Republicans, but perpetual votes for the war machine. In the second temptation, Satan tries to seduce Jesus to employ miracle, mystery, and dogma to bewilder human consciences and thus foster disbelief. In the third temptation, Satan urges Jesus to become a king and imperialist, to turn to political oppression. Satan wants Jesus to militarize and exploit human beings, like David and Solomon did.

Each circumstance offers Jesus a suggestion to play autocratic warrior with other lives, to enshrine the ego and to control the lives and deaths of others. Each temptation, in short, offers Jesus a suggestion to do all that God would never do.

What about our own temptations? Why are they precisely like what tempted Jesus to false power?

Before considering an answer, some thoughts about sin and powerlessness.

First, a word about sin, that mysterious adherence to evil about which we are often confused and unreflective. We know sin chiefly by its central characteristic, which is injustice to God, our neighbors, ourselves, Creation. Sin disrupts and destroys relationships in an altogether devastating and enslaving way. Furthermore, sin is first social and political. Only later is it personal, a condition often ignored by the bureaucratic church. We learn violence and abuse of neighbors from social sources like television, movies, parents, peers, and newspapers. We learn words like "nigger," "faggot," and "Commie," and we strike out at the people we think embody such pejorative terms.

Then there is the powerlessness of Jesus and the disciple, the powerlessness of Calvary and the cry of abandonment Jesus makes from the cross. How does one understand such powerlessness? Why doesn't Jesus come down from the cross, as the tempters suggest? And why doesn't he agree to accept Satan's bidding in the desert? Two views occur to me. The first is to see powerlessness as the lot of the suffering servant, victimized and without choice, totally dependent on God, relying on pure faith. Second, however, is to see powerlessness as a manifestation of perfect nonviolence, the powerlessness of Jesus as it emerges from John's Gospel, the true power of powerlessness chosen to control every phase of his life and sacrifice.

> No one has taken [my life] away from me, but I lay it down on my own initiative. I have authority to lay it down, and I have authority to take it up again.
>
> John 10:18

In the second view, of course, is the model for aligning oneself in faith and nonviolence to the power of God.

And so, what of our own temptations? What tempts me as I sit imprisoned for a Plowshares witness undertaken by five dear friends and me on February 12, 1997?

First, there is a temptation to ageism, knowing and experiencing how the culture sloughs off the elderly as expendable. If one attains sixty-five years—or seventy-three as I am now, one may be "out to pasture." Surely, polls of those people now attaining the age of fifty or sixty indicate that they do not intend to put their lives on hold at a certain age or "retire" from work and productivity, but it was a commonplace in my generation to be making toys for grandchildren or soaking up Florida sunshine, not boarding battleships and airplanes, hammer and vial of blood in hand—not beating swords into plowshares and being held for months or years in jail.

My response to the temptation of ageism is complicated. My health is good, I exercise, and I do not intend to retire—or perhaps, I should say, give up. But Jesus is the example, and I will keep on keeping on. And in my line of work, it can be discouraging. I have devoted my life to radical action for peace. I understand that people in the peace movement are weary, that the odds against us seem, at times, insurmountable. There is a great temptation to abandon the United States and the world to politicians, war-makers, and capitalists who use their wealth and power to torment the poor, ravish the environment, and destroy hope.

Activists feel overwhelmed by the apparent power of the empire and say, "But they have too much money, too many laboratory drones blueprinting the next doomsday obscenity. There are just too many of them. They are too powerful. They control business, universities, the military, the police, the World Bank, the International Monetary Fund. You are right, Berrigan. The empire is mighty—too mighty for a small, underfunded, and sometimes very tired peace movement."

Yes, the empire resembles a vast insane asylum, but I see no reason to give up hope. After all, doesn't our history reflect one long, never-ending struggle against genocide, slavery, exploitation of women and children, unsafe working conditions, long hours and poor pay? In short, Americans have always fought against the violent injustices of capitalism, facing impossible odds and finally bringing about change. The peace movement can do it, too. Brave men, women, and children of the past went hungry, were beaten during strikes, were locked out of their factories, and were fired from their jobs in the struggle for decent working conditions.

And so there is my answer to the temptation to quit. Who am I to give up the struggle? Why on earth should I give up hope, when so many people continue to suffer from hunger, homelessness, and myriad forms of violence in every corner of the empire?

How dare any of us give up on the United States and the world?

Life Becomes Light—and Life

by Philip Berrigan

Through him was life and this life was the light of the human family.

John 1:4

It is interesting to consider how the lives of my son Jerry, now in his early twenties, and his friends will develop. Their experiences are very different from mine and likely to continue to be.

Back in the sixties, for example, when I was in my forties, I was an ordained Josephite priest, a veteran of the civil rights movement, and a World War II veteran turned pacifist with ten years of nonviolent experience behind me. I had served time in jail for resisting the Vietnam War, written books, and studied theology. But I was still floundering, often confused, wondering just what more I could do to resist militarism.

Jerry was born in the 1970s. He and his friends missed what I experienced, but they know more than I knew back then. Above all, they know what they must do and have already engaged in acts of resistance at ELF, the Navy's extra-low frequency system for alerting Trident submarines, at a land mine factory in Minneapolis, and at the Pentagon. They have taken action at assorted other hell holes.

Perhaps Jerry's insight and determination are due, in part at least, to his never having served in the empire's army. I say so, because it may be difficult for those who have never been in the service to grasp just how debilitating that experience is. I recall struggling, even as late as the sixties, to recapture my heart and soul from the United States Army. When I served during World War II, I didn't consider myself a hero, but later I couldn't seem to break from the armed services. Something held me in a state of abeyance, and I was in thrall to the military code. I was stuck in time, unwilling or unable to break free of war as I had experienced it during World War II. Military life had left me intellectually and spiritually impaired. I had done my duty according to the conventional idea of the times, and I became a veteran with a preordained mind set (or so it seemed). And I was left with scars that, for the most part, I didn't know how to acknowledge.

I reflect on how Jerry and I are the same and how we are different as I consider the Gospel of John. John begins his Gospel with a synopsis of what is to follow, and he boldly asserts that God is life. God created life in its stunning diversity and beauty. God continues Creation, a miracle we have come to understand as a hundred billion galaxies across three hundred billion light years of expanding space. God sustains Creation by concurring with all life and by sharing life with us. Grace is what we call God's sharing.

When we consider the book of Genesis, we find that God created us in the divine image and likeness. God is truth and love in Genesis, that is to say, God is thought and volition. Genesis proposes that we are in a fallen state, with an attraction to evil nearly as intense as our attraction to good, and gaps in our human makeup manifest themselves to put us at odds with light or truth. Our minds do not comprehend reality as it is.

Enter the life of God. How does the life of God become light to us? There is an example in Mark's Gospel. Scholars say that the middle section of Mark's Gospel is a "discipleship catechism," opening and closing with cures of the blind—the blind man of Bethsaida and the blind Bantimaeus. Mark shows that literal blindness can be healed and his metaphorical meaning shines through: if they can be healed of their blindness, we can be healed of ours. We can see the light. We can experience God's grace. We can oppose the expectations of Genesis. We can make twisted action straight and violent action nonviolent. We can take action instead of remaining inactive.

The healing of God remedies the spirit first, requiring faith and repentance. Then the body is healed:

> It is the spirit that gives life; the flesh profits nothing.
>
> John 6:63

God grants forgiveness in every healing, and it works two ways—restoring one to God as a daughter or son and restoring one to humanity as a sister or brother. Furthermore, when God's grace heals our dead sight, we see by degree usually, like the blind man of Bethsaida. Slowly, little by little, life takes on a new perspective as we begin to see reality as it is: God, neighbor, ourselves, Creation. Slowly, ever so slowly, we discard infancy and adolescence to assume the duties of adulthood.

Duties broaden in concentric circles until they include the world—the bombed, starved, tortured, homeless refugees, victimized. In a word, we become "keepers" of the "least of these," attempting to do justice and good for them where we can, but more importantly, engaging the evil that persecutes, crushes, and kills them. "I will not kill, and I will prevent others from killing," as Buddhist thought would express the idea. It is a realization that came to Jerry and his friends sooner and according to a different path than it came to me, but the light came all the same. Confronting evil is the ultimate test of God's life, which should become light for us. Life is there, and light depends on us. We must want our blindness healed in order to be given light.

It is like arising from sleep, like waking up, another frequent metaphor in Christian scripture. The word of God tells us that life is too precious to live any other way but awake. The truth or light keeps us awake. We need the light to shine on ourselves certainly—on our fears, illusions, and denials. But, just as urgently, we need light to shine on our government and its darkness of lies, secrecy, covert operations, and mass murders. Jerry and his friends have already awakened to this truth.

Here is a truism: it is much easier to start a war than to end one. Similarly, it is much easier to build a war economy than to convert one to peace. Our war economy is the bone and sinew of national life. How does the United States phase out its Number 1 business?

It doesn't, of course. Not without massive conversion to nonviolence by its people, not without massive nonviolent uprising. Here is no excuse for lassitude or inaction. Here, instead, is a spur to begin on an individual and communitarian basis. Surely, the Cold War hasn't ended. We have merely shifted its madness, pitting a war with ourselves, running an arms race with ourselves. We spend $625 billion annually for killing and war. We have expanded NATO into eastern Europe with weapons sales, airfields, communication and control centers. We have a frenzy of new weapons systems, from the B-61-11 earth-penetrating nuclear war bomb to an arsenal of ships. President Clinton lifted the ban on weapons sales to Latin America.

Is the world safer after the Berlin Wall and the collapse of the old Soviet Empire? No. Soviet occupation of eastern Europe has been replaced by NATO expansion into Poland, the Czech Republic, and Hungary. Today, nuclear anarchy reigns in Russia, where there are multiple possibilities for civil war. Our export of lunacy, blood lust, and terror will continue as long as we cling to our nuclear arsenal, as long as we waffle on every serious arms agreement, as long as we remain on nuclear alert, as long as the American public remains fearful and dormant. Dormant: not awake, in the metaphor of scripture.

Dietrich Bonhoeffer, profound opponent of Hitler's terror, warned against cheap grace. One may also warn against cheap peace. William James, the philosopher, writes of a condition that is the "moral equivalent of war." He insists that peace is a nonviolent counterpart of the spirit, structure, and cost of war. The prospect of building the counterpart boggles the mind. It is an enormous and complex task, the equivalent of nonviolent revolution.

But Jerry and his friends appear to be up to the task, and we are right to take up the hammers with them. What must we learn about building a nonviolent spirit, structures of just peace, and resources that will pay anything for peace and nothing for war? Here is the challenge.

Through him was life and this life was the light of the human family.

John 1:4

Baptism as Presentation

by Philip Berrigan

Behold, this child is destined for the fall and rise of many in Israel, and to be a sign that will be contradicted. And you yourself a sword will pierce, so that the thoughts of many hearts may be revealed.

Luke 2:34-35

To Luke, author of the third Gospel and Acts, we are indebted for lovely, majestic accounts of the birth and early years of Jesus Christ. After his circumcision, Mary and Joseph take Jesus to the Jerusalem Temple to "present" him—give him back to God, so to speak. The gesture and ritual have a stunning truth in them—an acknowledgment that God gives the child, that the child belongs to God, so the parents must "present" the child or give him back to God.

Moreover, the presentation has added meaning, for it implies mission. This child was the Messiah, Emmanuel or God with us, sent from God to save the world, rescuing it nonviolently from its hubris, deceit, greed, and blood lust. This child would restore God's sovereignty in justice, equality, and peace.

Simeon and Anna appear, ecstatic with thanks for this child. God had promised that they would see the Messiah before death. This child and two elderly people gather all people to their midst—young and old, female and male, Jew and Gentile, black, white, brown, yellow. The prophets Simeon and Anna discern the meaning of his presentation and mission, seeing him destined for the "fall and rise" of many,

a light of revelation to the Gentiles, and the glory of your people Israel.

Luke 2:32

There is another consequence to mission—oblation, the act of offering or sacrifice. God "sent" Christ and gave him a mission. Christ accepted the mission, ratified it by offering himself, gave his *yes.*

For God did not send God's son into the world to condemn the world, but that the world might be saved through him.

John 3:17

The works that the Parent gave me to accomplish, these works that I perform testify on my behalf that the Parent has sent me.

John 5:36

The one who sent me is with me. God has not left me alone, because I always do what is pleasing to God.

John 8:29

There is another duty implicit in the *yes* of oblation—that of sentry. Christ paraphrased the sentry's duty in his parable of the Good Shepherd. Of all the Hebrew prophets, Ezekiel best describes the prophet as watchman.

But if the watchman sees the sword coming and fails to blow the warning trumpet, so that the sword comes and takes anyone, I will hold the watchman responsible for that person's death.

Ezekiel 33:6

The sword is a metaphor for any human injustice that causes needless suffering, injury, or death—war, nuclear testing, famine stemming from war, economic oppression, rape, genocide, death squads, torture, toxins in the environment, unsafe working conditions, or unemployment. At such threats and others, the sentry sounds the alarm, becoming a defender of people and, sometimes, the first line of defense. All Christians share the life of Christ as prophet, and the prophet is essentially a watchman.

For roughly thirty years, I have witnessed against war-making corporations—Dow Chemical, General Electric, and General Dynamics, to name a few. But never in my wildest imagining thirty years ago did I envision what is happening today—the corporatizing and globalizing of the American economy. Commonly today, corporations boast of their own "statelessness," relegating government to mere police, military, and housekeeping functions. In fact, corporations now rival America's super power or imperial status as threat to justice and peace. Washington commands the nuclear strike force and conventional killing machines. But the corporations are economic terrorists, totalitarian and rapacious. They share certain characteristics.

1. Accountability to a transnational financial system—This system, with all financial markets integrated into a single, computerized system, is the world's primary governance system.

2. Profit—Obsessively central to the corporate vision. Assets and the rate of profit must grow.

3. Aggressiveness—The corporate mind believes that competition is fundamental to human nature.

4. Individualism—Me-firstism on a corporate scale. Corporations are inherently selfish, always choosing profit over public welfare.

5. Pecking Order—Decisions come from the top down, because the world is comprised of leaders and followers, and inequality and conformity are facts of nature.

6. Technological compulsion—Must increase efficiency and boost profits, hence, a constant hunt for technological innovation.

7. The world as market—The corporations envision the world's peoples as homogeneous consumers.

8. Expand or die—The corporations habitually stress the future because of their need to grow. Their abstraction from present and past makes them ephemeral and vulnerable.

9. Abuse of Nature—There are basic contradictions between corporatism and nature. Nature is merely a resource to supply raw materials for commodities.

One superpower and a clutch of transnational corporations—twin threats to the world's people. Let every faithful, just person become a sentry and sound the alarm.

Faith Equals Love

by Steven Baggarly

Whoever hears my word and believes in the One who has sent me has eternal life and will not come to condemnation, but has passed from death to life.

John 5:24

We know that we have passed from death to life because we love our brothers and sisters. Whoever does not love remains in death.

1 John 3:14

John's two passages equate faith with love. He presents hearing, believing, and loving others as parallel activities. Faith is not a neutral belief in the invisible but is a belief that God is transforming the world into a sisterhood and brotherhood, a work that is also ours. Only through working for justice for the most vulnerable members of the human family can we believe in God. Both faith and love mean co-creating a new world with God.

A central paradigm of the Judeo-Christian tradition is God and Moses cooperating to liberate the Hebrews from slavery in Egypt. God speaks to Moses from out of the fire:

I have witnessed the affliction of my people in Egypt and have heard their cry of complaint against their slave drivers, so I know well what they are suffering . . . therefore I have come down to rescue them . . . come now! I will send you to Pharaoh to lead my people, the Israelites, out of Egypt.

Exodus 3:7-8, 10

In the example, God witnesses afflictions, hears cries, and acts. I believe God continues to intervene in the world on behalf of poor and oppressed people through people with the faith and love to join in the struggle.

Since the splitting of the atom, all of life is shackled to the whim of the few who control nuclear weapons. But, as developer of the bomb and perpetual leader of the nuclear arms race, the United States suffers the deepest spiritual and moral slavery to the weaponry. Stories like the following, told by a young Nagasaki survivor, carry the cry of agony that must be heard in order to know the suffering the United States is ever ready to unleash upon the world.

Fujio Tsujimoto was six years old when the United States dropped an atomic bomb on his home town. He was on his grade school playground at the time and recorded his memories a few years later.

> Suddenly there was a loud explosion. The other children were fooling and quarreling too loud to hear it, but I grasped Grandmother by the hand and ran with her toward the air raid shelter.
>
> "Enemy flyers, enemy flyers," a warden shouted. Horrified, the rest of the people stormed wildly toward the entrance of the cellar. Grandmother and I, who were at the front of the crowd, ran into the farthest corner.
>
> There was a dazzling glare. A powerful gust of wind smashed me against the cellar wall. After some time, I looked out of the cellar. Everywhere people lay thickly on top of each other, dead; only here and there one moved a leg or another raised an arm. Those who could still move crawled on all fours toward us in the cellar, which gradually filled with wounded.
>
> The row houses in the vicinity of the school were burning brightly. Our house, too, burned in a big blaze.
>
> My brother and my little sisters had come into the shelter too late. They were badly burned. They sat beside me and cried. Grandmother took the rosary from her kimono and prayed.
>
> I sat down at the entrance of the shelter and looked around, yearning for Father and Mother. Half an hour later, my mother did come. Her whole body was bloody. Mother had been surprised in the attack while she was preparing dinner. I'll never forget the joy I felt when I threw myself upon my mother. Full of worry, we waited for Father. He had gone away in the morning on warden duty.
>
> The people who were still alive died one after another. They groaned in pain. The next day, my young sisters died, and also Mother, our beloved mother. Then my brother. I believed that I also would die. Everyone that was with us in the cellar died. Grandmother and I, however, had been the deepest into the shelter. The blast had not reached us. Therefore, we remained alive, just we two.

Day after day, we searched in vain among the many dead for my father.

Only a few remained alive. These carried a lot of wood onto the playground and burned the corpses. My brother was burned there, too. Before my eyes, my mother became ashes.

Grandmother said to me that when I come to heaven I will see my mother again. Yes, but Grandmother is already old. She will soon go to heaven. But I, I am only a child and must live many, many years before I can be united with Mother, whom I love more than anything; before I can again play with my brother and talk with my small sisters.

I am now attending the Yamazato grade school once more. I am now in fourth grade. The playground is cleaned up now and many of my school friends play there. Those children know nothing about the fact that many, many of their comrades died and were burned to ashes here. Even I run happily around the playground with my companions. But, often and unexpectedly, images of that horrible day leap up before me.

Then I throw myself down on the piece of earth where my mother was burned. My fingers tear the ground. If one bores deeper with a bamboo stick, black ashes and charcoal come to the surface. When I look directly at the earth, suddenly the face of my mother is visible in it. I rage when I see my school friends walk on that ground.[1]

We have spent more than fifty years rationalizing omnicide and keeping the world a hair trigger from extinction. Rationalization has brutalized and numbed the American psyche. We are unable to recognize the evil or the demonic, even though it is palpable in nuclear weapons. In weighing Fujio's experience against John's passages, we remember that, biblically, faith equals love equals acting justly. Faith and love call us to an offensive of truth. That is how we should be instead of nervously living under the bomb.

As part of our response to the cries of suffering people, in an attempt to live faith and love in our day, we need to go to places like Bath Iron Works, where each Aegis destroyer under construction can single-handedly destroy thousands of Nagasaki playgrounds. Hundreds of such cogs in the imperial war machine are scattered all over this country. Faith in God and love for others requires acting against such a scourge on Creation.

Jesus and John assure us that whenever we put faith into action, eternal life begins. Active participation in the war makers' doomsday schemes or silence before them ignores the cries of the afflicted—including ourselves—and means spiritual death. Resistance to the machinery and mentality of omnicide just as surely signals resurrection amid the ashes.

Chapter 2

Dwelling among the Tombs: the Empire's Reign of Terror

by *Steven Baggarly*

So Pilate, wishing to satisfy the crowd, released Barabbas to them and, after he had Jesus scourged, handed him over to be crucified.

Mark 15:15

Pilate, Judea's Roman governor, sentences Jesus to death by cruci-fixion. Also implicated are the chief priests and the crowd, who, as part of a Passover deal, trade Jesus for Barabbas. The chief priests stir up the crowd who clamor for Jesus's death, and Pilate concurs. Jesus becomes the sacrificial Passover lamb—this time, God's firstborn will not be passed over by the angel of death.

Jesus is condemned through the collaboration of church and state. Just as his murder was both a religious and a political act, so would be a nuclear war. While the United States government, military, and arms manufacturers maintain a first-strike nuclear force and con-tinue the development of nuclear weapons, the churches keep a deaf-ening silence. By doing virtually nothing to discourage the dutiful tax payment and military enlistment of their members, churches lend divine sanction to daily preparations for mass annihilation. Churches are unwilling to breach the legal hedge protecting the weap-ons. Just as Jesus was sentenced to death then, so he continues un-der a death sentence now. Nuclear weapons constantly threaten to crucify all of humanity, the body of Christ.

Even with reductions since the end of the cold war, the destruc-tive force of today's nuclear stockpiles exceeds that of 750,000 Hiroshima-size bombs—more than sixteen hundred times the ex-plosive energy expended in World War II, some 1.7 tons of TNT for every woman, man and child on earth.[1] The United States and Rus-sia still deploy some 18,600 nuclear warheads between them, with fifteen thousand in reserve.[2] Their nuclear forces remain on high alert; the United States has 550 land-based ICBM's as well as the Trident submarine fleet ready to launch on warning.

Naval destroyers, including the USS *The Sullivans*, cruisers, and submarines, and Air Force B-2 and B-52 bombers can be readily nuclear-armed and sent around the globe. As a matter of policy, the United States government is always prepared to use or threaten to use nuclear weapons. During the Persian Gulf War, the navy kept six hundred warheads on ships and subs in the Gulf. A public verbal threat went out last year against Libya, in response to what proved to be an imaginary chemical weapons factory being built inside a mountain. NATO planes used depleted uranium penetrators, potent nuclear weapons, in Kosovo and Serbia. *The Bulletin of Atomic Scien-*

tists, taking the world political situation into account and its impact on the possible use of nuclear weapons, symbolically figures that the world is still only fourteen minutes from the midnight of global catastrophe.[3]

The very real possibility of a mistaken or unauthorized nuclear launch stands parallel to the constant threat of intentional nuclear exchange. In November 1979, a Pentagon computer took a war games tape for real and put all the American early-warning systems around the planet on alert. Three squadrons of nuclear bombers took off. If the alert had continued twenty more minutes, nuclear war would have erupted. Twice in June of 1980, a faulty forty-six-cent computer chip flashed warnings of Soviet missile launches. In one instance, B-52s taxied for takeoff, nuclear subs went on high alert, and launch keys in ICBM silos were inserted into launch slots before the error was discovered.[4] Presently, Russia's nuclear arsenal is decaying and often lacks replacement parts for old equipment. On several occasions, equipment malfunctions have switched Russian missiles to "combat mode," increasing the possibility of unauthorized launch. On January 25, 1995, Russian radar mistook a Norwegian scientific research rocket for a United States Trident launch and made every preparation for nuclear war short of the final command to launch.[5] As long as nuclear weapons exist, the world is only a hair trigger from destruction.

We can record a long history of nuclear weapons accidents, any one of which could have resulted in a nuclear detonation, instigating all-out nuclear war. On January 24, 1961, a crashing B-52 jettisoned two twenty-four-megaton bombs over Goldsboro, North Carolina. One broke apart on impact, and parts of the bomb were never found. On the other, five of six interlocking safety switches had been tripped. If the last switch had been released, an explosion eighteen hundred times more powerful than the Hiroshima bomb would have resulted. During the 1960s, B-52s crashed in both Palomares, Spain, and Thule Air Force Base, Greenland, their nuclear payloads either dropped or destroyed by fire. Both accidents released radioactive material. Because they were dangerously radioactive, thousands of tons of soil, ice, snow, and water had to be shipped to United States storage sites. Two nuclear-tipped antiaircraft missiles have been inadvertently launched. On September 19, 1980, an explosion at a Titan II missile silo near Damascus, Arkansas, blew off the 740-ton silo cover and hurled the nine-megaton nuclear warhead two hundred yards. In one of many accidents involving vehicles transporting nuclear weapons, a missile simply rolled off a truck and into the Tennessee River.[6] There have been more than 175 accidents involving United States nuclear weapons alone.[7] Doubtless, the actual numbers are higher—since accidents and mishaps, as well as brushes with unauthorized launch and mistaken launches, are kept classified unless disclosure is unavoidable.

The infrastructure of nuclear weapons programs is perilous as well. Decades of nuclear testing contributed to the cancer epidemic, produced birth defects near test sites, and have made us all carriers of radioactive particles. Exposed tailings at uranium mines around the world, accidents at nuclear power plants, and burned-out fuel rods with no burial place, all release radioactivity into the air and water.[8] Thousands of nuclear warheads and some twelve hundred tons of weapons-grade plutonium and uranium sit virtually unguarded in the former Soviet Union.[9] General Alexander Lebed, Russia's former national security chief, recently claimed that from fifty to one hundred of Russia's suitcase- or backpack-sized nuclear weapons are missing.[10] Such one-kiloton nukes (which the United States also has) each weigh between sixty and a hundred pounds and can take out much of a small city.

For fifty years, the specter of nuclear catastrophe has hovered over the world. American taxpayers have paid more than $5.5 trillion[11] to be at the forefront of the insanity. By not working for immediate disarmament of all nuclear weapons and then taking every precaution against their reemergence, the state, with support from the churches, continues to condemn Jesus. Clinging to nuclear weapons and United States world supremacy, our leaders unceasingly clamor for the people to side with the violent Barabbas and condemn the nonviolent Jesus. And the entire planet lives under the sentence of death.

Condemnation of Christ

by Susan Crane

Pilate then took Jesus and scourged him. And the soldiers twisted together a crown of thorns and put it on his head, and put a purple robe on him; and they began to come up to him and say, "Hail, king of the Jews!" and to give him slaps in the face.

Pilate came out again and said to them, "Behold, I am bringing him out to you so that you may know that I find no guilt in him."

Jesus then came out, wearing the crown of thorns and the purple robe. Pilate said to them, "Behold, the man!"

So when the chief priests and officers saw him, they cried out saying, "Crucify, crucify!"

Pilate said to them, "Take him yourselves and crucify him, for I find no guilt in him."

They answered him, "We have a law, and by that law he ought to die because he made himself out to be the son of God."

Therefore when Pilate heard the statement, he was even more afraid; and he entered into the Praetorium again and said to Jesus, "Where are you from?" But Jesus gave him no answer.

So Pilate said to him, "You do not speak to me? Do you not know that I have authority to release you, and I have authority to crucify you?"

Jesus answered, "You would have no authority over me, unless it had been given you from above; for this reason he who delivered me to you has the greater sin."

As a result of this Pilate made efforts to release him, but the Jews cried out saying, "If you release this man, you are no friend of Caesar, everyone who makes himself out to be a king opposes Caesar."

Therefore when Pilate heard these words, he brought Jesus out, and sat down on the judgment seat at a place called The Pavement, but in Hebrew, Gabbatha.

Now it was the day of preparation for the Passover; it was about the sixth hour. And he said to the Jews, "Behold, your king!"

So they cried out, "Away with him, away with him, crucify him!"

Pilate said to them, "Shall I crucify your king?"

The chief priests answered, "We have no king but Caesar."

So he then handed him over to them to be crucified.

John 19:1-16

August 6, 1997. Fifty-two years ago today, the United States dropped the atomic bomb on Hiroshima, Japan. Unable to make a public witness of repentance and reparation this year, I am in my jail cell, now a refuge for weighty reflection. I am reminded of the story of a German theologian walking through the ruins of Hiroshima a month after the bombing. As he approached the remnants of a small bridge, he noticed the shadow of a human being imprinted on its abutment. The person had been literally vaporized by the blast. Recalling the words of Jesus, "Whatever you did for one of the least brothers and sisters of mine, you did for me," the observer reflected that we had vaporized Jesus himself on those stones.

Thus reflecting, I realize that it feels right to be in jail today.

Consider the words of John at 19:1-16. In the passage, the chief priests of Jerusalem utter one of the most shocking statements in all scripture: "We have no king but Caesar." The statement marks the turning point in history, and the passage chronicles the weapons used to condemn the son of God to death: law, politics, and institutional religion. All are laid bare, and all the authorities involved are forced to make a public statement of their allegiance. Evil reaches its apex in history, but it did so at a price: exposure.

Imagine the place where the statement is made. It is daylight, about noontime on the preparation day for Passover. Priests have begun the ritual slaughter of thousands of lambs for a most solemn religious feast. Against the bloody backdrop, the chief priests and leaders make a stark choice. They choose fidelity to law and state and, thus, they reject God.

Rejecting God has deep roots in Israel's history, and Hebrew scripture repeatedly characterizes human sin as a preference for worldly kings over God. A particularly instructive example is found in First Samuel, the eighth chapter, where Yahweh (God) makes plain what will result from people's demands for a king: enslavement, comprehensive exploitation, and constant devotion to war. Nevertheless, the people persist, and Yahweh tells Samuel to grant their request, thus replacing with empire the system of local self-government by Israel's judges. It is a rarely mentioned fact in church liturgies and theologies at the turn of the millennium that kingship in Israel was born out of disobedience to God. After all, the contemporary church itself has a weakness for kings and the ways of empire.

On the day of Jesus's execution, humanity experiences the full impact of empire-building nurtured by disobedience to God. Temple authorities exchange Jesus—the messiah in Christian belief—for a Roman oppressor. Not even for a Judean king.

United States Christian churches treat it as an article of faith that we can have two kings, that simultaneously we can serve Christ and capitulate to the empire. Churches bless the empire's wars, and that is when the article of faith is most evident. The essential lie that allowed the chief priests to condemn Jesus to death is the same lie that perpetuates crucifixion today of war's innocent victims. At Hiroshima and Nagasaki, 150,000 people were incinerated by our flying ovens. Another 250,000 have since perished from the bombs' effects. In World War II, noncombatants made up fifty-two percent of those killed. In the Korean War, eighty-four percent of the deaths were civilian. In Vietnam, civilians accounted for ninety-one percent of the dead, and most of them were children. After the Gulf War, General Colin Powell said, "We don't know how many Iraqis died, and it doesn't matter." Among the commonalties linking such atrocities with crucifying Jesus are legality, political expedience, and the capitulation of religious authorities to the empire. In NATO action over Serbia and Kosovo, civilian casualties vastly outnumbered military casualties.

It is not possible to understand how Christ could be condemned, nor is it possible to understand how the contemporary world continues to condemn Christ—apart from the principalities and powers that produce the condemnation. Principalities and powers manifest themselves as

—law: "We have a law, and according to that law, he ought to die . . ."

—politics: "If you release this man, you are not a friend of Caesar."

—institutional religion: "We have no king but Caesar."

Living the life of Gospel faith confronts and opposes the principalities and powers. One lives the life of Gospel faith in constant conflict with the movements of such powers in the world. Consider:

> Finally, be strong in God and in the strength of God's might. Put on the full armor of God, so that you will be able to stand firm against the schemes of the devil. For our struggle is not against flesh and blood, but against the rulers, against the powers, against the world forces of this darkness, against the spiritual forces of wickedness in the heavenly places.
>
> Therefore, take up the full armor of God, so that you will be able to resist in the evil day, and having done everything, to stand firm.
>
> Stand firm, therefore, having girded your loins with truth, and having put on the breastplate of righteousness, and having shod your feet with the preparation of the Gospel of peace; in addition to all, taking up the shield of faith with which you will be able to extinguish all the flaming arrows of the evil one.
>
> And take the helmet of salvation, and the sword of the spirit, which is the word of God.
>
> Ephesians 6:10-17

When we fail to engage principalities and powers, we participate through the silence of complicity in the ongoing condemnation of Christ and crucifixion of Jesus.

With Hiroshima, Nagasaki, and fifty-two years of nuclear worship, the United States provides a clear, exposed, unequivocal statement to the world: "We have no king but Caesar."

Unless I Wash You

by Mark Colville

> Now before the feast of the Passover, Jesus knowing that his hour had come that he would depart out of this world to God, having loved his own who were in the world, he loved them to the end.
>
> During supper, the devil having already put into the heart of Judas Iscariot, the son of Simon, to betray him, Jesus, knowing that God had given all things into his hands, and that he had come forth from God and was going back to God, got up from supper, and laid aside his garments; and taking a towel he girded himself. Then he poured water into the basin, and began to wash the disciples' feet and to wipe them with the towel with which he was girded.
>
> So he came to Simon Peter. He said to him, "Lord, do you wash my feet?

Jesus answered and said to him, "What I do you do not realize now, but you will understand hereafter."

Peter said to him, "Never shall you wash my feet!"

Jesus answered him, "If I do not wash you, you have no part with me."

Simon Peter said to him, "Lord, then wash not only my feet, but also my hands and my head."

Jesus said to him, "They who have bathed need only to wash their feet, but are completely clean; and you are clean, but not all of you."

John 13:8

Luz, Keeley, Justin, and Soledad came to see me yesterday. Nothing calls forth the entire spectrum of emotions involved in resistance like a family visit in jail. It is by far the most anticipated event in my life as a prisoner, and it is the most joyous. Holding my wife and children brings a fleeting burst of normalcy into an absurd existence of forced separation. We spend the hour in a state of bliss as we reorient ourselves and reclaim our identity as a family. And in the process, we remember that it is by the strength of our love for one another, rooted in devotion to Christ, that we can endure persecution and even transform it into something life-giving.

On the other hand, visits also lay bare cold realities and the implications of the life we have chosen. For the past five months, I've not witnessed the day-to-day growth of my son, now sixteen months old, nor of his four- and six-year old sisters. They are in good hands, of course, with five other adults in our home community treating them as their own. Nevertheless, watching them play on the floor of the visiting room, I am aware that time is passing. My children are developing, learning new skills, and changing day-by-day, and I am missing out on precious moments. Similarly, my love for their mother, my wife, is mixed with longing and pain. Without question, our love has deepened, and our relationship has become stronger during the months I have been in jail. Yet we are denied the friendship, the daily conversations, the physical and spiritual intimacy we've shared for the past seven years. For now, and for the future, we must walk alone, and it leaves a deep and unfillable void for both of us.

Indeed, the love we feel for others—friends, family, children, neighbors, fellow resisters—that very love that makes our resistance possible can also increase our suffering and make jail more difficult to bear.

Such a jumble of thoughts and feelings naturally leads to uncertainties and to doubts. Looking around at my companions in the Plowshares action, I see two who have been doing Christian nonviolent resistance for the past thirty years, and at least two others who will probably spend the rest of their lives in and out of jails for crimes of peace against the empire. They are laying down their lives for the Gospel; if not in a bloody martyrdom, then certainly in one that involves years of struggle, mistreatment, separation from loved ones, anguish, and pain. Their witness is an inspiration and a discomfort demanding my response. Can I, too, follow such a path?

As we've studied John's Gospel together in jail for the past five months, we've come to realize that the central event by which Christian discipleship was understood in the community from which the Gospel of John arose was Jesus's washing of the disciples' feet, in Chapter 13. The event is nearly always misinterpreted in church liturgies today as an exhortation to humility and service, with never a mention of the inescapable fact that Jesus was commissioning his disciples to martyrdom (For a fine commentary on John 13, see *Becoming Children of God* by Wes Howard-Brook [Orbis, 1994], pp. 289-306). Jesus's action mirrors the anointing of Jesus himself by Mary, the sister of Lazarus at John 12:1-8. Jesus pointedly describes his anointing as preparation for his burial. By giving the same preparation to his followers on the night before his execution, Jesus suggests that to be a disciple is to give up one's life.

But Peter misunderstands. Perhaps he, like the contemporary, comfortable church, thinks Jesus is simply trying to place himself in a subservient role. Whatever the cause, Peter resists what his teacher does. Jesus's response is forceful, persuasive, and frightening, and it is directed at all would-be disciples: "Unless I wash you, you will have no inheritance with me." In other words, Jesus must anoint and thus commission his disciples to do the work of God.

Among North American Christians today, there appears to be an unspoken understanding that it is "out of bounds" for one to tell another what it means to follow Christ, to take up the cross. It is as if there were as many interpretations as there are Christians, as if the cross were a personal understanding between the individual and God. But the community of John didn't accept such an understanding, and they couldn't afford to. The original readers of John's Gospel were being hunted down, tortured, and killed by the Roman state that considered them evil and godless. Certainly, there was no room for ambiguity in their understanding of the sacrament of footwashing. For them, there was no question that faith in Christ meant resistance to empire, and that was the central purpose of their gathering as a community: to prepare each other for the cross, resistance, and martyrdom. Why, then, should our notion of discipleship be any different today, when we come up against an empire that is laying waste to the world and holding a nuclear gun to the head of all humanity?

Philip Berrigan says that jail is "the bottom line," and perhaps I am beginning to understand what he means. I've been here long enough now for any possible mystique of jail to wear off, long enough to struggle with some personal demons, long enough to work through some significant pain and loneliness. But I've also been here long enough to see the world differently, to gain some real perspective on the sickness of our society, to become a little impatient with friends and fellow Christians who see nonviolent resistance and jail as some peoples' "calling," but not theirs. As long as the American empire feeds itself on the blood of the poor and is ready and willing to destroy the entire world in order to protect its concentration of wealth and power, I no longer fathom how people in this country can think they are living a Christian life if it does not include resistance that risks real, substantive persecution. The cross and martyrdom are the essential part of the journey from nonviolent direct action through the empire's jails, and back again that all of us must come to terms with in the United States. It seems clearer than ever that it is the only journey.

In my own lack of readiness for this kind of life, I feel a kinship with Peter. He was not ready to have his feet washed, and even when he submitted, he did not understand. Yet Christ carried him and prepared him to be led where he did not want to go. In the same way I am trying, with some halting success, to extend my feet toward Christ.

We Ought to Prepare One Another

by Susan Crane

So when he had washed their feet, and taken his garments and reclined at the table again, he said to them, "Do you know what I have done to you? You call me teacher and Lord; and you are right, for so I am. If I then, the Lord and the teacher, washed your feet, you also ought to wash one another's feet."
John 13:12-14

Jesus, the master, the teacher, the incarnate God, becomes servant and washes the disciples' feet. The disciples, wrapped in Jewish scripture and culture from childhood, understand that washing feet is preparation for meeting God:

God spoke to Moses saying, "You shall also make a laver of bronze, with its base of bronze, for washing; and you shall put it between the tent of meeting and the altar, and you shall put water in it. Aaron and his sons shall wash their hands and their feet from it; when they enter the tent of meeting, they shall wash with water, so that they will not die; or when they approach the altar to minister, by offering up in smoke a fire sacrifice to God. So they shall wash their hands and their feet, so that they will not die; and it shall be a perpetual statue for them, for Aaron and his descendants throughout their generations."

Exodus 30:17-21

The disciples also remember that only six days before, when Martha and Mary were giving a dinner for Jesus, Mary took expensive, perfumed oil and anointed Jesus's feet. Judas had protested.

Therefore Jesus said, "Let her alone, so that she may keep it for the day of my burial."

When Jesus washes the disciples' feet, he commissions them, prepares them for their ministry, and makes them ready to approach God. He does for them what Mary has done for him, and all will be martyrs.

Scripture tells us to prepare one another, and so we should. The closest example of such preparation that I have experienced is preparation for a Plowshares action. We formed a community to prepare ourselves and each other for the witness. We metaphorically wash each other's feet by discerning, reflecting, and enduring, by giving hope, humor, encouragement, and food for the journey.

The journey, the preparation, has different, interrelated parts: spiritual preparation, study of the world situation, preparing our family finances, and getting our lives in order. We get our priorities straight and understand that our treasure is in heaven, which is to say that our treasure isn't this car or that dish or that house but is, instead, our relationship to our Creator. Material things are useful only if they help us do what we are called to do. Catholic Workers among us are way ahead of me in fathoming that thought. In order to prepare for the Plowshares action, I had to sell my car, rip up my credit cards, leave my teaching position, and sort through and get rid of years of accumulated stuff so that I could be free to be in jail. Because all of the stuff isn't treasure, it felt good to sort it all down into a few boxes that are still being kept by loving friends in Ukiah. Getting rid of stuff, I found, can be hard because we get inordinately attached to our money-making jobs and our things, but in other ways, it is the easiest preparation because it's mechanical. You can just do it.

Getting my spiritual life on the way to being ordered has been a much larger task. People who are brought up in the Roman Catholic church are fortunate because they learn about prayer and moral teaching and have such things stored in their hearts and minds, to be used as they choose. But I was not brought up in the church, and I had to start fresh.

Part of our preparation has been reading and understanding stories of people faced with the choice between obedience to God or obedience to the empire. The first story of civil resistance we discovered in the Bible is the story of the Hebrew midwives, Shiprah and Puah.

> *Then the king of Egypt spoke to the Hebrew midwives, one of whom was named Shiphrah and the other was named Puah; and he said, "When you are helping the Hebrew women to give birth and see them upon the birth stool, if it is a son, then you shall put him to death; but if it is a daughter, then she shall live."*
>
> *But the midwives feared God, and did not do as the king of Egypt had commanded them, but let the boys live. So the king of Egypt called for the midwives and said to them, "Why have you done this thing, and let the boys live?"*
>
> *The midwives said to Pharoah, "Because the Hebrew women are not as the Egyptian women; for they are vigorous and give birth before the midwife can get to them." So God was good to the midwives, and the people multiplied, and became very mighty. Because the midwives feared God, God established households for them.*
>
> Exodus 1:15-21

As far as the Pharoah of Egypt was concerned, Israelite slaves like Shiphrah and Puah were growing more numerous and powerful. Pharoah gave the Israelites difficult work in the masonry and fields. Then he told the midwives to let girls live but kill boys as they were born. The very figure of empire, the Pharoah, personally commands the midwives, two slave women, to do their work in a particular way.

How many of us have been summoned to the White House and given specific orders? Not anyone I know, although we are generally expected to pay taxes, register with the war department (if we are men), and obey the empire's laws. It must have been an intense and emotional experience for Shiphrah and Puah, and afterwards they probably went through a discernment process. Their chosen work is helping to birth new life, to assist during the tender time of childbirth when mother love is especially strong and miraculous. But they are ordered to do something completely opposite to that love: to kill new life as it is born.

It makes me think of the births of my sons Robin and Chet. Each was an intense, tender, love-filled event. Their dad, our community, and our midwife were there each time. Our midwife shared in the preparation, the labor, and the joy of birth. What an abhorrent thought, let alone the action, to hurt a child after the miracle of new life and love.

Scripture doesn't say, but surely Shiphrah and Puah asked each other, "Should we obey the Pharoah? How can we? Could I really kill a child? What will happen if I don't? Maybe we should escape or stop being midwives. Or maybe we should do what he says, even though it will be repulsive and immoral, in order to save our own lives. What would happen to my own children if I die? Don't my children deserve to have a mom's care?"

But ultimately Shiphrah and Puah demonstrate their fear of God. They don't want to do anything to offend God, the god of love and the life they knew. So they decide to disobey Pharoah. They decide to do civil resistance, to put God first. The women are brave, and the consequences for them would likely have been quite extreme.

Again scripture does not say, but Pharoah must have been angry when he realized that Shiphrah and Puah were not doing as he had ordered them. He wanted to decrease the strength of the Israelites, because he was afraid they would be too numerous and join his enemies against him. He was afraid for his life, his power, and his kingdom. He was accustomed to being obeyed, and the women were defeating his plan.

Scripture says that Pharoah has Shiphrah and Puah summoned to his presence. I can imagine him thundering, "Why have you acted thus, allowing the boys to live?"

But Shiphrah and Puah do not cower. Unafraid, they respond, "The Hebrew women are not like the Egyptian women. They are robust and give birth before the midwife arrives." Pharoah, seeing that he could not intimidate them, lets them leave.

As part of our washing of each other's feet—preparing for the Plowshares action—we study the story of Shiphrah and Puah. We learn to put God first, above the laws of the empire, and we learn not to be intimidated when we are brought into the courts of power. Also, we learn that women in dialogue with each other are strong, a unit. It's helpful to go as a community into the courts, the jails, the places of power.

Wash each other's feet.

We study about the events, present and past, that our media ignore or misrepresent. Our conscience has to be informed so that we know where we are in history.

Take, for example, the bombing of the Amariya shelter in Baghdad during the Gulf War. People slept there to be safe from bombing, and women, children, and elders were very likely to be there. The United States bombed the city of Baghdad early in the morning of February 13, 1991, and the shelter was full. A United States missile exploded through the roof, making a hole through cement six feet thick. Four minutes later, a second explosive went into the hole, incinerating twelve hundred women, children, and elders. The heat was so extreme that shadows of their bodies were left on the cement. Although there was some initial national press coverage of the Amariya bombing and the Pentagon has acknowledged the event, very little has been made of it in the national press.

When Steve Kelly, a Jesuit priest, and I went into Lockheed-Martin to convert Trident D-5 missiles being built there, we brought pictures of children whose mothers and siblings had died during the United States "surgical strike" on Baghdad. We did so to encourage workers to look into their own hearts, to see and to feel the consequences of their work, to imagine their own loved ones burning to death in a bomb shelter.

Our country killed the children, mothers, and elders in the Amariya shelter. Innocent blood was shed in your name and mine. To protect us? To defend our standard of living? Face to face with the child who stands next to a sign on his house where the names of his brothers, sisters, and mom are written, what do I say? What can I say to him about his family killed in that shelter when our bombs ripped through as they slept? For more than a year before we went to Lockheed-Martin, we kept the child's picture on our refrigerator and then we took it to Lockheed. We would do it again. Our country should have remorse, but it doesn't, so we provided a reminder of children killed by bombs built with the complicity of Lockheed-Martin, other weapons manufacturers, and the United States government and its taxpayers.

Would Shiphrah or Puah have killed those children in the shelter? Can I allow the government to kill in my name? Even today, sanctions continue against Iraq and are responsible for the deaths of more than a million Iraqis, mostly children—God's children, our children.

Wash each other's feet.

We reflect about sin, about our lives, about our own sin. We reflect about stealing, pride, and anger. With distaste, I realize that I have broken all of the commandments. And not only that, I am swimming with everyone else in a river of collective sin. Each of us is individually responsible for what we, as a nation, are doing. We participate in larceny, murder, and falsehoods. We don't have any remorse. Our first priority is war making. We deliberately choose to continue to make war, and that choice is gravely contrary to divine law. We praise and approve the military. We are accomplices in the injustice our military power and mass murder bring. The only way out, in response to our collective sins—all considered legal by our government, is to repent, withdraw my consent and compliance, and speak out nonviolently in word and action.

Like Shiphrah and Puah together and in the way Jesus commissioned the disciples, we work, reflect, and study together. We wash each other's feet. And then we act to uphold God's law, which is higher than the law of nations.

Of Words and Works: God and Empire

by Philip Berrigan

So Jesus, knowing all the things that were coming upon him, went forth and said to them, "Whom do you seek?"
They answered him, "Jesus the Nazarene."
He said to them, "I am he." And Judas also, who was betraying him, was standing with them. So when he said to them, "I am he," they drew back and fell to the ground."

John 18:4-6

Among the biblical realities given scant notice by Christians are the "works" of God. Yet "works" are one of the two wellsprings of faith, one of the two foundations of authority. We believe God because of the word of God and because of the works of God, or both.

Gandhi used to teach that we are what we think. More comprehensively, perhaps, we are what we *do*. Conduct is the measure of our lives. We take only our works with us to God.

Both the Hebrew and Christian scriptures reveal the majestic and sublime works of God. For example, creative deeds of God are related in Genesis 1; works about liberating the Israelites from bondage in Egypt in Exodus 7-11; feeding in the desert with manna and quail in Exodus 16; waters of Meribah in Numbers 20; the bronze serpent in Numbers 21; collapsing of the walls of Jericho in Joshua 6; strength of Samson in Judges 15; wisdom of Solomon in First Kings 3; Elijah saving the widow's son in First Kings 17; Elisha raising the Shunammite's son from death in Second Kings 4; Elisha curing Naaman the leper in Second Kings 5; God's speech to Job in Job 38.

Psalms 18, 19, 33, 65, 78, 103, 104, 106, 107, 124, and 150 continue the praise of God's works. "Give praise for God's mighty deeds, praise God for God's great majesty," says Psalm 150. The prophets Isaiah, Jeremiah, Ezekiel, Daniel, Hosea, Amos, Jonah, Joel, and Zephaniah are divine "works," embodiments of God's intense inspiration and strength.

As for Christian scripture, John's Gospel best illustrates the works of God and Jesus. John portrays Jesus as the apprentice and God as the artisan. Jesus does only the works that he sees his parent, God, doing, for example, at John 5:19. In his seven works, an evocation of God's perfection, Jesus parallels the creative works of God recorded in Genesis. Jesus thereby initiates a second Creation, a rebirth in God as adopted daughters and sons. The seven works with seven signs suggesting that Jesus enacts a new Creation and offers it to all are:

—wedding feast at Cana at John 2, when Jesus reinstates humankind as the partner of God

—healing of the royal official's son at John 5, when Jesus offers belief as curative

—healing the ill man at Bethsaida also at John 5, when Jesus shows compassion as worship of God

—multiplication of loaves at John 6, when Jesus's action is *analeptic,* that is a "gazing back" to the feeding with manna and *proleptic,* that is "gazing forward" to the Eucharist

—walking on water also at John 6, revealing Christ's mastery over nature

—healing a man born blind at John 9, showing Christ's mastery over our blindness

—raising Lazarus at John 11, showing Christ's mastery over death

When Jesus says

> *If I do not do the works of God, do not believe me, but if I do them, though you do not believe me, believe the works, so that you may know and understand that God is in me, and I in God.*
>
> John 10:37-38

> *If I had not done among them the works which no one else did, they would not have sin; but now they have both seen and hated me and God as well.*
>
> John 15:24

Jesus reasons at John 10:37-38 that the best yardstick of a life is works or conduct.

> *So then, you will know them by their fruits (works).*
>
> Matthew 7:20

Jesus pleads for faith. The word of God—and Jesus's word—should inspire faith, but if it doesn't, then Jesus's works or deeds should inspire faith. Faith reveals that God speaks and acts in Jesus.

Jesus indicts those unmoved by works at John 14:24. He reveals that those who are unmoved by works hate God and hate Jesus. Resistant to both word and works, people unmoved fear the plunge and risk of faith, fear the unknown geography of faith, and hate God and Jesus for requiring faith.

Before submitting to arrest by the military after Judas betrays him, Jesus teaches the last great work in Gethsemane. Luke describes the event as the "hour and power of darkness" at Luke 22:53, but John describes Jesus as always in control, even while on the cross. "I am thirsty," he says at John 19:28. Jesus thus echoes "I am who I am," the words of YHWH, the self-designation of God to Moses on Mount Sinai. Jesus asserts oneness with God and makes provision for our needs: "I am the bread of life."

John makes a point not stressed by Matthew and Luke, the synoptic writers who use Mark's Gospel as a source and then build upon it. John alone suggests deep complicity of the Romans in the arrest and murder of Jesus.

> So Judas got a band of soldiers and guards from the chief priests and the Pharisees and went there with lanterns, torches, and weapons.
>
> John 18:3

> Then, while he was still speaking, Judas, one of the Twelve, arrived, accompanied by a crowd with swords and clubs who had come from the chief priests, the scribes, and the elders.
>
> Mark 14:43

> While he was still speaking, Judas, one of the Twelve, arrived, accompanied by a large crowd, with swords and clubs, who had come from the chief priests and the elders of the people.
>
> Matthew 26:47

> While he was still speaking, a crowd approached and in front was one of the Twelve, a man named Judas. . . And Jesus said to the chief priests and temple guards and elders who had come for him, "Have you come out as against a robber, with swords and clubs?"
>
> Luke 22:47, 52

The Gospels make it clear that Jesus believed in the power of God's name. More than that, Jesus is God's name. He professes utter freedom in offering himself:

> For this reason God loves me, because I lay down my life so that I may take it again. No one has taken it away from me, but I lay it down on my own initiative. I have authority to lay it down, and I have authority to take it up again. This commandment I received from God.
>
> John 10:17-18

The incarnation and Jesus's full choice of his passion and death are also guarantees of our freedom. If God is rigid about anything, scripture implies, it is about never nullifying our freedom. The integrity of all our relationships depends on our freedom of choice. We choose the beloved community, scripture teaches, or we abuse our choice and create hell on earth.

The chief priests, Pharisees, and Romans got together to apprehend Jesus. They worked in a band, and here is an unappetizing truth: religion and politics in the world are the same thing. There never was a separation of church and state. We have the realities of the temple state of the Roman era with the established religion as chaplain to the state, and ultimately, the persecution of Christians by both church and state. As they uphold the law of government and war in the name of obedience to the commandment, today's churches are not different. Millions suffer and die because the churches are silent or endorse the repressive, warlike policies of governments.

Jesus believed and acted out of twin imperatives: to have faith and to do works. Jesus's first work was at Cana, where once and for all the human family was married to God. When Jesus stunned the Roman guard, his last work before the passion, Jesus acted in civil resistance.

In contrast to the matchless works of God, there are the works of the empire. We will mention only nuclearism and robbery of the poor, global poisoning, the Fortune 500, GATT, and NAFTA as exploitative works of the United States government. Military and CIA interventions of the past fifty years have killed millions, perhaps more than the seventy million who died in World War II. Here is a partial list: China, 1945-60; Italy, 1947-48; Greece, 1947-50; the Philippines, 1940s and 1950s; Korea, 1945-53; Albania, 1949-53; Iran, 1953; Guatemala, 1953-54; Syria, 1956-57; Haiti, 1959-63; Guatemala, 1960; Algeria, 1960; Ecuador, 1960-63; the Congo, 1960-64.

Also, Brazil, 1961-64; Peru, 1960-65; Dominican Republic, 1960-66; Cuba, 1959-80; Indonesia, 1965; Ghana, 1966; Uruguay, 1964-70; Chile, 1964-73; Greece, 1964-75; Bolivia, 1964-75; Guatemala, 1962-80; Costa Rica, 1970-71; Iraq, 1972-75; Australia, 1973-75; Angola, 1975-80; Zaire, 1975-80.

Also, Jamaica, 1976-80; Grenada, 1979-84; Morocco, 1984; Libya, 1981-89; Nicaragua, 1981-90; Panama, 1969-91; Bulgaria, 1990; Iraq, 1990 to the end of the century and beyond; Afghanistan, 1979-92; El Salvador, 1980-94; Haiti, 1989-94; Yugoslavia and the states of the former Yugoslavia, 1989-1999.

Fifty-five interventions in fifty years. More than one per year. So much for our claims as a godly nation. So much for our dedication to international law. So much for our works in faith as a manifestation of goodness on earth.

Worship in Spirit and Truth

by Mark Colville

John 4:7-27 (cited at pages 17 and 18)

Lots of people take up religion as a sort of hobby while they're in jail, similar to weight lifting, reading, or playing cards. Without doubt, the upheaval of incarceration leads people to take stock of their lives and even to make sincere efforts at changing their ways. Unfortunately, most of the time the transformation is limited and short-lived. When the crisis is over and the jail door opens, the Bible goes back on the shelf. The dominant culture and its values take over again,

and the last condition of that person is worse than the first.

Luke 11:26

I'm convinced that much of the blame for the situation can be attributed to the kind of religion being preached in jail: a fundamentalist, highly personalized, born-again Christianity. The focus is on personal guilt, personal forgiveness, and personal salvation. And there is little or no analysis of the myriad ways our culture fosters narcissism, promotes consumerism, and rewards violent behavior. Faith is reduced to the attempt to give up smoking, drinking, drugs, sex, and swearing. Inmates are encouraged to memorize and repeat slogans about Jesus, and there is no attempt to trace personal sin to systemic evil; no effort to use Christ's teachings to analyze institutional violence; no reaching beyond the self to a suffering world. Perhaps most disturbing is that there is no discussion about taking up the cross in defense of the poor, which was the only religion Jesus of Nazareth practiced. Indeed, some of the most violent, misogynistic, and self-centered people I've met in jail claim to be "born again."

Thus, "Christianity without the cross" is the preferred religion of the empire. The "me and God" approach to worship never challenges the status quo, never holds the purveyors of violence and injustice accountable to the Gospel. No surprise, then, that it is the prevailing worship in the empire's jails. And no wonder that, for many years now, the Central Intelligence Agency has been providing funding and support to fundamentalist churches that proselytize in Latin American countries but do nothing to resist the violent and oppressive governments in that region.

In John's Gospel, Jesus travels into the territory of a supposed enemy in order to expose and break the boundaries that prevent authentic worship of God. A close reading of his discussion at John 4:7-26 with the Samaritan woman at the well reveals Jesus's insistence that true worship consists in the transformation of self and world:

> Jesus told her, "Believe me, woman, the hour is coming when you will worship the Parent neither on this mountain nor in Jerusalem."
>
> John 4:21

In ancient Palestine, Jews and Samaritans were sworn enemies. Contact with Samaritans was considered to make Jews ritually impure, and for Jesus to speak with a Samaritan woman in public would have been an astounding breach of socially accepted conduct. The enmity between these two cultures had deep historical and religious roots, and the hatred frequently gave rise to violence. Perhaps a modern-day equivalent would be the Serbs and Croats in Bosnia, or the Tutsis and Hutus in Rwanda. The central location for Samaritan worship was Mount Gerazim, where it was believed that Moses had buried the vessels of the tabernacle. Just as the Jewish national identity was grounded in the Jerusalem Temple as the site of religious worship established by their ancestors, the same was true of the Samaritan national identity with regard to their holy mountain.

But Samaria's history was also one of occupation and enslavement by several different colonial powers, and this greatly affected the religious practice there. In their capitulation, the Samaritans had adopted the gods of empires that had subjected them. In fact, if we consider that the Samaritan woman with whom Jesus is speaking represents Samaria as a whole, it becomes clear that the five husbands he accuses her of having at John 4:18 represent five occupying powers the Samaritans had cooperated with over the years.[1] Their worship of God had repeatedly adjusted and conformed to empire. And their current relationship with Rome was evidence of their continued infidelity to their real "husband," the one true God.

When Jesus separates true worship from temple and mountain, he separates it also from nationalistic hopes and patriotic ideologies, false forms of worship. In questioning the Samaritan woman about her many husbands, he is asserting that fidelity to God and to empire are mutually exclusive pursuits. To accept one is to reject the other, and true worship is impossible without making a conscious, active choice.

How, then, is God worshipped in spirit and truth? Obviously, there are several schools of thought on the subject among Christians today, but few of them ring true when held to the light of God's word. Churchgoing, prayer and meditation, scriptural and spiritual reading, and avoidance of personal sin—all are useful, even essential in the development of Christian spirituality. Yet, how often they are confused with an actual relationship with God! The Hebrew scriptures and Gospels state clearly and repeatedly, from beginning to end, that there is only one way to know God: by love of neighbor, which consists in doing justice, resisting injustice, and defending the poor. There is, in fact, no distinction in the Bible between the words "love" and "justice." They mean the same thing. We also know that the only true image of God in the world is humanity; human beings are made in the image and likeness of God:

> Then God said, "Let us make humanity in our image, according to our likeness . . ."
>
> Genesis 1:26

It follows that our worship of God is indistinguishable from the way we treat others, especially our enemies. As Dorothy Day said, "We love God as much as the person we love the least."

In the life of Christ, we find the definitive expression of worship of spirit and truth—the cross. It is only in giving our lives over to self-sacrificing love, in pursuit of justice, that we can be free of the personal and structural demons that render God unknown.

Love of Enemies

by Philip Berrigan

> You have heard that it was said, "You shall love your neighbor and hate your enemy." But I say to you, love your enemies and pray for those who persecute you . . .
>
> Matthew 5:43-44

Americans obey the first part of the teaching of Jesus at Matthew 5:43-44 and reject the second. We don't love our enemies, and we take great pride in believing that no one would dare attack or persecute us.

Nonetheless, we must try to understand the profound significance of "love of enemies" and to link the survival of humankind and the planet to embracing and acting on the word. God's love, which alone makes love of enemies possible, is present in all human beings. Indeed, God's love is not a philosophical abstraction or biblical anachronism but a vital possibility, the measure of hope that guides us in the emperor's apocalyptic world.

What, then, is our choice? Either we enact love of enemies or we die by global poison or nuclear fire storm or both. We must clearly acknowledge the spirit behind weapons that technologize our ancient hatreds, violence, blood lust, and wars.

Love of enemies and Jesus's new commandment—". . . love one another, just as I have loved you" at John 15:12—paraphrase one another, because Jesus died for us while we were enemies:

> But God demonstrates God's own love toward us, in that while we were yet sinners, Christ died for us.
>
> Romans 5:8

We might also regard them as complements—the inexhaustible love of God bolstering our weakness so that we can love our enemies. Together, the teachings encapsulate and summarize the word of God containing faith, justice, and life itself.

Two parables clarify love of enemies and love of everyone as Christ loves us. The first is about the Good Samaritan:

> But wishing to justify himself, [the lawyer] said to Jesus, "And who is my neighbor?"
>
> Jesus replied and said, "A man was going down from Jerusalem to Jericho, and fell among robbers, and they stripped him and beat him, and went away leaving him half dead. And by chance a priest was going down on that road, and when he saw them, he passed by on the other side. Likewise a Levite also, when he came to the place and saw him, passed by on the other side. But a Samaritan, who was on a journey, came upon him; and when he saw him, he felt compassion, and came to him and bandaged up his wounds, pouring oil and wine on them; and he put him on his own beast, and brought him to an inn and took care of him.
>
> "On the next day he took out two denarii and gave them to the innkeeper and said, 'Take care of him; and whatever more you spend, when I return I will repay you.'
>
> "Which of these three do you think proved to be a neighbor to the man who fell into the robbers' hands?"
>
> And he said, "The one who showed mercy toward him."
>
> Then Jesus said to him, "Go and do the same."
>
> Luke 10:29-37

The second parable is about the Good Shepherd:

> And Jesus said, "For judgment I came into this world, so that those who do not see may see, and that those who see may become blind."
>
> Those of the Pharisees who were with him heard these things and said to him, "We are not blind too, are we?"
>
> Jesus said to them, "If you were blind, you would have no sin; but since you say, 'We see,' your sin remains. Truly, truly, I say to you, the person who

does not enter by the door into the fold of the sheep, but climbs up some other way, that person is a thief and a robber. But the person who enters by the door is a shepherd of the sheep. To that person the doorkeeper opens, and the sheep hear the shepherd's voice, and the shepherd calls the sheep by name and leads them out. A stranger they simply will not follow, but will flee from the stranger, because they do not know the voice of strangers."

This figure of speech Jesus spoke to them, but they did not understand what those things were which he had been saying to them.

So Jesus said to them again, "Truly, truly, I say to you, I am the door of the sheep. All who came before me are thieves and robbers, but the sheep did not hear them. I am the door; if anyone enters through me, that person will be saved, and will go in and out and find pasture. The thief comes only to steal and kill and destroy; I came that they may have life, and have it abundantly. I am the good shepherd; the good shepherd lays down life for the sheep. A person who is not a shepherd, who is not the owner of the sheep, sees the wolf coming, and leaves the sheep and flees, and the wolf snatches them and scatters them. The hired hand flees because the hired hand is a hired hand and is not concerned about the sheep. I am the good shepherd, and I know my own and my own know me, even as God knows me and I know God; and I lay down my life for the sheep. I have other sheep, which are not of this fold; I must bring them also, and they will hear my voice; and they will become one flock with one shepherd. For this reason God loves me, because I lay down my life so that I may take it again. No one has taken it away from me, but I lay it down on my own initiative. I have authority to lay it down, and I have authority to take it up again. This commandment I received from God."

John 10:1-17

In the first parable, extreme hatred—that of Jew for Samaritan or Samaritan for Jew—offers a foil for the love shown by an individual regardless of that person's ancient traditions of hatred. Context of the story is that Jews looked upon Samaritans as schismatics, and Samaritans saw Jews as religious oppressors. Samaritans had desecrated the Jerusalem temple of the Jews, dumping the bones of the dead there. Jews had destroyed the Samaritan temple on Mount Gerazim. Sometimes the adversaries would even kill one another on sight. In such an environment of deadly antipathy, Jesus the Jew taught his parable, and in his glory on the cross, Jesus became the Good Samaritan. By suffering to the extreme on the cross, Jesus redeemed the recalcitrant world from extreme suffering.

In the parable, brigands have robbed and beaten an unfortunate Jew, leaving him bleeding and half dead. Two Jewish religious functionaries, a priest and a Levite, see the victim and pass by. They do more than refuse to help him; they cross to the other side of the road and walk quickly away. A Samaritan, however, moved to compassion, tends to the poor man's wounds, takes him to an inn, and risks his own reputation with friends and family in order to save a Jew's life.

As for the Good Shepherd at John 10:1-18, the good shepherd lays down life for the sheep. In a sudden plunge of meaning, it becomes clear that the thief, wolf, and hireling personify the sheep because we are all thieves, wolves, and hirelings before Jesus, the Good Shepherd who died for us. Hebrew scripture offers:

> They have all turned aside, together they have become corrupt; there is no one who does good, not even one.
>
> Psalm 14:3-4

We were the scourge of the sheep fold, even killing the Good Shepherd by crucifying Jesus. Again, Hebrew scripture:

> Because he poured out himself to death and was numbered with the transgressors; yet he himself bore the sin of many, and interceded for the transgressors.
>
> Isaiah 53:12

Ironically, we do not often identify our actual enemies. They are not the people the empire encourages us to fear and hate, the people demonized in the empire's propaganda and the public relations vehicles of the weapons trade. Our real enemies are those who do us spiritual or physical harm or threaten to do so consciously or unconsciously. We can list enemies, beginning with the false self as Number 1 enemy, even as the Gospel does:

> If anyone wishes to come after me, that person must deny self and take up the cross and follow me.
>
> Mark 8:34

The false self exposes itself by anything not compassionate and just: egotism, greed, arrogance, bellicosity, racism, sexism. The false self prevents any acceptance of the cross and, thus, any struggle for liberation.

Other enemies are high officials of the empire: the president, vice-president, secretary of state, secretary of defense (who should be called secretary of war), joint chiefs of staff, the nuclear war-fighting party (the old Reaganite Committee on Present Danger)—all those who, under the figments of deterrence and national security, threaten humankind and the planet with the bomb. They are the "blind leading the blind" and have done more than threaten us with doomsday scenarios. They have, with devilish ingenuity, finessed us into paying with our tax dollars for the prospect of our own destruction.

Next on the list of enemies are the CEOs and executives of the war-making corporations like Lockheed Martin, Boeing, Northrop Grumman, Raytheon, TRW, and General Dynamics.

Politicians, generals, and arms dealers who strew the planet with terror, destruction, and death are the enemies of humanity, even though the emperor insists that the North Koreans, Iraqis, Iranians, Libyans, Cubans, and Serbs are the enemies. We are instead enjoined to love all people, even as God does:

> You have heard that it was said, "You shall love your neighbor and hate your enemy." But I say to you, love your enemies and pray for those who persecute you, so that you may be children of God who is in heaven; for God causes the sun to rise on the evil and the good, and sends rain on the righteous and the unrighteous. For if you love those who love you, what reward do you have? Do not even the tax collectors do the same? If you greet only your family, what more are you doing than others? Do not even unbelievers do the same? Therefore you are to be perfect, as your heavenly Parent is perfect.
>
> Matthew 5:43-48

The empire's own representatives may be startled by this concept of love. For example, twice during demonstrations at the White House when we were planning to pour blood on the pillars of the emperor's residence, Secret Service agents interrogated me. "Do you intend to harm the president?" they asked me.

"Of course not," I answered. "Christ requires that I love everyone." I did not try to explain that, while I view the emperor as the enemy of peace and social justice here and abroad, it doesn't mean that I wish to harm him. Nor would I do anything to injure the men and women who devote their lives to protecting the emperor.

I recall A. J. Muste's remark: "If I can't love Hitler, I am no Christian!" But how can we bring ourselves to love a mass murderer like Adolph Hitler or, closer to home, an emperor who lives in regal splendor while, just down the street, children live in rat-infested tenements, attend segregated schools, and go to bed hungry every night? How might we go about loving an emperor who professes love for children while condemning millions of young people, here and abroad, to a lifetime of hunger and misery? How can we love an emperor who talks endlessly about peace and social justice while supporting a new round of designing, building, testing, and using nuclear weapons?

We must love the emperor by exposing him through nonviolent civil resistance. We must love him by exposing him and the nuclear priesthood. That is the answer of the Plowshares folks, and that is my answer. We must cry out, loudly and clearly, that the emperor and his mighty army are preparing, every single day, for wars of mass destruction. We must tell all the world that more than a million and a half Iraqi children have died as the result of the emperor's Iraqi massacres, that high in the mountains of Guatemala the Mayan people are digging up remains of loved ones killed by United States-trained and United States-funded soldiers, that children of Nicaragua, hungry and ragged, rummage in garbage dumps because the emperor waged war against the Nicaraguan people.

Through civil resistance, like Jesus on the cross expiating our sins, we repent of the emperor's sins, take them as our own, take stock in our commitment to justice, and resolve to continue the struggle to love our enemies now and as long as we live. Through civil resistance, we enact our love for those who would tap our phones, intercept our mail, try us in kangaroo courts, and sentence us to prison. We thus demonstrate that Jesus did not offer us pleasant slogans but challenges that are sometimes painful, difficult, and even frightening to accept.

We are human beings, not saints, we Plowshares people. We know how easy it would be to succumb to bitterness and anger, to hate our enemies, and to curse those who persecute us. We are trying to live, to practice our belief that justice begins in our own hearts, that love is the measure of our own strengths and weaknesses, that while we are not perfect, we can and must live what we contend is true: that love is more powerful, more lasting, and more healing than hate.

Our models for love and compassion are the Good Shepherd and the Good Samaritan. May we honor them by remembering to be like them in all our actions as we cite the real enemies of the people and bring our civil resistance to the empire's bastions.

Chapter 3
They Will Hand You Over to Courts: Confronting Imperial Injustice

We Stand In Two Courts

by Susan Crane

Everyone who confesses me before others, I will also confess that person before my heavenly Parent. But whoever denies me before others, I will deny before my heavenly Parent.

Matthew 10:32-33

Jesus told his disciples they would be persecuted and handed over to courts to be denounced, insulted, and humiliated in front of leaders of state and state-sanctioned religion. Going on trial is a test of the disciple, just as it was in Jesus's time. God judges us according to our fidelity. We are challenged to be faithful in our actions and in our words, in all aspects of our lives, and that must include when we are tried before the powers of the state.

To be faithful in court, we need to understand just how the empire uses judges, lawyers, bailiffs, police, and federal marshals to perpetuate and legitimate violence and injustice. The courts are the yardstick, that is to say a measure of our contradictory and troubled society. In the courtroom, with all its contrived splendor—flags, proclamations, judges in flowing robes—one sees quite clearly that the laws of the state have little or nothing to do with justice. We see collusion between the courts and the powerful, and we witness time and again the myriad ways in which the judicial system is used to brutalize the poor, protect the rich, and perpetuate the empire's pathological violence.

The courts are not rooted in justice or mercy; they oppress the poor, protect weapons of mass destruction and condemn the peacemakers. Just looking around me in jail, I see women who are held for days on a twenty-five dollar bail, or for month after month on a $2,500 bail. While you are in jail, you can't do the normal things that would help your defense. Women are held in jail because their partners battered them, or because they are making a living in ways that our culture considers illegal, or because they themselves are considered "illegal." Poor women with addictions go to jail; women who have money go to a private rehab center and, thereby, bypass the "justice" system.

In the United States of America, there are nearly two million people in prisons or jails, the highest per capita ratio of any country in the industrialized world, with the possible exception of Russia. Most of the inmates are people of color. Most are poor and lack a formal education. Collusion between large drug dealers and the United States government has been well documented. The rich launder money and escape capture while the poor sell drugs on the street. Government officials invest in well-disguised schemes to make fortunes from cocaine, while the poor get sentenced to ten years in prison for trying to pass a minuscule amount of crack to an undercover agent. Meanwhile, white collar crimes—poisoning Mother Earth, exploiting and destroying the world's natural resources, clear cutting our forests, killing off entire species—are more often rewarded than punished. Building weapons that threaten to destroy the earth is considered heroic, or at the very least, gainful employment. Each and every day, year in, year out, the defense department, which we should call the war department, violates international law, yet no one from the Pentagon is hauled into the empire's courts, to be charged with a crime and sentenced to prison.

Ironically, the courts resemble churches and law is treated as sacred within such state-holy settings. Violence against prisoners is not only sanctioned but considered proper and morally right. Sadly, I've observed that even the more compassionate guards relish the chance to participate in violence against prisoners. Perhaps it helps explain why, though I have been in court many times, my guts churn each time I am led before guardians of the empire. Nevertheless, it is in the courtroom that we are given the opportunity to acknowledge God before others, to talk without shame about why we disarmed and converted weapons. When we go on trial, we are not alone. We have an advocate, the Holy Spirit, who helps us and stays with us, and we have the spirit of truth that acts as our defense lawyer.

Scripture describes two simultaneous courts, one earthly, the other heavenly. The outcome in the heavenly court depends on our faithfulness in the earthly court. In the earthly court, we refuse to renounce our witness by pleading guilty, nor do we feel ashamed of our actions, which we know to be based on love. We cannot agree to refrain from acting in the name of love to end the empire's race toward Armageddon, and we will never agree to pay "restitution" that will go to rebuilding or repairing weapons.

If the action reflects our faith, then it is important that we continue that faith in the empire's courtrooms and jails. We seek to speak truth to power in the courtroom and to set forth our motives, ideals, and faith, as clearly and honestly as we possibly can. We seek to speak truth to power so that judge and jury have the opportunity to know us not as saints or martyrs but as fathers and mothers, brothers and sisters, neighbors and friends, as human beings who act not out of malice or hate, but from a deep sense of love for our fellow human beings and for Mother Earth. At stake is our freedom and our integrity, neither of which the empire, though it might lock us away in cages, can ever take away.

Steven Baggarly put it beautifully when he told the court we are speaking for those whose faces we will never see, whose voices we will never hear, and whose screams we will never experience. He was speaking about the victims, past, present, and future of nuclear madness. He was speaking about the millions who have died from the effects of atomic testing, those who will die from atomic isotopes that have permeated our air, our food, and our water supply, and those who will die when the empire releases its atomic arsenal at one of its many enemies.

On the day of our trial, we rise early. The marshals shackle and chain us for the trip to the Portland Federal Building. I look around at my codefendants, who are all in good spirits. We approach the court as a community, acting and speaking for each other. We have chosen to represent ourselves, and we also have good legal advisers. We want to speak from our hearts and reveal the true nature of the court. We don't want to be bound by the rules lawyers have to follow. We want to press and probe, to speak the unspeakable. We know in our hearts that we are innocent, and we are certain the court will find us guilty.

We want to speak about international law and the Nuremberg Principles. Before the trial begins, Judge Carter disallows the defenses. We understand his position because other federal judges have acted in the same way, protecting the empire against the interests of ordinary people. Other judges have gagged defendants, finding them in contempt when they try to explain why they hammered on or poured blood over weapons. But we are Plowshares activists, not lawyers. We are not bound by the rules of Judge Carter's court. We are not "contemptuous" when we speak about God's love, the peril of atomic weapons, or the necessity to transform the empire into a place where the hungry are fed, the naked are clothed, and the homeless are housed.

Community is vitally important when we are going to trial. We work together, remembering our agreements, honoring our commitment to one another. Still, it is difficult to sit quietly in the courtroom, listening to the empire distort our motives, insult our integrity, and obscure the moral and legal issues about which not only this court, but the world's courts, ought to be talking. When I ask one navy witness if he has ever observed a Tomahawk or any other missile launched from his ship or whether he has viewed photographs of what the missiles really do to human flesh, Judge Carter points at me. "Now stop that," he shouts. "And sit down!"

It is difficult to back down from confrontations with the judge, because he must know, as Plowshares activists do, that treaties the United States signs and Congress ratifies become the supreme law of the land. According to the second paragraph of Article 6 of the Constitution, judges in every state are bound by such treaties. Yet, in Judge Carter's courtroom, we are not allowed to talk to the jury about laws which our own nation is obligated to obey.

The United Nations Charter prohibits crimes against peace. The Nuremberg Principles, which United States judges have used to try war criminals in other countries, prohibit weapons of mass destruction, wanton destruction of cities, villages and towns, inhuman acts against civilian populations. The Nuremberg Principles clearly and unequivocally state that obeying orders does not free anyone from personal responsibility for crimes against humanity. International law and the Nuremberg Principles not only give citizens the right to resist war and preparations for state-sponsored mass murder, they obligate us to take a stand, obligate us to refuse to pay for atomic weapons, obligate us to break laws that support the empire's plans to slaughter millions of our fellow human beings.

As the trial continues, in Judge Carter's courtroom and in our hearts, we remember Paul Miki, Franz Jaegersteatter, and Eleazar, all martyrs to the state. Our heroes and role models do what is good and truthful. They don't try to get out of consequences by tactical reasoning. They go to trial, to prison, and to their deaths speaking truth to power, asking only that the killing of the innocents stop.

At some point, we must call this charade to a halt. We must say "enough" to Judge Carter and the empire on whose behalf he seeks to send us to prison. When he refuses to allow Peter Weiss, our expert witness, to testify, we stand together with our backs to the court. In one terse sentence, Philip Berrigan explains our actions. "We will not participate," he says, "in this kangaroo court." With our backs to the judge, we read sections from scripture that have influenced us to act:

> You have heard that it was said, "You shall love your neighbor and hate your enemy." But I say to you, "Love your enemies and pray for those who prosecute you, that you may be children of your heavenly Parent, for he makes his sun rise on the bad and the good and causes rain to fall on the just and unjust. For if you love those who love you, what recompense will you have? Do not the politicians do the same? And if you greet your sisters and brothers only, what is unusual about that? Do not the stockholders do the same? So be perfect as your God is perfect."
>
> Matthew: 5:43-48

This is my commandment; love one another as I love you. No one has greater love than this, to lay down one's life for one's friends. You are my friends if you do what I command you. I no longer call you slaves, because a slave does not know what one's master is doing. I have called you friends because I have told you everything. I have heard from my Parent.

John 15:12-17

Marshals cuff us and remove us from the courtroom where our supporters are risking arrest by shouting: "Thou shall not kill!" They, too, are removed from the courtroom. The trial continues and we watch on a television monitor from a holding cell. The jury leaves and returns with one question: "Can the jury consider the fairness of the trial?" They do not ask about atomic weapons, international law, God's law, conscience, or what it means to be human. The empire's verdict is swift and absolutely no surprise: guilty as charged.

Our friend Jim Reale climbs the front of the federal building, stands on the portico and unfurls our Plowshares banner. How does God see us? How does God view Judge Carter and the jury? How does God see the empire's quest to keep the world in a constant state of nuclear terror? We have tried to be faithful to our belief in justice for all, not merely for the wealthy and powerful. We have acted on our conscience, knowing that the days ahead may prove difficult for ourselves, our friends, and our families. Prison is not where we wish to be. It is simply the price of acting out the words of beating swords into plowshares.

Moving from the Edge of the Abyss

by Steven Baggarly

words from his statement to the court at sentencing

During the Prince of Peace Plowshares trial in May, the United States federal judiciary, on behalf of the federal government, again asserted the legality of nuclear weapons, thereby upholding the death sentence it has long since passed on the entire world.

For more than fifty years, humankind has been condemned to live with the constant danger of nuclear war, accidental nuclear detonation and unauthorized launches, as well as the devastating effects of nuclear testing, uranium mining, and nuclear waste contamination. More than thirty times the planet has come within moments of a general launching of nuclear missiles. Terror, cancer, the squandering of vast human and material resources (some five and one-half trillion dollars, and counting) and an umbrella for countless military interventions worldwide, have been the rewards of the United States nuclear weapons program and United States nuclear policy. In this courtroom again today, everyone present, along with the rest of the human family, will be sentenced to life on a nuclear death row, with no stay of execution in sight, and the sentence only a hair trigger from imposition.

So I think of my son, Daniel, 6, my three-year-old niece, Hannah, my two-year-old nephew, Jesse, who is due to become a big brother today, and Rachel, 3, whose mom is in prison in Florida for a Plowshares action. I think of the kids in the Norfolk, Virginia, ghetto where I live—Antonio, Peaches, Marvin, Shalita, and Vernon Augustus.

I think of my grandmother and grandfather who have both moved into a nursing home since I've been in Cumberland County Jail. Though their bodies and minds have begun to betray them, they continue to be anchors for my soul.

I think of my spouse, Kim, with whom sharing life most closely has been a profound gift and a great joy. Living at Catholic Worker houses together for ten years now, we count scores of formerly homeless people we've had the privilege to live with as our family also—Julius, Conchita, Richard, Edwin, Maria, Marta, Stephen, Colette, Michael, and Eric—I could go on.

I name these people as they all are targeted by nuclear weapons and live their lives under sentence of death. All of them, and many more, bring me here. They are a part of me, and I carried them with me on Ash Wednesday morning aboard the USS *The Sullivans* as I helped begin the crucial work of converting swords into plowshares. For me, they are living proof that *all* people are made in the image and likeness of God, that all five billion of us on this planet share one nature, and that *The Sullivans'* sole purpose is to terrorize, torture, and burn to death people just like them around the world—from infants to elders.

Aegis missile destroyers built at Bath Iron Works are integral to United States global supremacy, whether as protection for carrier battle groups or as land attack or nuclear platforms. Among their armaments, they can each carry fifty Tomahawk cruise missiles, which have a range up to two thousand miles, and can be fitted with one-thousand-pound conventional warheads, scores of heinous cluster bombs, or two-hundred-kiloton W-80 nuclear warheads.

The next echelon of the conspiracy is the war department. It pieces together the weaponry, personnel, infrastructure, and propaganda necessary for first-strike nuclear war. Joint chiefs of staff are at the top of the pyramid; at the head, the secretary of war.

The ringleader of the nuclear strike force resides in the White House. He bears the gravest responsibility, as commander-in-chief, for this vast criminal enterprise, including all United States war industries and military bases around the world, which daily robs the poor, plunders and poisons the earth, and threatens to destroy all life on the planet.

Finally, it is courtrooms like this one which are linchpins holding the entire nuclear war-making conspiracy together. The judicial branch serves as the legitimizing agent for omnicide; the weapons are impenetrably protected by the hedge of law.

But the good news is that we do not *have* to live on the edge of the abyss. God assures us that this earth *can* become a sisterhood and brotherhood, that injustice *may* be undone, that domination *can* come to an end, that violence and hunger *can* become relics of the past, that we can all help God build a world devoid of swords and with Plowshares aplenty, a world worthy of its children.

Jesus assures us that what is done to poor and suffering people, to children, and to the enemy is done directly to him—that how we treat others is how we treat God. Yet, in this century, over two hundred million people have been killed in wars, more than in all of previous history, and hundreds of millions more have been maimed, raped, tortured, orphaned, or driven mad in the same wars. For half a century, we've lived on the nuclear precipice. Meanwhile, 1.3 billion people today don't have what they need to survive—enough food, water, or simple medical care. Eight hundred and fifty million of these go hungry. Each and every minute, world militaries spend $1.7 million while thirty children starve to death. In this courtroom today, the world is sentenced to more of the same.

Though the powers again have ruled *for* swords and *against* plowshares, the Hebrew prophets were right: there is *nothing* so urgent as beating of *all* swords into plowshares and the unlearning of war. Nothing is as vital as weapons of mass destruction, like the USS *The Sullivans*, being remade into tools beneficial to a blood-soaked, starving and desperate humanity. Nuclear weapons are history's greatest technological evil, the ultimate incarnation of imperial arrogance. Yet, even their disarmament is not difficult. The need is as real as the faces of those we love. And anyone can begin it with a single hammer blow.

Supporting the Prince of Peace Plowshares

by Mary Donnelly

Maine peace activists from many organizations offered support for the Prince of Peace Plowshares as soon as they knew about the action and through the trial, sentencing, and jailing. Mary Donnelly coordinated support efforts.

Seeds for support and organizing for their trial and subsequent sentencing began immediately after the Prince of Peace Plowshares action of Ash Wednesday, February 12, 1997, at Bath Iron Works, Bath, Maine.

Activists within and outside Maine came forth, encouraging individuals and social justice groups to get involved. An extemporaneous framework of communications emerged among supporters visiting Susan Crane and Steven Kelly at the Cumberland County Jail in Portland, Maine. In relation to previous disarmament witnesses in California, authorities held Susan and Steve at the Cumberland

County Jail after Bath police released the other Prince of Peace Plow-shares, Thomas Lewis-Borbely, Mark Colville, Steven Baggarly, and Philip Berrigan. Within days of their release, however, warrants were issued for their arrests. Aware that arrest warrants were issued, the four returned to Maine on February 25, 1997, with members of the extended Plowshares community to attend a mass at the Sacred Heart Church in Portland. The Prince of Peace Plowshares then traveled to Bath joined by supporters and the press for their arrest by the Bath police. The four were taken to Cumberland County Jail.

Two members of the extended Plowshares community, Ardeth Platte, OP, and Carol Gilbert, OP, both Dominican nuns who have themselves done Plowshares work and were living at Jonah House in Baltimore, remained in Portland. They began organizing Prince of Peace Plowshares support for the traditional Festival of Hope and upcoming trial and sentencing. Maine Veterans for Peace offered free office space and telephone in Portland for the initial organiz-ing. After long hours of work, Ardeth and Carol compiled a list of Plowshares supporters. Mailings to them contained information about the Prince of Peace Plowshares action and requested support. They left behind extensive information on resources from the Plow-shares community and outlined tasks for preparation of the Festival of Hope and support for the trial and sentencing. I was asked to take responsibility for organizing and my husband Mike was asked to be treasurer. Our efforts led to the formation of the Maine Plowshares Support Group.

Jail Visits

Scheduling visits for Plowshares families, supporters, and the me-dia took some coordination, as family visits came first. After becom-ing familiar with jail rules (always subject to change) and individual visiting hours for the six Prince of Peace Plowshares, I set up weekly and monthly charts to schedule visits. Families and friends called to sign up for visits at the jail. Many people, including journalists and television crews, had never visited a jail, and I spent much time walking people through the steps of jail rules, and how and when they could visit. This was no easy task because the jail administrator inconsistently applied rules and often changed rules without no-tice. Much of my time was on the telephone talking to the jail ad-ministrator to confirm and challenge stated jail rules and policy. People swarmed to the jail.

Communication with Prince of Peace Plowshares, families, and the extended Plowshares community took on many forms. News articles from newspapers and magazines pertaining to their action and arrest were clipped and sent to Prince of Peace Plowshares in jail, to their families, and to the extended Plowshares community. The Prince of Peace Plowshares were prolific writers. People took on tasks of typing their writing, contacting the press, and circulating their articles in several Maine newspapers and beyond. During the Lenten season, each Prince of Peace Plowshares wrote a series entitled "Letters from the Cumberland County Jail" for each Sunday in Lent reflecting on the Gospels' call to nonviolence and for peace. Pax Christi typed and mailed those letters to hundreds of churches and synagogues throughout Maine. Copies of all articles and letters were forwarded to Prince of Peace Plowshares, their families, and the extended Plowshares community. As writings appeared in newspapers and publications outside Maine, Plowshares supporters would send them to me. I made copies and moved them on to the extended community.

If the Prince of Peace Plowshares wanted to pass on information, needed information, or requested money for personal needs, they would call collect. I had daily conversations with the extended Prince of Peace Plowshares communities, supporters and legal advisers, keeping them informed of what was happening and asking for their input. Keeping communications open between the Prince of Peace Plowshares and the extended community meant that everyone received the same clear and up-to-date information. Otherwise, rumors and myths abounded. As the time of the Prince of Peace Plowshares trial and sentencing drew near, much effort went into obtaining reliable information from the lawyers and courts. Passing that information on to families and outside community was essential.

Resources and Donations

The key to organizing and getting people involved was maintaining an up-to-date list of supporters willing to do specific short and long term tasks. This database list constantly grew through the time the Prince of Peace Plowshares were in jail until their sentencing. I matched travelers arriving from a distance with supporters identified on the database as able to provide hospitality. Telephone trees were compiled by the Plowshares support group, and mailing addresses were generated from the database for news updates including announcements of trial dates, often with less than a week notice. As donations of money were received for Prince of Peace Plowshares support, I would add names to the database, deposit checks and write thank yous.

Festival of Hope

The Festival of Hope is a celebration the evening before the trial. Plowshares supporters from afar, as well as local people, gather to socialize and speak of resistance to warmaking and militarism. Three weeks before the Festival of Hope, a flyer giving the date, schedule, and map was sent to everyone on the database list. Peacemakers came together to celebrate with food, speakers, and music and to plan actions and activities to take place during the following days of the trial. It was also a time to discuss the logistics of how to move between two hundred and three hundred people in and out of the courtroom in some orderly manner. The Festival of Hope in Portland was organized by Pax Christi with support from the Maine Plowshares Support Group and others. It was held at the Woodfords Congregational Church, Portland. The Plowshares support group organized committees for food, hospitality, and program. More than two hundred people needed hospitality and food for the evening and for the days that followed. The hospitality committee arranged churches and private homes to accommodate them all.

Trial and Sentencing

The original date, May 5, 1997, set by the federal court for the Prince of Peace Plowshares trial never changed. That made it easier to organize the Festival of Hope the evening before and to plan activities for the trial. The culmination of all the previous organizing paid off as time came closer to the trial. We had lists of supporters and individuals with specific knowledge of previous trials, international law, and the necessity defense whom I could call upon when the Prince of Peace Plowshares requested information. The Maine Plowshares Support Group, including members of Peace Action Maine, Veterans for Peace, Women's International League for Peace and Freedom, Pax Christi, and others organized several activities outside the federal courthouse in Portland. I sent New England and Maine newspapers, Associated Press, alternative publications, and television and radio stations press releases with a follow-up telephone call, notifying them of the Prince of Peace Plowshares trial. As time got closer to the trial and the Prince of Peace Plowshares were developing their defense, we made calls to their legal advisers to arrange for their meeting together.

United States marshals requested a meeting with the Plowshares support group several days before the trial. The marshals were limiting attendance in the courtroom and wanted to assign a United States marshal to me (which I turned down). The marshals made it clear at the meeting that they would allow sixty people plus journalists in the courtroom during the trial. Subsequently, Plowshares organizers developed a fair plan to give as many people as possible time in the courtroom. As the trial progressed, the court rules changed and security became tighter. The marshals allowed only thirty instead of the promised sixty, and the courtroom was only half filled throughout the trial. People waited outside the courthouse for hours in bitter wind and cold reading Nuremberg Principles, circling the court with crime-scene tape, chanting, and drumming. Following the verdict of guilty for the six Prince of Peace Plowshares, police arrested fourteen people for acts of civil resistance both at the courthouse and the Bath Iron Works facility in Portland.

The wait for sentencing stretched from May to October 1998. The Plowshares support group organized activities for sentencing. The activities included a ceremonial march from the cathedral to the courthouse, readings from the trial of the Catonsville Nine, and wrapping the courthouse with crime scene yellow tape. Weekly vigils by the Maine Plowshares Support Group protesting Aegis Destroyers started at Bath Iron Works, Portland. Pax Christi, Maine, held their annual award dinner and honored the Prince of Peace Plowshares. Coordinating jail visits continued. Copying and distributing news articles and Prince of Peace Plowshares writings from jail continued. However, organizing for the sentencing itself was difficult because the court decided to hold an evidentiary hearing to establish damages and then divide the Prince of Peace Plowshares into two separate sentencing dates. The court announced multiple court dates with a minimum of notice, but I was able to notify the extended Plowshares community quickly by post cards and by telephone-tree calls. The turnout was large, and planned actions were successful. Following sentencing, police arrested several supporters for blocking the main gate at Bath Iron Works, Portland.

Plowshares Legacy in Maine

The Maine Plowshares Support Group continues to meet long after the Prince of Peace Plowshares left Maine and served their prison sentences. Support for the Prince of Peace Plowshares continues through individual correspondence and at probation violation hearings. However, the group directs support to its members in new acts of resistance. The group is currently protesting the sanctions and bombing of Iraq, the continued manufacture of land mines, the bombing of Kosovo, and, sadly, more launchings of Aegis destroyers at Bath Iron Works. The group acts independently but in concert with other local peace organizations. Activists in the group include members of other peace organizations including but not limited to Veterans for Peace, Peace Action Maine, Pax Christi, and WILPF.

Chapter 4

Take Up Your Cross and Follow Me:
The Cost of Waging Peace inside the Empire

by Mark Colville

Jesus sent out these twelve after instructing them thus, "Do not go into pagan territory or enter a Samaritan town. Go rather to the lost sheep of the house of Israel. As you go, make this proclamation: 'The kindom of heaven is at hand.' Cure the sick, raise the dead, cleanse lepers, drive out demons. Without cost you have received; without cost you are to give.

"Do not take gold or silver or copper for your belts; no sack for the journey, or a second tunic, or sandals, or walking stick. The laborer deserves one's keep.

"Whatever town or village you enter, look for a worthy person in it, and stay there until you leave. As you enter a house, wish it peace. If the house is worthy, let your peace come upon it; if not, let your peace return to you.

"Whoever will not receive you or listen to your words—go outside that house or town and shake the dust from your feet.

"Amen, I say to you, it will be more tolerable for the land of Sodom and Gomorrah on the day of judgment than for that town.

"Behold, I am sending you like sheep in the midst of wolves; so be shrewd as serpents and simple as doves. But beware of people, for they will hand you over to courts and scourge you in their synagogues, and you will be led before governors and kings for my sake as a witness before them and the pagans. When they hand you over, do not worry about how you are to speak or what you are to say. You will be given at that moment what you are to say. For it will not be you who speak but the Spirit of God speaking through you.

"Brother will hand over brother to death, and the parent the child; children will rise up against parents and have them put to death. You will be hated by all because of my name, but whoever endures to the end will be saved. When they persecute you in one town, flee to another. Amen, I say to you, you will not finish the towns of Israel before the Human One comes. No disciple is above the teacher, no slave above the master. If they have called the master of the house Beelzebul, how much more those of his household!"

Matthew 10:5-25

Jesus subjects the disciples to a much-needed reality check at Matthew 10. They are about to go into the world and engage it in the same way that Christ himself does: by confronting evil, casting out demons, living voluntarily poor and in community, bringing wholeness and healing into situations of brokenness and alienation. And what will be the result? They will be rejected, hauled into courts and beaten, betrayed by their own families, and universally hated.

Whoever will not receive you or listen to your words—go outside that house or town and shake the dust from your feet.

Matthew 10:14

But beware of people, for they will hand you over to courts and scourge you in their synagogues.

Matthew 10:17

> *Brother will hand over brother to death, and the parent the child; children will rise up against parents and have them put to death.*
>
> Matthew 10:21

> *You will be hated by all because of my name, but whoever endures to the end will be saved.*
>
> Matthew 10:22

From experience, the disciple will become like the teacher.

Today, the arrogance of privilege and comfort is nowhere more evident than in the pervading cultural attitude that we can be disciples of Christ and avoid persecution. Eagerly we accept the title of believer but rarely if ever at the expense of our good names, relationships, comforts, security, investments, or personal control over the future. Yet Jesus demands that disciples risk their names, relationships, comforts, security, investments, and personal control over the future, including the willingness to lay down their lives.

John's Gospel repeats the comparison of disciple and teacher:

> *Amen, amen, I say to you, no slave is greater than the master nor any messenger greater than the one who dispatched the messenger.*
>
> John 13:16

> *Remember the word I spoke to you, "No slave is greater than the master." If they persecuted me, they will also persecute you. If they kept my word, they will also keep yours.*
>
> John 15:20

Both times, Jesus prepares his friends to follow him to the cross. Understood, the foot-washing episode of John 13 is more than an example of humility and service. It is an extension of burial preparation performed with expensive ointment at John 12:1-8 on Jesus by Mary of Magdala. When Jesus washes the disciples' feet, he is plainly commissioning them to resistance and martyrdom, even if they will not understand until after his own crucifixion.

Jesus our teacher lived his entire public life in direct, constant, nonviolent confrontation with the established order, and he made it clear that anyone who wished to follow him must do the same. Persecution is one of the proofs that we are engaging the world as disciples, which is to say that we are living in active resistance to the demons that enslave the world: violence, selfishness, greed, oppression, war. And resistance, along with its attendant sufferings, is not an optional commitment, not simply one choice among many in a life of faith. It *is* the life of faith, and to avoid it is to avoid discipleship.

If we understand, however, that persecution is part of the Christian baptismal commitment, it then becomes essential to realize that the rest of the commitment is to joy.

Blessed are they who are persecuted for the sake of righteousness, for theirs is the kindom of heaven.

Matthew 5:10

So asserts the seventh beatitude, and its acceptance as an article of faith is foundation to any sustained commitment to nonviolent resistance. When we suffer in defense of the poor, we become one with Christ, brothers and sisters of Christ, children of God, and this union is the very source of joy. It is with joy that we are to make a clean break with the values of the domination system described by Walter Wink in *Engaging the Powers*, to put our lives in hock for the purchase of the pearl of great price. We are called to live lives that make no sense apart from the seventh beatitude.

And when we are able to live in such a way, we discover that there can be no greater freedom than jail. To proclaim Christ in the United States today is to blaspheme against nuclearism, the state religion that demands that we place our faith in weapons of ultimate violence. United States nuclear policy has made it a crime to love our enemies, yet we live under the assumption that the kindom of God belongs to those persecuted for the sake of righteousness. Our resistance, then, is nothing other than an act of rejoicing, and the measure of its authenticity is found in the amount of joy, peace, and freedom emanating from our jail cells. Like the disciples themselves, we must go forth rejoicing that we are found worthy to suffer shame for the sake of the name.

So they left the presence of the Sanhedrin, rejoicing that they had been found worthy to suffer dishonor for the sake of the name.

Acts 5:41

No Gap between Word and Action

by Susan Crane

And the word became flesh and made dwelling among us, and we saw the glory, the glory as of God's only child, full of grace and truth.

John 1:14

The word, God's speech, becomes incarnate. There is no gap between word and action. Yet we creatures have trouble uniting words and actions. We even have trouble getting our thoughts and words to reflect the reality of the world we live in.

Just as a mother loves her children, our Creator loves all of us on earth. We are all interrelated, brother and sister, connected in spirit. Yet we consider some people or some nations our enemies. When we think of others as our enemies, our thoughts don't stand the test of reality. As a consequence, our view of reality will be distorted. We begin to think, "I'm first. I'm going to get mine even if I have to walk over others in the process." So the effect is that we live in a madhouse. Our sense of reality is distorted, and since we can only speak about what we know, our words don't describe reality. Our talk is a jumble. All of us today, including young people, have trouble with reality. We have no moral compunction: we can't discern right from wrong. People are brutalized more and more from the top, and an increasing number of people become poorer without medical care, food, or shelter. Our nation's first priority is the military. As we continue to talk peace and make more death-dealing weapons, we get more confused and have trouble adjusting our minds to reality. Many Americans live in a cultural Disneyland.

Even when we go to worship in a place of God, there is a gap between our words and our actions. We pray for peace while we are indifferent to our national priority, which is war. But we have to keep our job, support our children, pay the bills . . . or is there another way? What are our obligations as humans? We can't serve love and war. It seems that community may be the only way our worldly and spiritual obligations can be met. Being compliant with a war-making state can only lead to despair. But community offers a way out as we forge new relationships based on love instead of competition and money, and where there is freedom to experiment with enfleshing the Gospel message.

The word becomes flesh. Our thoughts guide our words, our words guide our actions. If I think uncharitable thoughts, the thoughts will leak out into my words and body language. If I speak poorly about someone, others hear and feel it is okay to denigrate or hurt that person. The attacker would feel my consent and social force behind the punch. The first step to making someone an enemy is to slander that person. For our actions to have their origins in goodness, our thoughts need to be good and not guided by envy, jealousy, greed, or revenge. Nonviolence must be a matter of thought so it will end in nonviolent action. No wonder that some of us take a year or more preparing for a Plowshares witness. We want to act from love, to be motivated by nonviolence, to put on the armor of Christ, which is to say, put on love. We also do not want to imply that we are succeeding more than others, but we are engaged, collectively, in the struggle.

One morning, I was talking to a guard in the Cumberland County Jail. A veteran and a printer by trade, he was a good churchgoing man. He had thought he was getting a job at the jail that would allow him to teach printing, but the print shop never opened. Separately, the man argues that abortion and euthanasia are wrong but he feels that if someone crosses onto his property and threatens his family or if a country threatens to "over charge" for oil, then violence—killing—is justified.

"I worked hard for my family, and I'm not going to let some other country hold them hostage and force us to pay nine dollars a gallon for gas," he said. It would probably have been irrelevant to him that residents of many other countries, including the United States allies in NATO, pay as much and more for gasoline.

A woman at the jail, another prisoner who identifies herself as an atheist, expressed her agreement with the guard. In their view of reality, there were two choices: kill others or invite others to invade your home and kill you. On a national level, either we attack other countries or we invite them to overrun us.

But don't we want to treat other people and countries the way we want to be treated? Would we want another country to dictate the price of the wheat, lumber, or weapons we export?

To defend our standard of living means to perpetuate the poverty around us. We have some responsibility for the ever-increasing chasm between the poor and wealthy. Statistics are familiar: thirty-five thousand children die from hunger each day. The richer one-fifth of the world's people have four-fifths of the total world's income, while the bottom three-fifths of the world's people receive less than six percent. Individually, fortunes of the wealthiest 350 or so people are equivalent to the combined revenues of countries with forty-five percent of the world's population.

In the United States, weapons manufacture and export constitutes a good hunk of our economic wealth. The United States has cornered considerably more than half of the global arms trade, and thus, according to the Pentagon, has a reason to use more money to develop newer weapons.

The weapons protect our wealth and at the same time constitute a larceny from the people of the world. Bishop Raymond Hunthausen of Seattle has made clear why we are so heavily armed:

> We have to begin by recognizing that our country's overwhelming array of nuclear arms has a very precise purpose: it is meant to protect our wealth. The United States is not illogical in amassing the most destructive weapons in history. We need them. We are the richest people in history.

In the jail, as in the world outside, force and violence rule. The ideas of nonviolent defense, of living simply, or loving our neighbors appear foolish and naive. The values of the world, the jail guard and the prisoner, believer and atheist, find common ground: it is okay to kill.

And yet, the commandment remains: no killing, and the new commandment of Jesus remains: to love each other as brothers and sisters, to love regardless of the consequences, to love without limits. Such love is disarming. The challenge is to have it in our hearts and speak it in our words. The challenge is to put our words into practice.

Christ—and Everything Else

by Philip Berrigan

If God is for us, who can be against us—God who did not spare God's own son, but handed him over for us all, how will God not give us everything else along with him?

Romans 8:31

Somebody sent me a letter to the editor from a critic. This was the gist of the letter, as I recall: "Who gave you people a pipeline to God? History is full of the likes of you, whackos and fanatics who say they have a handle on God's will. To me, you're a group of hysterics and neurotics. Who says you can make your own laws? Who says you know better than the government?" And so on. The author wrote from Dover, New Hampshire.

I gave the letter some thought, because our friend had a valid concern or two. History is indeed full of religious zealots and ersatz prophets who claimed to be commissioned by God and to personify God's will. Such delusionaries have left their bloody footprints on continents, their victims numbered in the millions. Consider the Crusades, the Inquisition, the Thirty Years War—no fanatic like a religious fanatic.

Criticism today, however, is usually more temperate, ranging from uneasiness over "destruction of property" to the fear that the next step after attacks on war materiel is assault on military personnel. In other words, critics suggest that other protesters might learn from a Plowshares action done on an Aegis war ship and repeat the action; in the critics' mind, it would not be a good thing. Indeed, some critics go further to imply, protesters might board the ship and shoot young sailors in the name of disarmament, and that, of course, would not be a good thing. In fact, it is preposterous to imagine that non-violent activists would shoot young sailors.

We can neither anticipate nor prevent such wild scenarios, but we cannot stop Plowshares actions because of the possibility of mis-interpretation.

Disarmament is too critically needed for us to stop Plowshares actions. However, classifying us with fanatics and terrorists over-looks several factors. We have sought the will of God by accepting the nonviolent authority of the scripture, especially at Isaiah 2:4 and Matthew 5:44. Plowshares activists have distinguished conver-sion of war materiel from vandalism or maximum destruction pre-cisely because war materiel is the source of killing. It is analogous to Jesus overturning the moneylenders' tables in the temple. Likewise, we have resolved to stop a Plowshares rather than harm any person because every person is the image of God. We have tried to follow the nonviolent Christ and his command to disarm our hearts as well as our weapons.

Perhaps such efforts will satisfy our critic. If they don't, we can only advise continued study of the matter—and prayer.

Early in John's Gospel, at John 3:16, the community marvels over God's love of the "world"—Creation and its people. And Isaiah's God suffers with the desire to do more and more for the world:

> *What more was there to do for my vineyard that I had not done?*
>
> Isaiah 5:4

God loved us and the universe enough to become exhausted in the excruciating death of God's son. To this, Paul adds "everything else" besides. If God exhausted generosity by giving the son to die for us, will not God give us "everything else" as well? Paul asks the question. In the great gift of changing us for the better and turning the course of history—what of "everything else?"

Like Peter, we are eager to add, subtract, and tote everything up, to hold God to promises.

> *Amen I say to you, there is no one who has given up house or sisters or brothers or mother or father or children or lands for my sake and the sake of the Gospel, who will not receive a hundred times more now in this present age, houses and sisters and brothers and mothers and children and lands, with persecutions, and eternal life in the age to come.*
>
> Mark 10:29, 30

What's in it for me? There's a time-honored American question. Nonetheless, awareness of the "hundredfold" might inspire thanks-giving, might bring us to our knees in gratitude. Has God not given us life, denied to so many potential billions? Has God not given us a second birth in God as daughters and sons of God? Has God not given us the Holy Spirit, to teach us the life of Jesus Christ? Has God not given us God's word in the scripture—

a lamp for my feet and a light for my path?

Psalm 119:105

Despite all the distortion of the churches, has God not given us faith that is slowly creating a new order of nonviolence, justice, and peace? Has God not given each of us a unique personality, unrepeatable in the five and a half billion people on earth? Has God not given each of us the magnificence of Creation, including a hundred billion galaxies across three hundred billion billion light years of expanding space? Has not God given us the best of friends, safe homes by the score, communities of nonviolent resistance, Gospel nonviolence, and resistance to war, patriarchy, and imperialism? Has God not given us persecutions like misunderstanding, ridicule, risk, kangaroo courts, and prison—all opportunities to snuff out violence.

What should we make of a God who hands over a son to Calvary and would give us everything else besides, a God who would anguish over what more could be done for us? There should be no mystification about God, revealed as the one who leaves ninety-nine just to find one sinner, the lover of enemies, the Parent who forgives us prodigals, who numbers the hairs of our heads and knows what we need before we ask.

Lord, you have probed me, you know me: you know when I sit and stand; you understand my thoughts from afar. My travels and my rest you mark; with all my ways you are familiar. Even before a word is on my tongue, Lord you know it all. Behind and before, you encircle me and rest your hand upon me. Such knowledge is beyond me, far too lofty for me to reach.

Psalm 139: 1-6

If we knew the truth of God's goodness, our thanks would infuse our lives every waking moment. We'd give thanks to God, even for the next beat of our heart or our next breath, neither of which would happen without God's sustaining power. And since we'd be people of thanksgiving, our outrage would boil out over the ingratitude of our people. Ingratitude is at the root of injustice, at the root of military, economic, and ecological terrorism.

The scripture is precise—what we sow, we reap. And when we sow systemic violence, we reap the whirlwind.

For more than fifty years, there has been the astonishing assumption that both American nuclear warriors and the public have escaped free from the consequences of doomsday roulette with the

Soviets. The assumption is astonishing because it doesn't make sense. It doesn't make sense, in God's truth, that weapons create peace and that nuclear weapons create a larger peace. Our weapons, in truth, threaten us before they threaten others. They spiritually threaten us, and they spiritually threaten others. They physically threaten us, and they physically threaten others.

A few years ago, some robust citizens in the United States energy department leaked portions of a study commissioned by Congress in 1982 and done by the National Cancer Institute. It has since been suppressed by the government. The institute scrutinized American atmospheric tests from 1951 to 1962 and discovered that virtually 160 million people, the whole population at that time, suffered heavy exposure to radioactive fallout. The study estimated that seventy-five thousand cases of thyroid cancer resulted from atmospheric tests and that contamination was considerable. When measured against the later Chernobyl disaster, contamination measured could be seen as fifteen times greater. Save for those in Washington state and California, everyone was a "downwinder."

The government's reaction was lies and suppression—its usual stance when forced to confront its addiction to image and public relations. While the tests continued, officialdom claimed that exposure to radiation was the equivalent of one chest X-ray. Now, the Cancer Institute asserts that the average exposure was two hundred times the equivalent of an x-ray and, in some sections of the United States, two thousand or three thousand times the equivalent of an x-ray.

Who knows what other cancers owe their genesis to insane atmospheric nuclear tests? After all, a United Nations study claimed that the radioactive garbage ascended to the stratosphere and circled the globe. Are such tests, and others like them, the primary source of the present cancer epidemic? Who knows what food chains were poisoned by the tests, what air, soil and water polluted, what gene pools altered and weakened? What is the extent of pollution caused by the United States military, already known to be the world's greatest institutional polluter?

And what, exactly, are the fruits of imperial pride, greed, violence, and ingratitude? Will we ever really know? We need to ponder long and hard a God who has given us a son and "everything else." We need to ask ourselves how we treat and whether we love one another.

by Steven Baggarly

*The next day [John the Baptist] saw Jesus coming toward him and said,
"Behold, the Lamb of God, who takes away the sin of the world."*

John 1:29

Throughout John's Gospel, Jesus is identified as the Lamb of God. The title recalls the crucial role the lamb played in liberating the Hebrews from slavery in Egypt. The death of every first born was the tenth and final plague sent by God to Egypt when Pharoah refused to let the Hebrew slaves be free. Lamb's blood on the door post distinguished Hebrew households at that time and saved the Hebrew children. In commemorative Passover meals ever since, an unblemished lamb has been the center of the meal. The title also brings to mind Isaiah's suffering servant, who is

like a lamb led to slaughter or a sheep before shearers . . . and . . . who gives his life as an offering for sin.

Isaiah 53:7, 10

At his very first appearance, John the Baptist emphasizes both the sacrificial and redemptive nature of Jesus's life and death.

The Gospels describe Jesus's life as a progression from sheep to shepherd to Lamb of God. He grows up learning just as we do, from the example of others, by studying scripture, by listening to teachers, and by praying. During his public ministry, he is a shepherd, teaching others who God is, what God is doing and saying in the world. He is, in fact, the Good Shepherd who

lays down his life for the sheep

John 10:11

protecting them from the wolf, the thief, and the hireling. The Good Shepherd tries to hinder those who would kill the sheep, sacrifices himself for them, and becomes the Lamb. In becoming the sacrificial Lamb, he fulfills the role of the shepherd and teaches us how to shepherd.

The work of a shepherd:

Defend the lowly and orphan; render justice to the afflicted and needy. Rescue the lowly and poor; deliver them from the hand of the wicked.

Psalm 82:3-4

To freely give one's life on behalf of suffering people is what God desires, according to Jesus.

This is why God loves me, because I lay down my life. . . No one takes it from me, but I lay it down on my own.

John 10:17-18

The essence of both the shepherd and the lamb is active nonviolent defense of the oppressed against the oppressor and a willingness to suffer the consequences. We, too, are invited to become sacrificial lambs, exposing and de-legitimizing the violence of the powerful. We are thus invited to partake in building God's social order of justice and peace.

As we stood for arrest after hammering and pouring our blood on the USS *The Sullivans*, the Prince of Peace Plowshares hoped to attest to the task of the Good Shepherd and the redemptive witness of the Lamb of God. We willingly gave ourselves to arrest, trying neither to run away nor deny our participation. Rather, we attempted to shout it from the rooftops—that humanity can beat swords into plowshares, we can unmake the vast criminal enterprise known as war.

At best, we freely put our bodies into the machinery of mass destruction, hoping to gum up the works. Like real lambs, we are penned and herded, enduring sensory deprivation and the unnaturalness of living in a cage. We are paraded before a judge in the pay of the war makers for a charade of a trial, and we will spend a chunk of time in jail—not for committing a crime, but for doing what is right, good, and just. We are publicly misunderstood and held up for ridicule in the press as violent vandals, traitors, fools, betrayers of our own people and country or dismissed altogether as publicity-seeking leftovers from the 1960s.

The Prince of Peace Plowshares received a copy of a letter from a veteran living in Bath, Maine, who writes that he killed a lot of North Koreans for whom he had more respect than he has for us! If it were possible, the man continues, he would gladly put a bullet in each of us. At home, my spouse Kim receives an anonymous letter from a Norfolk man furious that we would waste his tax money. He hopes that not one cent of tax money is paying for her to be on the dole while I'm in jail. He demeans the hungry people with whom we share food, and calls her "deranged" for exposing our son to such "shit."

Those slings and arrows pale in comparison to the bloody martyrdoms so often suffered in the Third World. Yet they are part and parcel of trying to respond to Jesus's call to nonviolent resistance to the powers of death here in the First World. Nonviolent resistance to the powers of death means a lifetime of interruptions by jail and prison.

Jesus dies a martyr's death. The Greek word for martyr means "witness." By defending dispossessed and powerless people from institutions that crush them and by freely bearing consequences for his actions, Jesus also bears witness to the possibility of nonviolent trans-formation of the world. When Jesus, the unblemished Lamb, is murdered, his complete innocence blows the long-standing cover of violence as the necessary order. For a world where people believe in violence rather than in God, Jesus becomes the Passover Lamb and rescues the world from enslavement to a cruel master.

Growth from sheep to shepherd to Lamb of God is a human im-perative, and Jesus offers inspiration and truth as he perfectly dem-onstrates the way.

Healing Our Paralysis

by Philip Berrigan

Which is easier, to say to the paralytic, "Your sins are forgiven," or to say, "Rise, pick up your mat and walk!"?

Mark 2:9

Crowds press so much on Jesus that a paralytic's friends dig through an earthen roof and lower the stricken man to Jesus's feet. Their faith—God's will and their desire the same—move Jesus to heal the man's spirit:

Child, your sins are forgiven.

Mark 2:5

In their hearts at that moment, the scribes convict Jesus of blas-phemy, the very charge for which they will later murder him. But he turns the tables on them by challenging them.

Jesus immediately knew in his mind what they were thinking to them-selves, so he said, "Why are you thinking such things in your hearts? Which is easier, to say to the paralytic, 'Your sins are forgiven,' or to say, 'Rise, pick up your mat and walk?' But that you may know . . . authority to forgive sins on earth" —he said to the paralytic, "I say to you, rise, pick up your mat and go home."

Mark 2:8-11

I've heard it said that one way to measure a person's life is by her nonviolent struggle against evil—primarily all systemic evil.

In healing the paralytic, Jesus engages evil in three forms: the man's sins, his paralysis, and the self-righteousness and blasphemy of the scribes. The faith of the paralytic's friends provide Jesus with an occasion ripe for God's deliverance or healing—first of soul, then of body. Cure of his paralysis restores the man to full social stature. He can now walk, his condition of paralysis now removed. Finally, the scribes accused Jesus of what they themselves are guilty of, power over social indebtedness or sin.

The alarm and rage of the scribes about Jesus's act of forgiveness are justified, because he expropriates from them their control over sin. As guardians of the Torah, scribes in Jesus's day arrogated to themselves the keys to God's kindom long before Christ laid that responsibility on the church. They dared to define relationship to God according to an array of rigid and shopworn regulations and rubrics. All in God's name, of course, and all quite devoid of compassion and mercy.

Such power over debt to God or sin has a terrifying allure and ultimacy about it. It is literally the power of death over life. Theocracies practice it, oligarchies and empires certainly practice it, the church and synagogue practice it as well—usurping the sovereignty of the God of life in an altogether insidious and perverted fashion. Instead of teaching and living the guts of Biblical morality and ethics—compassion, justice, love of enemies, nonviolence, forgiveness, community, mercy, resistance, they seduce people to the foolishness and emptiness of rule, rote, and rubric. I recall the ingrained fear experienced during a time when a Roman Catholic committed "mortal sin" by missing Mass on Sunday, by eating meat on Friday, or by breaking one's fast and then receiving the Eucharist. Meanwhile, the church maintained a deafening silence about killing in war, about hatred toward blacks and strangers, about oppressing women, about usury, about complicity with the enormous tyranny of government and transnational corporations. A silence that is, in fact, largely intact today. Legalistic Roman Catholic practices and the attitude of the scribes of Jesus's time are remarkably similar.

Jesus's Gospel "healings" are acts of forgiveness—nullifying the burdens and ostracism of synagogue and society. His "healings" are mirrors of God's mercy and forgiveness, of God's loving kindness. God is the grieving father who forgets the misdeeds of his prodigal son, embracing him and rejoicing over his return at Luke 15:24. God is the shepherd who searches and searches for the lost sheep, and finding it, calls in neighbors for a celebration at Luke 15:7. The paralytic "walks"—restored as an equal and healthy person. No longer will neighbors look askance, wondering at the sins causing his paralysis.

It makes me think of when federal marshals came for two friends, taking them to federal prison. Our friends are victims of conspiracy to import marijuana. They never brought marijuana to Maine. They thought about doing it. A narcotics officer infiltrated them, and they were indicted, convicted, and sentenced, one to nearly six years, the other to four and one-half. Meanwhile, "legal" drugs like nicotine kill between 320,000 and five hundred thousand Americans annually; alcohol kills between a hundred thousand and two hundred thousand people during the same period. Illegal drugs like heroin and cocaine kill between six thousand and thirty thousand. Marijuana kills no one. Obviously, there is an enormous official effort to keep the price of drugs stable—by deploying the war on drugs; by hiring more police, narcotics agents, judges, probation officers; by encouraging citizen's groups to enact local "wars" on drugs; by doubling and tripling jail and penitentiary capacities. Apparently, the billions spent, the vast construction of prisons, and the expansion of anticrime personnel are viewed as good investments to define America's drug "problem" as consumption of cocaine, heroin, crack cocaine, and marijuana, while keeping cigarettes and alcohol legal. As one example, officialdom defines "sins" and blames the victim when it can, allotting Americans to the perils of smoking while ignoring the poisoning of tobacco by herbicides and insecticides.

Nearly without exception, the guardians of morality draw their credentials from the domination system—government, military, transnational corporations, banks, churches, synagogues, campuses, and media—all with a lucrative stake in the status quo. And therefore, the domination system has a rigid determinism, putting profits before people. It is ideological, violent, unjust. The domination system is a massive, powerful social coalition skilled in the application of carrot and stick. The carrot is a combination of lies and bribes, the stick familial disgrace, media ridicule, social ostracism, indictment, and imprisonment when one resists the lies and bribes.

I recall vividly being immediately distanced from and morally condemned by my Josephite confrères and the Archdiocese of Baltimore when several of us poured blood on 1A draft files in the Baltimore Customs House in October, 1967. The same rote rejection happened in May, 1968, when we burned draft files at Catonsville. The same resistance to the empire's violence, the same knee jerk reaction.

Yes. The domination system dares to define the debt code, dares to define "sin." One who publicly resists the military and economic oppression of empire has "sinned"; one who publicly resists first strike nuclear weaponry has "sinned"; one who publicly resists the "625 billion annual financing of past, present and future wars has "sinned"; one who publicly resists the world's 350 billionaires while the world's poor starve has "sinned"; one who rejects Caesar and chooses God has "sinned." It is what happened when Jesus healed the paralytic: the scribes convicted Jesus of blasphemy. And, likewise, the domination system convicts resisters of sin.

The scribes were right at least on this count:

Who but God alone can forgive sin?

Mark 2:7

Indeed. And who will choose the empire's "forgiveness" as it perpetuates idolatry, blasphemy, criminality, and complicity in lies, bribery, and murder?

Sleep and Death

by Philip Berrigan

As they were stoning Stephen, he called out: "Lord Jesus, receive my spirit!" Then he fell to his knees and cried out in a loud voice, "Lord, do not hold this sin against them," and when he said this he fell asleep.

Acts 7:59, 60

I sat by his bedside and watched his last moments. The priest had come and gone; he had confessed his sins and received the sacrament of the sick. His lucidity of mind astonished everyone, for the pain was terrible, coming and going, gripping him in spasms.

His family had said good-bye, his wife and children pressing forward tearfully to kiss him and take his hand. Composed, he spoke softly to each, as though to say, "Parting is wrenching, but something greater beckons."

For six years, he had battled rectal cancer, which had spread inexorably. Once a large muscular man, he had become a husk, his gaunt frame outlined beneath the sheet.

One of his daughters murmured the Psalm 130: "Out of the depths, I call to you Lord . . . " His breathing grew faint, hung on for a minute or two, finally stopped. He had fallen asleep.

In that room of sorrow and muffled sobbing, I thought of the little daughter of Jairus and Christ's blunt statement to the mourners before driving them out:

Why this commotion and weeping? The child is not dead, but asleep.

Mark 5:39

I thought of Stephen, the first Christian martyr, and of his horrible torture and death by stoning. Yet Luke wrote of it calmly and briefly: "He fell asleep!" Stephen was a victim of the temple/state mob; my friend with his cancer was a victim of the nuclear war-fighting mob. Both endured torture—one sudden and crushing; the other prolonged. And both "fell asleep"—calmly, peacefully.

My friend was an "atomic veteran"—one of the thousands of officers and GIs who witnessed atmospheric testing of the bomb at the Nevada Test Site in the '50s. During his final illness, he confided much to me: officialdom knew of the dangers of radioactivity to which they exposed unfortunate soldiers. They said, "The risks were acceptable!" But they weren't, and my friend was the last of his battalion to survive.

The martyr Stephen,

> *a man filled with faith and the Holy Spirit,*
>
> Acts 6:5

was one of seven deacons chosen by the disciples to tend the material needs of the community. But Stephen did more. He also unequivocally and fervently preached the word.

Chapters 6 and 7 of Acts offer more insight.

What infuriated the temple/state mob was not Stephen's recall of Israelite history, but his contention that grace and truth came through Jesus Christ, replacing and transcending the law of Moses. The charges against Stephen, oddly enough, were true—he had elevated Jesus to a stature above Moses. And, therefore, he challenged the whole temple/state bureaucracy, including the Torah and Talmud.

> *But he, filled with the Holy Spirit, looked up to heaven intently and saw the glory of God and Jesus standing at the right hand of God. And he said, "Behold, I see the heavens opened and the human one standing at the right hand of God."*
>
> Acts 7:55, 56

Stephen here speaks obliquely of a new Creation and implies a new law, a familiar law:

> *Love one another as I have loved you.*
>
> John 15:12

His vision and declaration equated Christ with God, Christ's authority with God's authority. The mob could not tolerate such subversive blasphemy. He had to die.

The odious and brutal practice of stoning was constant in Israelite history and tradition. The Book of Numbers tells of a man caught gathering wood on the Sabbath and the whole community stoning him to death at Numbers 15:36. Israel stoned Achan to death at Joshua 7:25 for possessing banned goods. The Judeans prepared to stone Jesus at John 8:59 because he equated himself with God. Paul was stoned outside Lystra and left for dead at Acts 14:19.

What can one liken to stoning? It has some similarity to being beaten to death with clubs. In stoning, however, the blows come from heavy stones—often thrown with hatred and fierce velocity. Stones batter and shatter the head and trunk and, eventually, become lethal. A person is first knocked unconscious, and then, very shortly, killed. Like Jesus did, Stephen prayed for his executioners, then "fell asleep."

Why would the Bible describe death as "falling asleep" while the culture describes death as death? As a commentary on a life lived for God and others, I suppose. If one lives compassionately and justly, one "falls asleep" as physical life ends. If not, one dies.

My brother Dan used to comment on death as he experienced it at Saint Rose's Cancer Hospital for the terminally ill in Manhattan. Of the scores whose deaths he attended, the poor invariably made the transition with composure and dignity. The rich left this life with frequent dread and unrest. The old maxim seemed verified: "one dies as one lives." One "falls asleep," the other "dies."

I think of the unknown innocents everywhere, who die as martyrs like Stephen; of those consciously offering their lives for others, like the nuns and Jesuits in El Salvador, like the Trappists in Algeria. I think also of those whose lives have been savagely ripped from them—the hundreds of thousands of East Timorese, villagers in Algeria terminated by fundamentalist fanatics. Such victims lived ordinary lives, some of them faithful and noble lives. Their blood seeds the world with justice and hope.

I think of the agony in Colombia, with a worse record of imprisonment, disappearance, torture, and death than the bleakest days of madness and death in El Salvador and Guatemala. The "dirty war" there, sustained by "immunity" for torture and assassination, catalyzed by the "war on drugs" policy of the United States, has killed more than thirty thousand Colombians suspected of sympathy for the guerrillas, and has driven over a million Colombians from their homes. In the Phoenix Program in Vietnam sponsored by the CIA and National Security Agency—and now shades of it in Colombia—we liquidated more than sixty thousand village chiefs, labor leaders, monks, critics of the war, and teachers.

Drug lords in Colombia have four million acres available for the cultivation of coca and opium. Opium production now makes Colombia one of the three top world producers of heroin. Even guerrillas cultivate coca and opium and run their own processing labs—to buy guns and supplies.

Meanwhile, martyrs testify against the demonism of war, assassination and economic rape. Alvaro Ulcue of Colombia was an Indian priest, intent upon relieving the oppression of his people. His hunger and thirst for justice led to conflict with large landowners, who killed his sister and injured his parents. In 1984, he was shot and killed by two hired gunmen of the landowners. He left this epitaph: "If I must die, I would like my body to be mixed in with the clay of the forest like a living mortar, spread by God between the stones of the new city."

Juan Fernando Porras, a Colombian doctor, was accused of support for the guerrillas. Human rights workers found his body, arms and hands wide in the form of a crucifix, scalped and with several bullet wounds in his head. He was so badly mutilated that identification was made mainly from his hands.

Some can easily imagine martyrs like Alvaro and Juan praying for their executioners as Jesus and Stephen did. And "falling asleep."

On Treachery and Betrayal

by Philip Berrigan

> *His betrayer had arranged a signal with them saying, "The man I shall kiss is the one; arrest him and lead him away securely." He came and immediately went over to him and said, "Rabbi." And he kissed him.*
>
> Mark 14:44,45

Mark's rendition of events just before the Passion is full of grandeur, contrast, and anguish—namely, the anointing of Jesus by Mary at Bethany, Judas's sellout, the Last Supper, Peter's bravado exposed, the Agony in the Garden, Jesus's arrest after Judas's kiss.

By contrasting the enormously significant action of the woman anointing Jesus for death and burial, Mark makes a feminist statement in the story at Bethany followed by the traitorous action of Judas. A woman recognizes Jesus's divinity and anoints him with precious oil even though it brings her the ridicule of onlookers; she is elevated by the truth of her act. A man trusted to be treasurer of the apostles betrays Jesus's humanity (and, thus, his divinity) by identifying him to the Romans, who reward the man with money; later, he is destroyed by the falsehood of his act. Mark will make another feminist statement—male disciples will scatter like sheep but women will stand at the cross at Mark 15:40. Women, politically least or last in the Jerusalem of Jesus's day, become the greatest or first.

"If you don't sell yourself, somebody comes and buys you" is a statement about virtual reality in the empire. Is there any current counterpoint to imitating Judas, selling oneself for thirty pieces of silver, and in the process, betraying Jesus? Does that murderous act of treachery resonate only in the dust bin of history, or are there modern variations?

The incidents that Mark relates are fantastic in their contrast between unconditional love and discipleship, pomposity, cowardice, and degradation. Giving the apostles his flesh and blood as a seal upon partnership in his death and resurrection, Jesus institutes the Eucharist. Almost immediately, Peter boasts of his fidelity to Jesus, and Jesus predicts Peter's threefold denial. But Peter will not be silenced:

> *"Even though I should have to die with you, I will not deny you." And they all spoke similarly.*
>
> Mark 14:31

The "one"—Judas who actually betrays Jesus—later becomes "all." Judas sells Jesus out; the others abandon him.

Who can describe Jesus's likely revulsion and terror, as he leaves Peter, James, and John to pray in Gethsemane? One interpreter says, "The Greek words depict the utmost degree of unbounded horror and suffering." Jesus's mind reviews in tiniest detail the torture, abandonment, crucifixion, and death awaiting him. He additionally reviews our crimes, sins, injustices—mass murders, rapes, homicides, extortions, larcenies, scapegoatings—all the rejections of God that he will vanquish in his death. Luke says Jesus's sweat became blood dripping to the ground at Luke 22:44. Jesus admits his profound distress to Peter, James, and John.

> *My heart is ready to break with grief.*
>
> Mark 14:34

We have little real understanding of betrayal—of God, of others, of ourselves. Our perceptions remain dull despite life around us, despite drug cartels, white collar thieves, and politicians who invariably betray one another. To a degree, however, we understand betrayal when it happens to us. Nevertheless, we are largely unconscious when we practice it.

In an earlier essay, "Christ's Temptations—and Ours," I discuss the temptations of Christ, concluding that they are also our temptations. We are seduced into wrongdoing by our desire for economic, political, and religious power—over others and over ourselves. When we impose power upon people instead of working to organize power for, with, and by people, we betray them. And we also betray ourselves. We don't seize the "now" of the Gospels, we don't see the face of Christ in the poor, we don't exploit the opportunity to serve and nourish others.

When we impose economic, religious, or political power upon people instead of working to organize power for or with or by people, we betray them. And we betray ourselves. We don't seize the "now" of the Gospel, we don't see the face of Christ in the poor, we don't exploit the opportunity to serve and nourish others.

I am reminded of the fear and rage I felt when Boyd Douglas "gave me up" to the FBI in 1970. I had met Douglas at Lewisburg Penitentiary. He went daily to Bucknell University for class, and he was the only prisoner allowed to do that. He carried my letters to Elizabeth, my wife, and brought in her letters—all contraband. The prison authorities caught him and called the FBI, who threatened him with another charge and sentence. He thereupon betrayed Liz, me, and others. Out of the debacle came the wrath of J. Edgar Hoover, who wanted to put my brother Daniel and me behind bars for life. The Harrisburg "conspiracy" trial lasted for five terrible months. Hoover lost his gamble. We were acquitted of the government's absurd charges.

Douglas certainly betrayed me, and he collapsed like a paper bag in a rainstorm when the FBI squeezed him. I was so sensitive to what he had done, even to the point of hiding my own indiscretions. He was, after all, an inveterate con artist, and I had trusted him. I had to reflect deeply on the betrayal of Judas to plumb the dimensions of his betrayal of Jesus and to grasp the duplicity of Boyd Douglas when he betrayed others and me.

Millions of deaths from war, from nuclear testing, from food as a weapon, from urban homicide, from death rows, from torture rooms and prisons and death squads—all are betrayals of God and neighbor. Whenever we betray God, we betray one another. Whenever we betray one another, we betray God. Hiroshima, Nagasaki, the 38th Parallel, Vietnam, Baghdad, Yugoslavia, East Timor, and far too many more. At every turn, we betray each other. At every turn, we betray God.

Until we wake up from our deadly sleep, appalled and nauseated by our capacity for betrayal, we stand in line with Judas, our hands outstretched for thirty pieces of silver. With Judas, we receive the Eucharist and then depart to lead the soldiers to Gethsemane. With

Judas, we greet Jesus with a kiss and see him taken to torture and death.

Whatever you did for the least of my sisters/brothers you did for me.
Matthew 25:40

A Demon in the Synagogue

by Steven Baggarly

Then they came to Capernaum, and on the sabbath he entered the synagogue and taught. The people were astonished at his teaching, for he taught them as one having authority and not as the scribes. In their synagogue was a man with an unclean spirit; he cried out, "What do you have to do with us, Jesus of Nazareth? Have you come to destroy us? I know who you are—the Holy one of God!"

Jesus rebuked him and said, "Quiet! Come out of him!" The unclean spirit convulsed him and with a loud cry came out of him.

All were amazed and asked one another, "What is this? A new teaching with authority. He commands even the unclean spirits and they obey him."
Mark 1:21-27

Engaging the Powers by Walter Wink has contributed greatly to our discussion of the devil and demon possession. Wink suggests that the world ethos is best characterized as an ethos of domination. The unquestioned belief that some people have the right to dominate others undergirds five millennia of social organization based on ranking. Domination is the paradigm for relationships in politics, race, economics, gender, religion, and beyond. Wink calls it "all pervasive exploitation of the many by the few," the domination system, and offers it as a clarifying translation of what New Testament writers call "the world."

As Wink explains, the domination system is marked by inequality, the use of force, and maldistribution of wealth; moreover, it dictates cultural values. Into this world of domination comes Jesus, proclaiming a domination-free system, the kindom of God. The kindom is essentially egalitarian and nonviolent, a sisterhood and brotherhood, free from oppression, victimization, and hunger.[1]

"Satan" is the spirit of the domination system, and it is this spirit that howls in the synagogue in response to Jesus teaching the kindom. The kindom clashes with scribal teaching that theologically justifies the social stratification of rich over poor, men over women, clean over unclean, clergy over laity, learned over uneducated, free over slave, and physically-able over physically-impaired. In the synagogue on the Sabbath (Galilee's holiest place and time), Jesus's teaching exposes the scribes as beneficiaries of and apologists for a religious structure in league with the spirit of domination rather than with the spirit of God. The same holds true for contemporary United States churches. To the extent that they adhere to the values of domination, they too are possessed. As much as they align themselves with the power structures, rather than opposing violence and exploitation of the powerful, they are a haven for demons. Unless they are working for an order free of domination, they are instruments of Satan.

The supreme manifestation of domination has always been state military power. To understand the spirit of United States churches with regard to domination requires a sober reading of the meaning of empire. Since emerging as a world superpower after World War II, the United States has been on a constant war footing in order to maintain its position. It has military bases in thirty countries and military missions in more than sixty. Our government has trained not only armies but also secret police, paramilitaries, and death squads around the world. Many such groups have shored up brutal regimes of "anti-Communist" client states from Guatemala to Indonesia to Zaire, promoting United States-controlled transnational corporations, banks, and cultural imperialism.

The United States trains troops in 110 countries (including those of many governments to whom Congress has cut off aid because of dismal human rights records).[2] In 1996, United States Special Forces engaged in 2,325 missions in 167 countries.[3] The Central Intelligence Agency, the National Security Agency, and other covert government agencies have spared no effort in subverting foreign governments at odds with our ideological and business interests, quashing dissent in the far reaches of empire.[4] One ex-CIA official estimates that the agency breaks ten thousand laws a day worldwide in sovereign nations. The United States has intervened in or invaded other countries some fifty times since 1945, including during three major wars, and has deployed troops around the world more than two hundred times for political influence.[5] Since 1945, considerably more than thirty-five million people have been killed in wars, millions directly by the United States military, and even more millions courtesy of United States weaponry, training, and advice.

To preserve the empire since 1945, the United States government has spent more than fourteen trillion dollars on war. It will spend another $627 billion this year (including interest on the military share of the national debt) on past, present, and future wars[6]—more than the rest of the world combined. The United States also leads the world in arms research, production, export, and giveaways, flooding the world with weapons and arming both sides in many of the world's three dozen current wars. The United States government resumed sales of high tech weapons to Latin America in 1997, just as wars and political killings in several countries finally slowed. Most ominously, we in the United States still have twelve thousand nuclear warheads, including 2,300 at launch-on-warning status. We spent thirty-five billion dollars in 1997 on stockpile upkeep, research and development of new warheads, and maintaining first strike capabilities. The cornerstone of the United States empire has always been its readiness to use its weapons of mass destruction. If it one day becomes vital to national security, United States officialdom stands prepared to participate in the murder of the entire human family and the undoing of Creation itself.

Functioning in the midst of the largest killing machine in the world, United States churches are meant to be the leaven of the nonviolent kindom. Yet they overwhelmingly accommodate the government's global domination, giving a spiritual rubber stamp to United States nuclear terrorism, interventionism, and militarization of the planet. Churches customarily either align themselves wholeheartedly with the war game as the lesser of evils or, with their silence, lend divine sanction to imperial crimes. Churches renege on their prophetic mission to confront the powerful for abusing the poor and powerless, and to act against domination and brutality. Instead, they prefer cultural myths of redemptive violence over the Gospel.

Father George Zabelka, Roman Catholic chaplain to the airmen who dropped the atomic bombs on Japan at the end of World War II, later came to understand the spirit of his church's silence:

> The morality of the balance of terrorism is a morality that Christ never taught. The ethics of mass butchery cannot be found in the teachings of Jesus. In Just War ethics, Jesus Christ, who is supposed to be all in the Christian life, is irrelevant. He might as well never have existed. In Just War ethics, no appeal is made to him or his teaching, because no appeal can be made to him or his teaching, for neither he nor his teaching gives standards for Christians to follow in order to determine what level of slaughter is acceptable.[8]

The churches sit on the Gospel, which Wink calls, "the most powerful antidote for domination the world has ever known." The churches, like the synagogue of Jesus's day, are possessed, though much more lethally.

Yet, Jesus's very first public action in Mark, there in the synagogue, shows a way out. He casts the unclean spirit out of the man, healing him on the Sabbath and violating law and order. In going to the heart of the social order and nonviolently breaking laws used to legitimize domination, Jesus reveals the strategy for subverting the systems of domination and making room for the kindom.

A primary responsibility for United States churches is to work for the dissolution of our empire. Throughout the Judeo-Christian scriptures, from Egypt to Rome, empire is the antithesis to Gods' work in the world. These vast accumulators of wealth and military power are the premier enslavers, the polar opposite of who Jesus is and what he does. The dissolution of empire will likely not appear at the ballot box as a votable issue, so the task is to bring the cross to bear against it. The means will include boycotts, tax refusal, strikes, noncooperation, civil resistance, hunger strikes, and many other nonviolent actions that even the poorest and weakest person can employ against military, corporate, and government entities. The ripple effect would touch every other justice issue both here and abroad. Though it may mean enduring pain, destitution, and even death, it is our only hope to be on the side of history where God is so firmly planted, our one chance as a people to join the human race, to be family rather than mere benefactors to the world's poor and despised. As the churches work toward such ends, they can be the leaven of the kindom and begin to exorcise their demons.

Chapter 5

Who Are My Mother and Brothers? Family and the Empire

by Philip Berrigan

There was no needy person among them, for those who owned property or houses would sell them, bring the proceeds of the sale and put them at the feet of the apostles, and they were distributed to each according to need.

Acts 4:34

In a conversation on community one day, a friend said: "Those early Christians had it right! More than fifteen years in community, we have lacked for nothing—enough money for our work, wholesome food, comfortable housing, warm clothes, the best of medical care, education impossible elsewhere."

"Yeah!" someone else said. "It was because they welcomed the Holy Spirit."

Now, that's helpful. I had never heard it put that way. They welcomed the Holy Spirit who taught them about the life of Jesus Christ, his teaching, his deeds, the cross. He did live in community with the disciples. He did live as a poor, homeless person. He did hold things in common with his friends. Judas kept the "bag," a little money for their necessities. Clearly, possessions were no obstacle to the cross.

When I was at the federal prison at Danbury, our community of prisoners read about the Gospels' emphasis on community, and we also read about Gandhi's devotion to the ashram or community. In fact, after independence and the partition of Pakistan, up until his assassination, Gandhi prepared to rebuild the new India through communities of prayer and action.

Our vision included all of the above when we began Jonah House in 1973. Besides theory, however, an issue of pure practicality arose—how to survive in resistance, when the empire was virtually unanimous about war?

After innumerable meetings and a great deal of prayer, we settled on nonviolence, community, and resistance as philosophical convertibles, as meaning the same thing from different reference points. Slowly, we began to understand that nonviolence inevitably means communities of resistance—since truth—that is, nonviolence—requires that one live as the whole should live in sisterhood/brotherhood. One should defend the whole against those who threaten it, including empires, transnational corporations, and wars.

Confusion within the churches exists over such notions, so the notions deserve restatement. Nonviolence must give spirit to be community, both interpersonally and politically, both in the face they show one another and in the face they show to the world. Moreover, community must first represent the human family, embodying up close its unity and destiny in God. Also, it must defend the human family by nonviolent resistance. The first requires nonviolence, the second resistance.

Furthermore, if community is to reflect the sovereignty of God and the sisterhood/brotherhood, its members must live voluntarily poor, in strict equality of the sexes and in service to the poor.

Again, community should have both an internal and an external life—the internal relationship between its members, the external relationship with society and the world.

Internally, we learned but slowly and painfully, especially me. My violence displayed itself in egotism, arrogance, and dominance. I used to seethe when others didn't meet my expectations, didn't work as hard, or didn't resist as single-mindedly as I did. Consequently, I often bent the bruised reed and quenched the smoldering wick mentioned at Matthew 12:20. Always, the model was me, but my blindness prevented me from seeing it.

At Jonah House, we practiced voluntary poverty, because in God's order no one owns anything and because the institutionalization of greed is behind most of the world's misery. We also knew that possessions are a tenacious spin-off of one's ego—an obstacle to the cross and to resistance. Minimizing wants and disciplining needs can be liberating, especially when provided by the work of one's hands.

Next, equality of the sexes is critical. The age-old patriarchy is an idolatry and a curse, rigorously untrue and unjust. To patriarchy one can largely trace hatred, war, racism, ethnocentrism, corporate capitalism, and ecological devastation in the world. There are matriarchal societies where war is engaged only reluctantly, matrilineal communities where physical violence is virtually unknown.

To us, service of the poor is a Gospel imperative, because we are all poor in God's sight and because what we do for the poor, we do for Christ, as illuminated at Matthew 25:40. Yet despite our best efforts, we cannot completely identify with the poor. Our white faces and privileged training prevent it. Such privileges rescue us from the insult of discrimination and often provide food and opportunity not available to the poor. Among Plowshares people, there is a long-standing realization that only in prison can we become one with the poor, prisoners among prisoners.

Let's turn now to the external relationships of community, to society and the world. Jonah House persisted in resistance to the Vietnam War through 1973, 1974, and the early months of 1975. We did civil resistance at the White House and at the Vietnamese Overseas Procurement Office, which funneled military aid to the Saigon regime, our puppet in South Vietnam.

Then, on April 30, 1975, the United States was driven out of South Vietnam and Saigon collapsed. We surmised rightly that the American empire would lick its wounds, regroup and intervene elsewhere. The Book of Revelations appears to apply:

> I saw that one of its heads seemed to be mortally wounded, but this mortal wound had healed.
>
> Revelations 13:3

Healing the "mortal wound" came in the form of announcements by Schlesinger, the secretary of war; Kissinger, the foreign policy adviser, and President Ford. They said the United States possessed a nuclear first strike counterforce capacity. It had to mean that the nuclear warriors had been secretly readying the technology for between ten and fifteen years. Counterforce was a statement to the world that the third Asian defeat in thirty years—in China, Korea, and then Vietnam—in no wise reduced the United States to a paper tiger.

The Vietnam defeat drove our war makers into hysteria and madness. They matched the deranged doctrine of counterforce with an insane domestic plan to protect the public during nuclear exchange. Millions of ordinary Americans would wait out the holocaust in limestone, coal, or granite mines located near population centers. There was little reckoning that a nuclear war would turn the mines into gigantic mass graves.

Jonah House began a mini-campaign to expose this psychotic scheme by digging a grave first on the White House lawn. Then, in early 1976, we dug several graves on the parade ground at the Pentagon. For the remainder of the 70s, we concentrated on the Pentagon—the most powerful institution in the world with assets three trillion dollars plus, a massive bureaucracy with but one aim: to find more efficient ways of killing people. The Pentagon had been largely ignored by the "movement"—some claimed that an evil miasma engulfed it and its thirty thousand civilian and military personnel. We did civil resistance at the River, Mall, South and Tunnel entrances, chaining doors shut, blocking entrances, splashing pillars with blood, forcing employees to walk over bodies and through blood—anything to suggest symbolically the consequences of their bloody work.

In 1980, two notable resistance events happened: the year of action at the Pentagon and the first Plowshares witness at General Electric Plant #9 in King of Prussia, Pennsylvania.

Every week, from New Year's Day to December 31, 1980, a new community from a different state appeared in Washington, D.C., for training and action at the Pentagon. In the end, the militants represented more than forty states from as far away as Alaska, and most did civil resistance on the Friday of their state's week. Friends offered an Episcopal Church on 16th Street NW in Washington as a base, and it was there that the FBI waged an intense campaign of "dirty tricks" against us, trying to drive us away from the Pentagon. To camouflage their venality, the FBI used black agents/mercenaries, so we would tend to blame people from an adjacent African American neighborhood. During 1980, these provocateurs raped a young woman, holding her companion at knife point, vandalized our cars, robbed us, sexually harassed women, and terrorized us at gun point. We learned of their "dirty tricks" when an acquaintance, microfilming at the FBI Building, located the church file that specified every attempt to drive us away from the Pentagon.

The series of actions culminated with a thousand peace people encircling the Pentagon. Scores arrested.

In September, a new chapter opened as community attention shifted from the war department to first strike weaponry. Bob Smith from the Brandywine Peace Community and John Schuchardt, then from Jonah House, suggested a disarming action. The idea followed two years of demonstrations at Plant #9, where General Electric manufactured the Mark 12A reentry vehicle for our Minuteman IIIs. Bob and John suggested using Isaiah 2:4 and the words "swords into plowshares," clearly an inspiration by the Holy Spirit, as scriptural authority. Response was quick, and eight of us resolved in faith to attempt disarmament. We had only a floor plan of the plant and no idea where to reach the Mark 12A. Our fears that we would not be able to reach the missile, however, proved groundless. We entered the plant and distracted the guard. Within ten seconds John Schuchardt located the Mark 12A in a "non-destructible" testing room. We disarmed two of the terrible devices.

That was the first of more than sixty Plowshares witnesses, most of them symbolically disarming first strike nuclear weaponry, most of them happening in the United States but also some in Australia, England, Sweden, the Netherlands, and Germany. When Plowshares people build well on faith and love, building staunch, cohesive communities and leaving the intangibles to God, we find that nothing can protect the demonic instruments of war from those determined to disarm them. The instruments of war are too anti-human and anti-God to be protected.

So goes a thumbnail sketch of our community. In community, events and imperial politics were pondered, ideas and tactics hammered out, faith appealed for and enfleshed, support and logistics offered, consequences sustained. Without such communities of faith, resistance would be a mental exercise, an illusion.

In fact, greater deeds beckon. If they are understood and enacted, they will come from community.

> *Amen, Amen I say to you, whoever believes in me, will do the works that I do, and will do greater ones than these . . .*
>
> John 14:12

> *How good it is, how pleasant*
> *where the people dwell as one . . .*
> *There the Lord has lavished blessings,*
> *Life for evermore.*
>
> Psalm 133, 1:1-3

Testifying to Truth

by Steven Baggarly

> *Pilate said to him, "Then you are a king?"*
> *Jesus answered, "You say I am a king. For this I was born and for this I come into the world, to testify to the truth. Everyone who belongs to the truth listens to my voice."*
>
> John 18:37

Testifying to truth means working for justice in a world rife with injustice. To be instruments of God's love, it is essential to speak and act truthfully at the very center of worldly power, where the mechanisms of violence and lies produce large-scale evil. Moses testifies to the truth before Pharaoh, as do the Hebrew prophets before the kings of Judah and Israel, as Jesus does before Pilate. Such testimony is inevitably good news for poor and oppressed people and bad news for the rich and powerful. Truth tells the powerful that their control over the lives of others has to be relinquished, that they have no right to exact subservience, to coerce anyone, or to abuse nature. By doing so, they oppose God. They must step down.

One bears such a message knowing it can lead the powers to every imaginable kind of retribution. Though most of the names are lost, there are many people around the world who belong to the truth and testify at great risk against the abuses of the powerful and for the lives of the people. Here are a few examples.

Colombia has been our hemisphere's premier slaughterhouse over the past ten years. Courtesy of vast amounts of United States weaponry, training, and advisers, the Colombian military, paramilitaries, and death squads are responsible for most of the political violence that has claimed more than twenty victims a day since 1988. Crucifixion, burning with blow torches, and dismembering conscious people with chain saws are but a few of the horrific tortures endured by Colombian peasants and those concerned for them.[1] Two of the concerned, Elsa Alvarado and Mario Calderon, worked for a Jesuit-sponsored human rights office that keeps track of the political killings. On May 19, 1997, gunmen broke into their Bogata apartment, killing them and Alvarado's father. Elsa was able to hide eighteen-month-old Ivan in a closet at the last minute. When police arrived, they found Ivan sitting between his parents' bullet-riddled bodies. Alvarado's mother survived, too, through crippled from being shot point-blank in the head nine times.[2]

In late 1996, the *Philadelphia Inquirer* ran a series about Tibetans who spoke truth to their Chinese overlords. One story follows a group of Buddhist nuns who not long ago in a town square passed out leaflets calling for Tibetan independence. All the women were arrested, and for some it was not the first time. They were taken to the local prison and given the usual treatment—they were immediately beaten and gang-raped by Chinese guards before a crowd of male Tibetan convicts who cursed the women and cheered the guards. Weeks of torture followed before their release.[3] A critic of Chinese government policy and proponent of human rights, Wei Jingsheng, has spent all but six months of his last seventeen years in prison and just began another fourteen-year sentence. For much of his time in jail, trustees have been specifically assigned to harass him and make his life miserable.[4]

While no longer marching under the watchful eyes of the Argentine military, after more than twenty years, the Mothers of the Plaza de Mayo continue to call the powerful to account for the thirty thousand lives lost during the military dictatorship's "dirty war" in the 1970s and 1980s. Any governmental critic was then targeted for disappearance, and thousands were thrown out of airplanes into the ocean, drugged and naked, from thirteen thousand feet. Mothers whose family members were "disappeared" continue to identify military, political, and religious authorities who participated in or helped to cover up the carnage.[6]

In 1988, Aung San Suu Kyi left her husband and two children in England to return to her native Myanmar, formerly known as Burma, to tend to her dying mother. Her father had been a national hero, assassinated on the eve of independence in 1947. Popular unrest against twenty-six years of political repression turned into a bloody military coup while Aung San Suu Kyi cared for her mother, and the hero's daughter became a leader of the opposition to the new military junta. From 1989 to 1995, she was on house arrest. When released, she immediately resumed her struggle, at times still restricted in her movement and under constant surveillance.[7]

In 1991 in East Timor, a Mr. Galhus, then twenty-eight, sold "Free East Timor" tee shirts at a demonstration against Indonesian occupation of his tiny, oil-rich country. He was arrested and interrogated by Indonesian security forces who beat him until his face was unrecognizable. Each time he refused to answer a question, they pulled out a fingernail by grinding a finger under a chair leg. Minus all ten nails, he was released after six months. His sister says that since getting out he has been mentally unstable. When the people of East Timor courageously voted for independence in 1999, the Indonesian military cracked down and slaughtered thousands. Indonesia had invaded East Timor in 1974 with United States weapons and support and embarked on a genocide, killing a million people in order to resettle the island with Indonesians.[8]

In 1995, Nigerian poet Ken Sara WiWa and fifteen others were arrested by the military dictatorship for leading nonviolent resistance against the transnational oil company, Royal Dutch Shell. Pollution from Shell's drilling and refineries at the Niger River delta has devastated the ecology and caused widespread illness, yet Shell refuses to clean up or redress local grievances.[9] In collusion with Shell, the government convicted Sara WiWa and the other activists on trumped-up charges and hanged them all.

People like these—who fully realize what may happen to them when they speak and act in truth and then choose to do so in spite of the risk—witness to the very best that is in human beings. Such people are on the side of right, nonviolence, selflessness, and hope. They are to be emulated. While we in the United States grow rich from political repression, exploited labor, cheap resources, and arms markets of the Third World, such people take up the cross in opposition not only to the local tyrants but to their imperial backers—us—as well. Our sisters and brothers in resistance show us clearly what testifying to the truth and following Christ means today. As a First World person, it is the least I can do to gather with others to hammer on an instrument of mass crucifixion.

by Mark Colville

Yesterday I got a pile of mail, including several drawings and colorings by my daughters, Keeley and Soledad. Keeley actually drew a crucifix and wrote her name and Jesus's name on it. The figure on the cross, too, appears as if it could be Jesus or it could be Keeley herself. At six years old, she is living at a depth that I struggle to understand.

I also received a letter from a longtime companion in the journey. It is a deeply moving reflection on our friendship and his love for me, Luz, and the children. He reminds us of his unconditional support for us and of his personal position of difficulty with jail witness (particularly separation from family). He writes eloquently, and he obviously took much serious prayer time to pull his thoughts together. It is a letter I will keep and always treasure.

My friend's point of difficulty is that he doesn't think God would ever will him or his family to endure the hardships of physical separation brought on by a lengthy jail sentence. His place as a husband and father is with his family, and that is where he can best serve God—in loving and supporting and being present to them. By implication, he says he questions the rightness of our Plowshares action based on that understanding.

My only problem with his position is that I read the letter three times, and I can't find the cross in it, at least not the cross as I understand it.

Christianity is supposed to be centered around the cross. It is supposed to be about suffering. Not suffering for suffering's sake, but redemptive suffering, acting for justice, embracing the consequences, healing the world by affiliating ourselves in solidarity with the afflicted. In Spanish, the word solidarity is also used as a verb, *"solidarizarse,"* which essentially means "to solidaritize oneself." I believe the Spanish captures the concept of Christian vocation much better: not simply to identify with the poor in mind and heart, but also to actively place ourselves alongside them through unity of experience. The rich man in the gospels understands and goes away sad:

> *As he was setting out on a journey, a man ran up, knelt down before him, and asked him, "Good teacher, what must I do to inherit eternal life?"*
>
> *Jesus answered him, "Why do you call me good? No one is good but God alone. You know the commandments: 'You shall not kill; you shall not commit adultery; you shall not steal; you shall not bear false witness; you shall not defraud; honor your father and your mother.'"*

He replied and said to him, "Teacher, all of these I have observed from my youth."

Jesus, looking at him, loved him and said to him, "You are lacking in one thing. Go, sell what you have, and give to the poor and you will have treasure in heaven; then come, follow me." At that statement his face fell, and he went away sad, for he had many possessions.

Mark 10:17-22

An official asked him this question, "Good teacher, what must I do to inherit eternal life?"

Jesus answered him, "Why do you call me good? No one is good but God alone. You know the commandments, 'You shall not commit adultery; you shall not kill; you shall not steal; you shall not bear false witness; honor your father and your mother.'"

And he replied, "All of these I have observed from my youth."

When Jesus heard this he said to him, "There is still one thing left for you: sell all that you have and distribute it to the poor, and you will have a treasure in heaven. Then come, follow me."

But when he heard this he became quite sad, for he was very rich.

Luke 18:18-23

The cross on which Jesus hung was a political reality. As a particularly shameful and brutal form of execution, it was one empire's systemic expression of violence against those who should stand against the empire. The churches have emasculated the symbol of the cross by removing it completely from its political nature. That's why we misuse the symbol so much. We talk about a backache, a tough childhood, an addiction, a sick mother, and we call those things "the cross." But they are not the cross. They are sufferings, to be sure, and they are not insignificant. To bear them patiently builds virtue. But they are not the cross. The cross is the suffering we take on in birthing the kindom of God in the world. It is "solidaritizing ourselves" with the poor, who suffer daily from systemic evil, injustice, and war. And we don't solidaritize ourselves by handing them a sandwich in a soup kitchen (although that, too, can build virtue). We do it by taking on the systemic evil, in confrontation

with the principalities, with the powers, with the world rulers of this present darkness

Ephesians 6:12

and by joyfully accepting the sufferings that doing so brings.

Of course, we rarely talk about the cross in terms of joyful suffering in solidarity because, at the turn of the millennium, suffering is un-American. It's what the other people do who are not as lucky as we are. Suffering is supposed to be done in private so as not to make others uncomfortable. And it certainly isn't something we want to make ourselves available for. We literally want to avoid suffering at all costs. So we insist on a wasteful life style that impoverishes the rest of the world, and we are ever prepared to defend that wasteful life style with violence. That is why our understanding of the cross is so pitiful, confined to the simple acceptance of the sufferings that happen to come our way.

> For Jews demand signs and Greeks look for wisdom, but we proclaim Christ crucified, a stumbling block to Jews and foolishness to Gentiles, but to those who are called, Jews and Greeks alike, Christ the power of God and the wisdom of God.
>
> 1 Corinthians 1:23

A Plowshares action strikes me as a particularly good way for a family, especially an educated white family living in the modern empire, to take up the cross. It solidaritizes us with many families in this world who are separated by war, hunger, economic crisis, unemployment—all of them direct results of policies, especially the arms race, of the United States government. So we personally take on the responsibility for doing what the empire won't do, never will do on its own. Disarm. And for that, we get imprisoned. Not in a jail from which people never return and are never again seen, as in so many countries whose militaries we arm, but in a comparatively controlled and safe environment. And we are separated as a family—physically separated—usually not by an incredibly long distance and certainly not by national borders that people like migrant workers and refugees have to sneak across. But we say good-bye to one another with the well-founded expectation that it is not good-bye forever. Again, how many families are torn apart in the blink of an eye by our bombs, bullets, and land mines with never the chance to embrace and shed tears together? How many others flee their homes in the night or get on an overcrowded raft with a slim chance of reaching the other shore? Their good-byes carry no promises.

Yes, in the light of the realities of three-fifths of the world's people, what we do seems a feeble, inadequate attempt to walk the way of the cross. But it is an attempt, in community, accepted voluntarily and suffered together. It is a prayer, a concrete expression of hope for the world, a refusal to let empire, violence, and sin have the last word. And, perhaps, if we can embrace it with joy, it will lead to something deeper.

Being away from Luz, Keeley, Soledad, and Justin (and David and Steve and Demetrius, our extended family in the Catholic Worker) does not feel right or natural or fulfilling. In fact it isn't right or natural or fulfilling. Neither is the cross. But I have never felt closer to my wife and kids, and I've never felt more strongly that we as a family are living the way God wants us to live.

by Steven Baggarly

An argument arose among the Disciples about which of them was the greatest. Jesus realized the intention of their hearts and took a child and placed it by his side, and said to them, "Whoever receives this child in my name receives me, and whoever receives me receives the one who sent me. For the one who is least among all of you is the one who is the greatest."

Luke 9:46.48

Luke and Matthew each relate narratives of Jesus's birth and infancy. With the birth of Jesus in a stable, God completely takes on the human experience. Almighty God, Creator of the universe, alpha and omega, God whose name is too holy to pronounce, is born into poverty, into a tiny human body. He is totally defenseless, at the mercies of his parents, passersby, wild animals and cold, heat, hunger, and thirst. Ironically, he embodies not the warrior God so many expected but instead arrives unarmed. Matthew then describes the government's pursuit of Jesus and its slaughter of Bethlehem's children. Before he's old enough to talk, Jesus and his family are heading for the border as homeless refugees. In our passage from Luke, Jesus assures us that he still moves through the world in the guise of children:

Whoever receives this child in my name receives me, and whoever receives me receives the one who sent me.

How we treat children is how we treat God.

How are children "received" in today's world? For the past thirty years, ninety percent of war casualties have been civilians. Children are often the main casualties and are much more likely than soldiers to be casualties of war. From 1984 to 1994 alone, more than 1.5 million children were killed and more than four million were maimed, blinded, disabled, or brain-damaged in wars worldwide. More than one million were orphaned or unable to locate their parents, twelve million were left homeless, and ten million were made refugees as the result of wars. Some two hundred thousand children were recruited to become soldiers or take an active part in war. During those ten years, one out of every two hundred children in the world was traumatized by the effects of war, needing help to overcome emotional distress.[1] Just as Herod hunted for Jesus, so do world leaders still consider children to be legitimate military targets.

In a world of plenty, children die hunger-related deaths at the rate of 250,000 each week. In 1995, eleven million children died before they were five, among them two million deaths that would have been preventable by immunization. Despite extensive documentation about how malnutrition hinders cognitive development, 180 million children around the world are malnourished. Seven hundred thousand are blind because of a lack of vitamin A.[2] And every minute, while thirty of the world's children die hunger-related deaths, world militaries spend $1.7 million.

In the United States, the wealthiest nation known to history, one of every five children lives in poverty. One in two African American children and one-third of all Hispanic children are born into poverty. Children are the fastest growing segment in a United States homeless population of nearly three million. In 1996, 11.3 million children through age eighteen had no health insurance, 3.1 million children were reported abused or neglected, and fourteen children a day died of gunshot wounds.[3] In Maine, where we were imprisoned in Cumberland County Jail after our Plowshares action, forty percent of the children go hungry sometime during any given month. At the same time, Maine taxpayers will shell out $194 million towards the expansion of Bath Iron Works whose parent company, General Dynamics, raked in six hundred million dollars in profits during 1997 and 1998.

Since the Gulf War, United States-enforced sanctions against Iraq have made food and medicine scarce, leading to the deaths of more than 650,000 Iraqi children.[4] One million Iraqi children under five, or thirty-three percent, are chronically malnourished,[5] and more than six thousand die each month as the result of the sanctions. When asked about the death toll, United States Secretary of State Madeleine Albright said, "It is a difficult decision to make, but we think the price is worth it." Killing children is ultimately a matter of policy, whether it persists because of vested interests in the gross maldistribution of the world's resources or as collateral damage to power politics.

Jesus condemns all of it when he brings a child amid the disciples who are lost in posturing and bravado. There is no sentimentality as he brings the child to his side. Being a child is dangerous. For so many children then, as now, abuse, prostitution, forced labor, homelessness, malnutrition, and lack of access to simple medicines, sanitation or education are part of everyday life. For hundreds of millions of children, the world is a harrowing and murderous place.

Bringing the child to his side, Jesus explains that a true community will exist for the sake of children. As God relinquished status and power to become human, the disciples' humanity hinges on their willingness to forego dominance over others and serve those most vulnerable. In a world that relentlessly pursues military power, economic affluence, and patriarchy, Jesus calls his disciples to make children's concerns central. No matter how many patriotic parades they've marched in, how often they've pledged allegiance to a flag, or how many hours spent playing "war," children desire peace and disarmament. No child rejoices when parents, older siblings, uncles, or aunts go off to war to kill other parents and kids or when a loved one returns seriously maimed, deranged, or in a body bag.

The children Kim and I know personally play a large role in our decision to participate in a Plowshares action. We try to raise our son, Daniel, by moral example, and we know the importance of living what we believe. We felt that we couldn't dramatize our op-position to all violence more clearly than to take a hammer to a weapon like the USS *The Sullivans* which can instantly make millions of children into war casualties. We have felt the profound tragedy that is the death of even one child. While we were part of the Los Angeles Catholic Worker community, a three-year-old Mexican girl, Maria Carillo, died from cancer. We were privileged to be with her and her mom when she died. The destitution and desperation of the children in our Norfolk ghetto neighborhood distinctly cries out for swords to be beaten into plowshares, for Creation's bounty to be put at the service of the most vulnerable rather than the engines of destruction. We understand the very existence of atomic weapons as a declaration of war on the world's children, and we committed ourselves to turning nuclear swords into plowshares.

Luke last mentions children when Jesus reprimands his disciples for hindering children trying to approach him:

> For the kindom of God belongs to such as these. Amen, I say to you, whoever does not accept the kindom of God like a child will not enter it.
>
> Luke 18:15-17

To live the Gospel is to put ourselves in the position of what children endure, to become children, as God did. Breaking the empire's laws that sanction the killing of children and their families may mean that we, too, will suffer. We, too, may be of no account in the world, our voices unheard.

Using household hammers, we attempt to see with children's eyes, and to indict people who target them for mass destruction and steal their bread. Our hammers are a call to refashion the world we have into one worthy of its children.

by Steven Baggarly

Jesus spoke to the crowds in parables . . . to fulfill what had been said through the prophet: "I will open my mouth in parables, I will announce what has lain hidden from the foundation of the world."

Matthew 13:34-35

Jesus spins a series of parables about the kindom of God in Matthew's thirteenth chapter. Four parables—the briefest—serve as possibilities for meditation on two of the most frequent concerns about doing a Plowshares: whether parents of small children should participate, and the effectiveness of a Plowshares action.

When considering whether to do a Plowshares, our starting point is a world in which all children are targeted for extermination. My son Daniel, niece Hannah, friends Antonio, Peaches, Shalita, and all the kids in our Norfolk, Virginia, neighborhood and throughout Hampton Roads are top priority Russian targets because of their proximity to the home port of the navy's Atlantic Fleet. Likewise, the children of Washington, D.C., Moscow, Beijing, and all points between are reachable by nuclear-tipped ICBMs in minutes. The infrastructure and offspring of nuclear weapons are also potentially dangerous. Accidental missile launches, meltdowns, or leaks at nuclear power plants or waste repositories, and malfunctioning plutonium-powered satellites are constant threats to the lives and well-being of the next generation.

Jesuit Father Richard McSorley says,

> The taproot of violence in our society today is our intent to use nuclear weapons. Once we have agreed to do that, all other evil is mild in comparison. Until we squarely face the question of our intent to use nuclear weapons, any hope of large-scale improvements in public morality is doomed to failure.

Acceptance of nuclear weapons also fuels the descent of America's neighborhoods into war zones, a total culture of violence and abuse, murder and mayhem in which our children grow up. As long as nuclear weapons exist as an instrument of or for United States foreign policy, and as long as we are willing to accept the consequences of a nuclear attack—torture and death of hundreds of millions of children—local efforts to bolster respect for life will be instantly subverted.

Before Daniel was born, I seldom took note of the children around me. With an abiding sense of awe, I grew with him, and now wonderment replaces my unawareness of the lives of little people. Proportionately, my sense of the evil inherent in even the simplest weapon has deepened. That parents, politicians, health profession-als, educators, and all people do not do everything in their power to disarm every weapon and prevent new ones from being made seems unconscionable. It is outrageous that we the people give govern-ment and corporations the power to threaten to end all life in a nuclear holocaust. That we are willing to subject our children to this terror for even a day bespeaks profound spiritual death. It is a contemporary version of original sin that normality should mean at any moment the incineration, vaporizing, flash-burning and radia-tion poisoning of the world's children.

Two of Jesus's parables help show the way out.

> *The kindom of God is like a treasure buried in a field, which a person finds and hides again, and out of joy goes and sells all that one has and buys that field. Again, the kindom of God is like a merchant searching for fine pearls. When one finds a pearl of great price, one goes and sells all that one has and buys that field.*
>
> Matthew 13:44-46

Selling everything to gain a treasure is a metaphor for taking up the cross in hopes for the kindom. To interrupt life, to take to the streets, to convert weapons of mass destruction, requires giving all that we have. During my time in jail, my family has identified with these parables like never before, having quite literally given up what we have—each other—for the sake of the kindom.

One articulation of the kindom we pin our hopes on came out of the 1995 United Nations World Conference on Women in Beijing. "The Women's Creed" stated the goals of the gathering:

> *The Women's Creed*
> Bread. A clean sky. Active peace. A woman's voice singing somewhere. The army disbanded. The harvest abundant. The wound healed, the child wanted, the prisoner freed, the body's integrity honored, the lover returned . . . labor equal, fair, and valued. No hand raised in any gesture but greeting. Secure interiors of heart, home and land so firm as to make secure borders irrelevant at last.

Here is a vision of God's nonviolent kindom. In a just and peace-ful world where everyone and all Creation are afforded dignity and respect, the kindom is both pearl and treasure. It is the world Kim and I want Daniel and his generation to grow up in, to live in, and to hand on to their children. It can come any time, anywhere, and God always calls us to help bring it about right now. So we make scripture our own and wield Isaiah's hammer.

As I sat in jail, some people asked, "How can you do this as par-ents of a small child?" Here's the rejoinder: "How can we not do this as parents of a small child?"

"But, what difference does it make? The weapons are still there. We can't change it. There's always been war and there always will be!" is the reply we often hear. Jesus tells two more parables demonstrating that pursuit of the kindom is no jousting with windmills.

> The kindom of God is like a mustard seed that a person took and sowed in a field. It is the smallest of all seeds, yet when full grown, it is the largest of plants. It becomes a large bush, and the birds of the sky come and dwell in its branches . . .
>
> The kindom of God is like yeast that a woman took and mixed with three measures of wheat flour until the whole batch was leavened.
>
> Matthew 13:31-33

Metaphorically, in the two parables, Jesus describes the efficacy of the cross. There is no doubt that by shouldering the cross and, thus, taking on the empire and its gargantuan killing machine, we will be the losers, objects of ridicule in a brutal theater of the absurd. It appears foolish to give everything for a kindom which exists sight unseen. Yet, it is precisely Jesus's humiliating death on the cross that redeems the world. We believe that, as surely as a seed becomes a plant and leaven raises bread, active nonviolent resistance will sow the seeds of the kindom. During our stay in Cumberland Country Jail, we caught a glimpse of how the kindom works.

Our remaining in jail when most of us could have been out on personal recognizance moved people in the local community to take to the streets. Weekly vigils are held at Bath Iron Works Repair Facility in Portland, which services both Aegis destroyers and cruisers. There have been vigils at Bath Iron Works Open House in Bath, at the federal courthouse, and at the jail. There was street theater through downtown Portland on Hiroshima Day. When we weren't allowed to offer any defense during the trial, local and out-of-town friends joined us in courtroom resistance. When the verdict came down, nonviolent civil resistance took place at Bath Iron Works in Portland and outside the courthouse, resulting in arrests and jail. Another action took place at sentencing. The simple act of sitting in jail stirs the hearts, minds, and spirits of others who want to end the reign of terror of omnicidal weapons. I know that I was moved by three Plowshares groups acting in Virginia and North Carolina over the last six years. They sacrificed and endured jail that the world might be a better place for our son and all little ones.

The mustard seed in the parable yields a bush for the "birds of the sky [to] come and dwell in its branches." Jesus takes the reference to the imperial power of the "high trees," Egypt at Ezekiel 31:6, and Babylonia at Deuteronomy 4:7-9, 17-19 and applies the references to God's kindom. Implicit in his appropriation of the phrase is the audacious claim that the mustard seed of the kindom is mightier than any empire. God will

> bring low the high tree, lift high the lowly tree . . .
>
> Ezekiel 17:24

Gandhi offers the same thought in different words:

> Nonviolence . . . means the pitting of one's whole soul against the will of the tyrant. Working under this law of our being, it is possible for a single individual to defy the whole might of an unjust empire, to save one's honor, one's religion, one's soul and lay the foundation for that empire's fall or its regeneration.

Margaret Mead concurs. "Never doubt," she writes, "that a small group of committed people can change the world; indeed, it is the only thing that ever has."

Using parables, Jesus announces what has been hidden from the foundation of the world: that taking up the cross creates a partnership between the human and the divine that leads inexorably to the advent of the kindom.

Who Are My Mother and Brothers ?

Mark Colville

> Then his mother and his brothers arrived, and standing outside they sent word to him. A crowd was sitting around him, and they said to him, "Behold, your mother and your brothers are outside looking for you."
>
> Answering them, he said, "Who are my mother and my brothers?" Looking about at those who were sitting around him, he said, "Behold my mother and my brothers! For whoever does the will of God, that one is my brother and sister and mother."
>
> Mark 3:31-35
>
> While he was still speaking to the crowds, behold, his mother and brothers were standing outside, seeking to speak to him. Someone said to him, "Behold, your mother and your brothers are standing outside seeking to speak to you."
>
> But Jesus answered the one who was telling him and said, "Who is my mother and who are my brothers?" And stretching out his hand toward his disciples, he said, "Behold my mother and my brothers."
>
> Matthew 12:46-49

There are perhaps no teachings in the Gospels more difficult to understand, or to live by, than those addressing the relationship of disciple to family. The devotion to bloodlines is clearly seen by Jesus to be at odds with devotion to the cross, and several examples serve to expose the conflict. For instance, what are we to make of his words at Luke 14:26:

If anyone comes to me without hating father and mother, wife and chil-dren, brothers and sisters, and even her own life, she cannot be my disciple?

How is it that a would-be disciple is told not to attend the funeral of his own father at Matthew 8:21-22? What is the source of the division Jesus promises to sow in households at Matthew 10:34-36 and Luke 12:49-53 or the reasons for predicted betrayals of disciples by family members at Luke 21:16 and Matthew 10:21?

To begin to get at some answers, it is helpful to reflect on what the Gospels reveal about Jesus's relationship with his own kin. I think the best insight can be gained from a brief interaction which takes place while Jesus is ministering among a large crowd and disputing with the Pharisees at Mark 3:31-35 and Matthew 12:46-49. His mother and brothers appear and send word among the gathering that they wish to take him aside for a private talk. Mark places the scene in the family home, and describes his relatives as thinking Jesus is crazy and needs to be taken away. Jesus's response amounts to a repudiation of kinship as the determining factor in the new life of the discipleship community. It is also an announcement of how the new community is to be organized: "Whoever does the will of God is brother and sister and mother."

As important a role as family or bloodline plays in contemporary culture and individual development, to the world of ancient Pales-tine its influence was all-encompassing. As Ched Myers explains, in *Binding the Strong Man*

> The extended family structure determined personality and identity, controlled vocational prospects, and most importantly facilitated so-cialization. [In Mark's Gospel], kinship is the backbone of the very so-cial order. Jesus is struggling to overturn . . .

To place following Christ as a higher priority in such a society was not only to risk the emotional pain and suffering of alienation from loved ones but also to threaten one's own social status and liveli-hood as well.

The problem with the primacy of kinship is that it limits our sphere of concern and responsibility to the boundaries of bloodlines. It is impossible actively to implement Christ's teachings—love of en-emies, denial of self, acceptance of the cross—within such bound-aries and the social pressures they exert upon the individual. If one's true identity as a child of God is based on following Christ, then the deference to family and bloodline can be understood as an exten-sion of the false self, the self one must learn to deny. The entangle-ments so common to family dynamics are usually based on ego, psychological dependence and coercive, controlling relationships.

The family becomes an idol when devotion to it interferes with one's readiness to resist violence, injustice, and systemic evil—to deny self and take up the cross. Jesus clearly perceived family and devotion to family as a grave threat to discipleship, and his perception is reflected in his uncompromising demand for total devotion to the Gospel.

The family Christ proclaims is inclusive and places those on the periphery—the poor, the stranger, the outcast—squarely in the center. Christ's idea of family is therefore a subversion of the social order by justice. The new community is gathered around, doing the will of God—which is nothing other than discerning and embracing the cross. Here is the only kind of communal life advocated by God in the New Testament, the only kind of life that each of us is called to live. Dispensation with bloodlines makes possible a return to the Garden of Eden, where we are all children of the same parents, Adam and Eve, with God as our Creator. True community, based on love, equality, inclusivity, nonviolence, and shared resources, is both the origin and the destiny of human existence.

As members of families in this context, we are obliged to ask ourselves some hard questions. Why do I consider my own children more important than other children? Do I perceive my identity as spouse, parent, son, or daughter, an exemption from taking up the cross in ways our times demand or as an encouragement to do so? Can a family truly be called Christian if it doesn't hold the practice of nonviolent resistance as a central value? How can we overcome the limitations of nuclear family life in order to respond to the Gospel mandate of universal love and inclusive community? How can we place ourselves in solidarity with families all over the world who are victimized by our nation's war making and economic exploitation?

To address such questions is to begin to place family relationships in their proper perspective. Yet, as with all things related to Christian faith, it is fruitless to try to get at the answers by reflection only. We must also be willing to act.

The personal experience of moving out from nuclear family life into a Gospel-based community has illuminated paths of discipleship which my wife, three children, and I never imagined could be open to us. It has enabled us to understand the true nature of family. In community, our love and interdependence extends beyond bloodlines to a wider circle, with the cross in the center. We learn to give and find the support needed to live in resistance to the powers of this world, even when our resistance leads to jail. And along the way, we believe we are raising up children who will be better-equipped than we are to cast out injustice.

Bloodlines have no meaning and can make no claim in the reign of God. It is a hard but essential teaching in the attempt to recognize who our brother, sister, and mother truly are.

The Two Foundations

by Mark Colville

> *"Why do you call me, 'Lord, Lord,' but not do what I command? I will show you what someone is like who comes to me, listens to my words, and acts on them. That one is like a person building a house, who dug deeply and laid the foundation on rock; when the flood came, the river burst against the house but could not shake it because it had been well built. But the one who listens and does not act is like a person who built a house on the ground without a foundation. When the river burst against it, it collapsed at once and was completely destroyed."*

Luke 6:46-49

With the simple analogy of choosing a foundation for a house, Jesus speaks about the necessary unity of hearing and acting. In many ways, centuries of Christian theology contradict Jesus's words about the person who builds on rock. Theology considered at the heart of Christianity tends to concern itself with orthodoxy or what Christians are supposed to believe. Only in the past thirty years or so, since Vatican II, with the rise to prominence of theologies of liberation, has the focus begun to shift back to the central concern of the Gospels—clearly spelled out at Luke 6:46-49. It is orthopraxies, or what we are supposed to do.

The Christian based communities of the Third World, where Liberation Theology arose, have developed and clarified a concept that seems to get to the heart of truly Gospel-based Christian practice. It stems from the notion, implicit in the foundation analogy, that the meaning of scripture can be comprehended fully only in the attempt to live it. Following scripture is a circular process of hearing/reflecting/acting. Hearing the word of God and reflecting on it within our life context inevitably leads to action, to implementation of the word. Action in turn leads to a deeper, better informed hearing and reflection, which leads back to a more faith-based action and so on. Thus, our lives are constantly being exposed to evaluation in light of Jesus's words and deeds, and our reflection on the Gospel is never done in the vacuum of the abstract. Here is the foundation of faith, built on rock, based on hearing God's word and acting on it.

For the past several years, I have participated in a communal life based on the scriptural model of discipleship. Beginning with a commitment to the Works of Mercy, a shared life of voluntary poverty, prayer, and nonviolence, we have opened our home as a Catholic Worker house of hospitality for the poor. When sitting in jail, I continually marvel at how the experience of community discipleship has radicalized my perspective on what it means to follow Christ. One example is the intensity of discomfort I feel with the system and its victimization of people, now that victims are regularly landing on our doorstep in search of help. The urgency of confronting the injustice and violence routinely done to people, particularly the poor, has never been more prominent in my reading of scripture.

When we give food, clothing, or shelter to the poor, we are doing nothing more than giving back to them that which has been unjustly taken from them. Performing such service is not a burden but a privilege. Indeed, service to the poor is a privilege we don't deserve if we are not actively engaged in defending them against the theft of their property, their rights, and their very lives. And if we are not defending them, then we are cooperating in the systematic oppression of the poor by making their exploitation easier. Catholic Worker life has impressed this conviction upon me, and it is a conviction that weighed heavily on my decision to join in a Plowshare action.

To clarify, I will use the example of working in a shelter for the homeless, which many of us have done over the years. We believe that housing is a human right. We know that right is systematically denied to millions of people in the United States. Throughout the United States, good, selfless, hard-working, caring people staff shelters for the homeless. Nevertheless, even the best shelters don't restore the rights of the poor. They warehouse the poor. Most shelters are little more than jails for those who are forced to live in them. They are temporary dumping grounds for those the empire has written off as throwaway people. We volunteer in a shelter, hoping to do some good, to offer some solace to those who daily suffer from police brutality, hunger, and random acts of state-sponsored violence. Yet how easy it is to go home feeling good about ourselves, thinking we are following Jesus while never addressing the fact that our service is also serving the purposes of a government that couldn't be bothered with housing the poor. Meanwhile, shelters have become a permanent solution to homelessness, and Christians have allowed this to happen by neglecting to connect their service substantively to justice.

In Matthew's Gospel, just before that writer's version of the two foundations analogy, Jesus makes an astonishing statement:

> Not everyone who says to me, "Lord, Lord," will enter the kindom of heaven, but only the one who does the will of my God in heaven. Many will say to me on that day, "Lord, Lord, did we not prophesy in your name? Did we not drive out demons in your name? Did we not do mighty deeds in your name?" Then I will declare to them solemnly, "I never knew you. Depart from me, you evildoers."
>
> Matthew 7:21-23

I believe Jesus's statement can be understood only as referring directly to the cross. Clearly, it is not enough just to do good deeds or even "mighty deeds" in God's name. There are many virtuous and beneficial things we can be doing, but if we want to be identified with Christ—if we want to be known by Christ—our lives must be about the cross.

And what is the cross, if it is not directly confronting the powers of this world and their laws, as Jesus did, in defense of the poor, the outcast, the exploited? For him, this resulted in running afoul of Roman and Judean authorities. He was accused of lawlessness and denounced, persecuted, tortured, and finally, executed. In the twenty-first century, the cross must involve resisting the killing machine, our nation's unbridled, legalized commitment to weapons, death, and ultimate violence. And as with Christ, our action is political, illegal, and nonviolent. Hammering swords into plowshares is, at its root, an act of defending the poor. We dismantle weapons that are built by the theft of resources from those who most need them, weapons that entrench and enforce a scandalously unjust global distribution of wealth. Hammering swords into plowshares is an outright rejection of the diabolical and false form of security that comes from domination, exploitation, and the preferential option for violence. Hammering swords into plowshares is the kind of action that builds a solid foundation for a life of true discipleship.

Chapter 6

Coffin Ships and Truth to Power: Inside the Empire's Jails

Yokes and Burdens

by Mark Colville

Come to me, all you who labor and are burdened, and I will give you rest. Take my yoke upon you and learn from me, for I am meek and humble of heart; and you will find rest for yourselves. For my yoke is easy, and my burden light.

Matthew 11:28-30

"I'm just doing my job." I have heard that phrase so many times since my arrest at Bath Iron Works that it has come to sound like a mantra. Notably, it was once on the lips of a jail guard who spent an hour and a half searching my eight-by ten-foot cell, purportedly looking for contraband. As I waited in the doorway, he carefully examined all of my personal items—books, letters, Bible, clothing, bedding, family pictures, toiletries.

Such violations become routine indignities in our daily lives in jail, usually involving a bodily search that requires us to strip naked. On the occasion mentioned, I was moved to respond to the comment, "I'm just doing my job." I told the guard that he was doing far more than some ordinary job. Indeed, I said to him, "Your job is to humiliate and demonize, and when you do that, you place your own humanity at risk." He responded with a blank stare, indicating neither agreement nor disagreement, allowing no space for dialogue, showing no sign of comprehension.

I have grown—ironically, perhaps—to feel sympathy for corrections officers. They are trained to abuse people and are rewarded for cultivating adversarial relationships with prisoners. Their superiors mistrust guards who are kind and non-confrontational. Those who irritate, provoke, demonize, and humiliate prisoners advance in their careers. The guards' work is a unique form of enslavement, because it saddles them with the burden of administering punishment on those whom the system persecutes, jails, and demonizes. Lawyers and judges may be more responsible for the suffering in jail, but they maintain an air of respectability because their roles extend only to condemnation and judgment. Jail guards don't have the same luxury. They do the dirty work. Human beings are not created to imprison, abuse, punish, or oppress each other, and when we do such things, we surrender some of our own humanity. Doing such work cannot help but undermine the quality of the oppressor's life.

It can be frightening to admit the extent of control our jobs and careers exert in our lives, not just through the amount of time we devote to them, but also how much they mold our identities, outlooks, and allegiances. Any farmer would know that a yoke, when placed around the neck of an ox or horse, serves a threefold purpose: it places the animal under control so that it cannot deviate from the work in front of it, it attaches the animal to a burden, and it can also be used to unite more than one animal in common purpose. In Matthew's Gospel, Jesus applies the image of a yoke to human life when he says:

> Come to me, all you who labor and are burdened, and I will give you rest. Take up my yoke and learn from me, for I am meek and humble of heart; and you will find rest for yourselves. For my yoke is easy and my burden light.

To submit our necks to the yoke of Christ is, first of all, to stake our lives on love of God, love of neighbor, love of enemy. When love becomes the guiding principle of life, all of our pursuits, including work and career, must be measured by the standard of how they fulfill Christ's mandate to love. Such discernment leads to non-cooperation. We refuse weapons building and military service, but the implications extend elsewhere. How, for example, do we reconcile faith in a loving God with work in a legal system that is imprisoning people at a higher rate than any other nation in the world? Three percent of the United States population—about five and a half million people—are in jails, prisons, or on parole. They are overwhelmingly minority and poor, and the prison industry is one of our nation's fastest-growing. Can a person conscientiously take a job in such an industry?

When our lives become directed by the command to love as Jesus loved, we find ourselves attached to the burden of resistance. Not only must we non-cooperate with the culture of death, we are also obliged to stand against it with nonviolence. It means going to places where death is planned and prepared; where—using money stolen from the poor to buy raw materials and pay workers' wages—weapons of unspeakable evil are built. In such places, Christ is crucified. Bath Iron Works in Maine, Electric Boat in Connecticut, the Pentagon, the White House, and CIA and NSA headquarters are among the hundreds of places where people can and must go to make a public confession of faith. If we do not go there, we give consent by silence to the crimes of empire and we refuse the liberation of the cross.

The yoke of Christ binds us to communal relationships with other people in a commitment to justice and truth. We form communities around the simple vocation that is our baptismal commitment: hearing the word of God and acting upon it. And our shared life makes the hearing and acting more possible.

The yoke that Jesus invites us to is, in real terms, nothing less than the yoke of freedom. And, as his own life and death make clear, the freedom Christ intends for us is a violation of the empire's laws. In his letter to the Romans, Saint Paul identifies human law as the perpetuation of sin. He says faith in Christ crucified is freedom from both sin and law. The crucifixion, after all, was not a miscarriage of human justice. It was the fulfillment of the law. The end result of the law is the execution of God. To come to terms with that fact is absolutely necessary as we attempt to follow Christ daily in a nation where nuclear war is also legal.

History shows that the crimes of empire—war, impoverishment, oppression, genocide—are always made possible by the cooperation, capitulation, and silence of good, ordinary people. The dominant systems and structures in our lives are fabulously adept at yoking us to a war-based economy and then coercing us to divorce notions of personal morality from the public, social, or global spheres. That is why the ovens used at Auschwitz could be built by respectable, patriotic, churchgoing people who were struggling to put food on the table. At Bath Iron Works, the slaughter of Iraqi children today and the nuclear holocaust of tomorrow are quietly being made possible by the same kind of good people. And in Cumberland County Jail, where we spent so many months, they are keeping human beings in cages. The end result of such pursuits is spiritual and physical death, the perpetuation of empire, the selling of humanity for a pay check. God's reign will become fully realized in history only when good, ordinary people refuse to bear such burdens.

Following Christ is not simply about avoiding sin. It is about doing justice. To assume fully the yoke and burden, we must leave behind all commitments that mitigate against it. In taking off the yoke of the world, the domination system, the yoke of untruth, we experience liberation, and liberation makes Christ's yoke both easy and light.

The Demon of Unbelief

by Mark Colville

When they came to the disciples, they saw a large crowd around them and scribes arguing with them. Immediately on seeing him, the whole crowd was utterly amazed. They ran up to him and greeted him. He asked them, "What are you arguing about with them?"

Someone from the crowd answered him, "Teacher, I have brought to you my son possessed by a mute spirit. Wherever it seizes him, it throws him down; he foams at the mouth, grinds his teeth, and becomes rigid. I asked your disciples to drive it out, but they were unable to do so."

He said to them in reply, "Oh faithless generation, how long will I be with you? How long will I endure you? Bring him to me."

> *They brought the boy to him. And when he saw him, the spirit immediately threw the boy into convulsions. As he fell to the ground, he began to roll around and foam at the mouth. Then he questioned his father, "How long has this been happening to him?"*
>
> *He replied, "Since childhood. It has often thrown him into fire and into water to kill him. But if you can do anything, have compassion on us and help us."*
>
> *Jesus said to him, "If you can. Everything is possible to one who has faith."*
>
> *Then the boy's father cried out, "I do believe, help my unbelief!"*
>
> *Jesus, on seeing a crowd rapidly gathering, rebuked the unclean spirit and said to it, "Mute and deaf spirit, I command you: come out of him and never enter him again!"*
>
> *Shouting and throwing the boy into convulsions, it came out. He became like a corpse, which caused many to say, "He is dead!" But Jesus took him by the hand, raised him, and he stood up.*
>
> *When he entered the house, his disciples asked him in private, "Why could we not drive it out?"*
>
> *He said to them, "This kind can only come out through prayer."*
>
> Mark 9:14-29

The United States military budget in the United States amounts to spending nine thousand dollars per second or seven hundred million dollars per day on war making. *The National Catholic Reporter* trumpets the information below the headline:

Quaint Plowshares Disturb Business As Usual

The article characterizes our nonviolent disarming of a billion dollar nuclear hell-ship (for which, by July 20, 1997, we had already spent more than four months in jail) as "archaic, indeed mad," "charmingly eccentric," and "wildly Christian in an austere, single-minded way." The editorial attempts ironically to praise the Prince of Peace Plowshares!

On deeper reflection, I realize that I am annoyed because the editorialist is right. With two million people in United States jails, one could count on two hands and perhaps a foot those doing time because they are people of faith who are disturbed—indeed disgusted— by their government's spending nine thousand dollars per second on killing. The national consensus on violence has produced such a cultural paralysis that the very idea of noncooperation is considered anachronistic. At best, usually, it is understood as a throwback to the sixties, a worshipping of values and ideals that were born, lived briefly, and died in one tumultuous decade. Such a view fails to acknowledge that social action—that is, opposition to injustice in the United States—neither began nor ended with the sixties. Abolitionists, labor organizers, civil rights activists, and women's rights advocates were crusading for justice long before the sixties. Moreover, the quest for social and political justice will continue, whether the media choose to report it accurately or not.

I can only conclude one of two things: either I am reading a most unusual translation of the New Testament or most of what passes for belief in Christ these days has absolutely nothing to do with the cross. The crisis of faith today, oxymoronically, is that there is no crisis of faith. Hence, even within the faith community of Roman Catholicism to which we belong, resistance to empire is far from a central concern. It is deemed odd. Nevertheless, if we listen to the Christ of the Gospels, the failure to resist is nothing other than the failure to believe.

Through the healing of a boy with a deaf and mute spirit Jesus points directly to the disease of faithlessness and its symptoms. For those who are listening, he diagnoses the illness of our own day and age. It is important to understand, before continuing, that all healings and exorcisms performed by Christ in the Gospels are symbolic. This is not to say that they didn't happen. Rather, it is to say that their descriptions always point beyond the individual to the larger community and to the social reality. The afflictions of one are the afflictions of many, and to ignore the social implications of the healing episodes is to entirely miss the messages behind them.

Thus, on closer examination, we find that the central focus of this story is not the boy's healing, but the unbelief of the disciples. In two preceding episodes, Peter is rebuked for his inability to articulate an understanding of the cross:

> He began to teach them that the Human One must suffer greatly and be rejected by the elders, the chief priests, and the scribes, and be killed, and rise after three days. He spoke this openly. Then Peter took him aside and began to rebuke him. At this he turned around and, looking at his disciples, rebuked Peter and said, "Get behind me, Satan. You are thinking not as God does, but as human beings do."

Mark 8:31-33

Three disciples are chastised by a voice from heaven for their failure to listen to Jesus:

> Then Elijah appeared to them along with Moses, and they were conversing with Jesus. Then Peter said to Jesus in reply, "Rabbi, it is good that we are here! Let us make three tents: one for you, one for Moses, and one for Elijah." He hardly knew what to say, they were so terrified.

Mark 9:4-6

Both incidents concern questionable faith, and confronted with a deaf and mute spirit in the boy, the disciples of questionable faith are unable to drive it out. Symbolically, the demon itself can be understood as the paralysis of unbelief. Symptoms of deafness and muteness represent the failure to hear, understand or articulate Christ's mission and message. It renders the disciples and the boy's father impotent before the power of evil.

It is known that in the early days of Christianity, baptism was considered more than simply a sacrament of initiation into the community of believers. It was also a rite of exorcism. Living by the values of the dominant culture was understood as being possessed by demons, and a person was thought to be unable to hear or understand Christ's teachings while still under the demon's influence. There is even evidence that people were not allowed into full communion with the church unless they could provide proof, through deeds which pointed to a counter-cultural life-style, that their demons had been exorcised.

How nice it would be if we could recover and revive such a tradition. Unfortunately, today's churches are filled with people whose baptisms have not freed them from the spirits of deafness and muteness which render us so scandalously lacking in responses to the world's evil.

The turning point of the story about the deaf and mute spirit is Jesus's intervention, prompted by the stunningly heartfelt plea of the boy's father: "I do believe, help my unbelief!" His statement captures poignantly the condition of all who struggle to follow Christ, plagued by doubt and tempted toward despair. It also provides the key, the way out, the bridge from unbelief to faith. As Jesus plainly explains at the story's climax: "This kind can only come out through prayer."

"I do believe, help my unbelief!" How many people in our time dare to pray in such a way and mean it? Who will dare to pray their way out of cynicism, apathy, inaction, and despair? Who will ask God to help them stop spiritualizing the cross and personalizing belief? Who will allow into their prayer the souls of two hundred million people killed in wars this century, so that we may finally end our complicity in nine thousand dollars per second spent on killing?

And who will continue to follow the nonviolent Christ when the path leads through the empire's jails?

Jesus told us:

> Whoever says to this mountain, "Be lifted up and thrown into the sea" and does not doubt in her heart but believes that what she says will happen, it will be done for her.
>
> Matthew 21:21

138

When the demon of unbelief is cast out, we know that the transformation of self and world is possible. We know that the mountain of violence, nuclearism, and empire can be cast into the sea. When the demon of unbelief is cast out, we know that the cross is the revolution.

We also know that our actions are much more than how they are understood, interpreted or packaged by a cynical world and the press. Our actions are actually a participation in the redemptive event. And so, we Prince of Peace Plowshares act to change the world, and our deeds become a prayer that the world might not change us. When we pray, we exercise belief, we access the power of God, and we refuse submission to the demon of unbelief.

Chapter 7

Be Not Afraid: Creating Hope Within the Emperor's Apocalyptic World

by Steven Baggarly

"I am the way, the truth, and the life. No one comes to God except through me."

John 14:6

God speaks to Moses on Mount Sinai from the burning bush, telling him to go to Egypt and lead the Hebrew people out of slavery. Moses asks God's name so he might relate it to any inquiring Hebrews. God replies,

I am who I am . . . This is what you shall tell [them]: I am sent me to you.

Exodus 3:14

Jesus makes many "I am" statements in John's Gospel, and the passage above is one example. Sometimes he identifies himself with a simple "I am," as at John 4:26; 6:20. Other times he speaks to the depths:

Before Abraham came to be, I am.

John 8:58

If you do not believe that I am, you will die in your sins.

John 8:24

When you lift up the Human One, then you will realize that I am.

John 8:28

Always he depicts himself as sent from God who fulfills every human need:

I am the bread of life.

John 6:36

I am the light of the world.

John 8:12

I am the resurrection and the life.

John 11:25

I am the good shepherd.

John 10:11

I am the vine, you are the branches.

John 15:5

When soldiers come to arrest Jesus, he calls himself "I am," and they fall to the ground at John 18:6. Throughout the Gospel, by using "I am" phrases, Jesus identifies himself with the God who spoke to Moses from the burning bush. For Christians, Jesus is, in fact, arrived in the flesh, the very God of the universe, God of the ancestors, who liberated the enslaved Hebrews. He states it even more plainly:

143

Whoever has seen me has seen God.

John 14:9

and

God and I are one.

John 10:30

God's way, truth, and life are all most fully revealed in Jesus, according to the text. Jesus's way is ultimately to Jerusalem and the cross. Jesus journeys to Jerusalem, the heart of social domination, where he nonviolently confronts violence. He knows that power rests upon violence and that power harbors the evil empire, the enemy of the poor, weak, and outcast. Thus, he also nonviolently confronts the empire and its minions who will crucify him. He then accepts the backlash that comes to him because he has spoken truth to power. Even though it results in death dealt viciously to him by those in power, Jesus takes the necessary way, the path to truth, life, and justice.

As truth, Jesus is the reality of God. His life and teaching define who God is and what God does. He shows his disciples how to reconstruct the world through unsentimentally pursuing love of neighbor as self, treating others as one likes to be treated, and loving even one's enemies. He teaches about hungry, thirsty, cold, homeless, sick, and imprisoned people, saying that

What you do unto the least of my brothers and sisters you do unto me.

Matthew 25:40

He lives compassion for poor and suffering people, healing and feeding them, confronting authorities who benefit from their misery, and breaking laws that bring them death rather than life. Indeed, lawbreaking sets the rhythm of Jesus's life, which includes healing on the Sabbath, eating with sinners, freely moving between leprous and general society, picking grain on the Sabbath, treating women as equals, driving money changers from the temple, and closing down its commerce. He makes claims of kingship or sonship of God (both titles exclusively the property of Caesar under law). When his own life is at stake as a result and self-defense seems justified, he commands Peter to put away his sword. And he lives his teaching to the end, forgiving his murderers as he hangs on the cross. Gandhi rightly called him "the greatest nonviolent revolutionary who ever lived."

Jesus is the life, his is the life to imitate. Amid a confused and hopeless society, the way and truth of his life radiate empowerment and purpose. God not only calls us to live the life of Christ but enables us to do so. John illustrates when Jesus heals a man born blind, who then identifies himself with the same "I am" at John 9:9 as Jesus. He is elevated to status as a child of God, on a par with Jesus. He, too, can do God's works and be God's presence in the world. Jesus promises that God's power is available to everyone:

Whoever believes will do the works that I do and even greater.

John 14:12

The power is faith expressed in active nonviolence. By nonviolence we mean the pursuit of justice governed by love. After Jesus, his disciples will form communities of nonviolent resistance empowered to renew the face of the earth.

Persistent nonviolence transforms everything; it can even topple powerful and brutal governments. Since World War II, nonviolent movements have ousted colonial rule in India and Ghana. In the Philippines, Iran, and Latin America, dictators have been unseated by people filling the streets in nonviolent protests like general strikes; and, in 1989, Poland, East Germany, Hungary, Bulgaria and Czechoslovakia all gained freedom from Soviet control through nonviolent means. Again, as Gandhi said, "Love, though the humblest thing in the world, is also the most powerful force imaginable."

Violence is the primary Biblical concern. Through disobedience to God in the Garden, violence enters Creation. Cain kills Abel, and history's blood bath begins. All kinds of violence are mentioned. The Bible tells of mass drowning, murder, assault, assassination, gang rape, infanticide, starvation, human sacrifice, ethnic cleansing, torture, massacre, and total war. The Hebrew scriptures serve not only as an account of the often bloody history of the Hebrew people and Israel, but also as a metaphor for the human condition, a commentary on prosperity, slavery, empire, and exile that illuminate the stories of all people.

Israel, in whose Creation myths all things are pronounced "good" and whose covenant with God includes a ban on killing, repeatedly falls into idolatry and becomes like other nations, often trusting in the sword and projecting human violence on God. Israel's understanding of military fortunes as evidence of God's favor or judgment reveals a culture that sees God's hand in absolutely everything. Israel exposes human proclivities to invoke God and religion to garner support for conquest and to hold God responsible for the unconscionable horrors that people freely inflict upon each other. In broad strokes, the Hebrew scriptures portray the world as it is, fraught with violence, oppression, and suffering, conditions that seem to implicate even God.

In the desperate human landscape of Hebrew scripture, we hear scattered prophecies of peace and justice. In fulfillment, almighty God comes in the person of Jesus, calling people to build the nonviolent kindom, where no one dominates anyone else and vulnerable and suffering people are given first consideration. Even he is lynched. Yet with the legal murder of God's own self, every age-old justification for injury and killing is exposed as a lie.

With the dawn of the nuclear age, the reign of violence seems insurmountable. The choice facing us today, as Martin Luther King, Jr., put it, is no longer between violence and nonviolence but between nonviolence and nonexistence. We live amid the ultimate violence, unparalleled idolatry, and blasphemy of nuclear weapons. Current stockpiles can destroy the entire planet a dozen or so times. Yet, since 1980, some sixty Plowshares actions have witnessed to the vulnerability of even nuclear components and delivery systems to disarmament's hammers. For the sake of the billions of people crushed under the imperial heel, symbolic yet real blows have been dealt to those metal gods that demand the awe and servitude of all creation.

The "I am" of the burning bush finds fulfillment in the way, truth, and life of Jesus. Determined nonviolent resistance to injustice points the way to freedom from where we are.

The Genius of Forgiveness

by Philip Berrigan

And if he wrongs you seven times in one day and returns to you seven times saying, "I'm sorry," you should forgive him.

Luke 17:4

Who has experienced a prison strip search, where a guard demands that one strip naked to peek into one's orifices? It is a degrading, humiliating experience. I have experienced a thousand strip searches.

And I had better forgive guards and penal policy makers.

Who remembers responding to three-minutes-to-nuclear-midnight during the Reagan era? We set up a phone tree coordinating trips to the Pentagon, where we expected to die in a nuclear fire storm. It would have been one last witness against the psychopaths of the nuclear war-fighting party.

I remember well. I also remember my outrage at politicians, generals, arms hucksters—those most guilty of the ultimate exhibition of social pathology. Should we talk about public enemies? Or war criminals? What social crime rivals holding entire populations hostage to the BOMB? To holding even creation itself hostage?

I had better forgive such blind, ruthless functionaries.

In Matthew's Gospel, Jesus tells the parable of a king settling accounts with his servants:

> *Then Peter approaching asked him, "Lord, if my brother sins against me, how often must I forgive him? As many as seven times?"*
>
> *Jesus answered, "I say to you, not seven times but seventy times seven times. That is why the kindom of heaven may be likened to a king who decided to settle accounts with his servants. When he began the accounting, a debtor was brought before him who owed him a huge amount. Since he had no way of paying it back, his master ordered him to be sold, along with his wife, his children, and all his property, in payment of the debt.*
>
> *"At that point, the servant fell down, did him homage, and said, 'Be patient with me, and I will pay you back in full.'*
>
> *"Moved with compassion, the master of that servant let him go and forgave him the loan. When that servant had left, he found one of his fellow servants who owed him a much smaller amount. He seized him and started to choke him, demanding, 'Pay back what you owe.'*
>
> *"Falling to his knees, his fellow servant begged him, 'Be patient with me, and I will pay you back.' But he refused. Instead, he had him put in prison until he paid back the debt.*
>
> *"Now when his fellow servants saw what had happened, they were deeply disturbed and went to their master and reported the whole affair. His master summoned him and said to him, 'You wicked servant! I forgave you your entire debt because you begged me to. Should you not have had pity on your fellow servant, as I had pity on you?' Then in anger his master handed him over to the torturers until he should pay back the whole debt.*
>
> *"So will my heavenly Parent do to you, unless each of you forgives one another from the heart."*
>
> Matthew 18:21-35

The sense is clear. God forgives us enormous sins or debts and expects us to forgive one another for immeasurably lesser offenses. Jesus adds weight to the parable when he answers Peter's question, "Lord, if my sister or brother sins against me, how often must I forgive them?" Jesus finally answers Peter's question from the cross. The first of seven "words" is of forgiveness:

> *God, forgive them for they know not what they do.*
>
> Luke 23:34

I am beginning to understand that Jesus's forgiveness of sins was the ultimate revolutionary act, because it took from the state the power of death, restoring it to God. In the same fashion, when we extend mercy and forgiveness to another, the violence of sin stops in us. We take it into ourselves, where grace, the life of God, destroys it. It stems from Calvary—Jesus killed sin, law, and death on the cross to rise victor over them in the Resurrection. When we forgive, Jesus's risen life in us kills the offenses of others against us. Furthermore, our forgiveness—personal, interpersonal, and political—allows us to join the nonviolent revolution of Jesus.

Forgiveness has political aspects. Jesus's healings were essentially acts of mercy and forgiveness that resulted in the restoration of physical and spiritual health. Disease and disability were not God's will for humanity; humanity chose disease and disability in Eden. Human beings then chose to to ostracize the blind, diseased, and paralyzed. When Jesus restored a victim to social status by physical healing, he restored the order preferred by God. Through each healing act, he caused a political outcome. Further, human societies achieve cohesion and survivability by violence. They are born in violence. They reject God, wage war, or undertake violent revolution. Sometimes, societal violence enacts the death penalty and centers on a victim upon whom the social order heaps its sins. Such scapegoating echoes the ancient Hebrew practice of symbolically loading a goat with the community's sins and driving the goat into the wilderness. The act rids the society of sin and thus saves the social fabric from being torn apart.

When we take upon ourselves the social burdens of the victim by becoming the victim, as Christ did, lending our voice, our hands, and our freedom in civil resistance, we break the scapegoating mechanism because we take violence upon ourselves, absorb it, stop it, terminate it. Nonviolence provides a voluntary scapegoat as victim.

Furthermore, it is the will of God for people to live in community as Jesus did. It is the will of God to live in communities that embody the eventual unity of the human family, communities whose truth of nonviolence withstands the age-old reliance on lies and bribes, communities whose resistance defends and rescues the whole body, communities that guarantee the needs of the human family by voluntary poverty.

Finally, it is the will of God that we become people of the word—eager to know God, determined to live the divine will.

In temporary rebellion against having been moved peremptorily from one jail to another, I awoke one morning in jail with a suffocating sense of the blahs, of uselessness and ennui. For a moment, I entertained the question: "What the hell am I doing here?

I had been in prison for eight months in Maine, and I knew I would go for sentencing on October 27. Prison time for me, since

1967, then added up to nearly eight years, ninety-four months. I was seventy-four years old. A treacherous question whirled in my heart: "For what?"

To add to the blahs, the future looked ominous. We knew that the government intended to break up our communities, mainly Jonah House, and to stop Plowshares. Michele Naar-Obed, due for release from federal prison in Florida a week after our trial, was forbidden to return to Jonah House in Baltimore. When she did return, she was immediately rearrested and sentenced to more time in prison. Realizing that Jonah House is a vibrant, strong, indefatigable resistance community, the government decided quite consciously to harass and persecute us.

For a time, their repression went unchallenged because we didn't have anyone in a position to challenge them in their loathesome courts. And so we couldn't ask publicly, "How dare this government tell us where we can live and not live? How dare they take us from our right to worship? How dare they force us into work not of our choosing, like slaves or members of a chain gang?"

We have repeatedly told the court that we won't pay fines and restitution, that we won't serve supervised release. Yet it is virtually certain that a judge, whose career reflects reverence for the empire, will sentence us to both.

By all appearances, all doors are slammed on us. Subjecting us to endure prison is not enough to satisfy the empire's wrath. It reminds me of the Vietnam era, when oligarchs resorted to dirty tricks, kangaroo trials, prison, and murder to assert control.

Before, we possessed a long-standing hope: accept the consequences of disarmament so as to win freedom to return to family, community, and work. That hope seems gone. The empire will tolerate no reminder that it is destroying itself and its people. I see now that such hope is a facet of the thirst for normalcy. I want to live my last days in some measure of peace.

The spirit of God helps as always when I "wait" for God, as the psalmist advises. I recall a portion of the prayers beginning the old Latin Mass:

What shall I render to God for all the things rendered to me?

Psalm 116:12

Well, the fact is, I've rendered virtually nothing, despite my many actions and years in prison.

The story is told of a speech Frederick Douglass gave near the end of the Civil War. For the first time, he called for the gun. "Now is the time!" he said.

Then a clear voice rang out from the audience: "Frederick, Frederick. Isn't God still God?"

Maybe it's pay up time. Maybe the persecution will broaden and intensify. I think of what Christ said to Jairus before raising his little daughter from the dead:

Don't be afraid. Just believe!

Mark 5:36

And forgive. Yes. Just forgive, believe, and trust. Amen.

Feeding the Multitudes

by Susan Crane

When the apostles returned, they explained to him what they had done. He took them and withdrew in private to a town called Bethsaida. The crowds, meanwhile, learned of this and followed him. He received them and spoke to them about the kindom of God, and he healed those who needed to be cured. As the day was drawing to a close, the twelve approached him and said, "Dismiss the crowd so that they can go to the surrounding villages and farms and find lodging and provisions; for we are in a deserted place here."

He said to them, "Give them some food yourselves."

They replied, "Five loaves and two fish are all we have, unless we ourselves go and buy food for all these people." Now the men there numbered about five thousand.

Then he said to his disciples, "Have them sit down in groups of fifty." They did so and made them all sit down. Then taking the five loaves and the two fish, and looking up to heaven, he said the blessing over them, broke them, and gave them to the disciples to set before the crowd. They all ate and were satisfied. And when the leftover fragments were picked up, they filled twelve wicker baskets.

Luke 9:10-17

The story of feeding the multitudes is one of many scripture stories about justice, about sharing the earth's resources and products that we make.

One of the first such stories is found in Exodus when the Israelites are journeying in the desert. They are hungry and begin to grumble. In response, God sends them manna in the morning and quail at night. But there are rules about the manna. The people are told to pick up the manna in the morning and take what they need for all the people in their tent. If they gather too little or gather too much, when they go to weigh it out, they will always have the right amount.

They are told not to hoard it but to gather it fresh each day except on the sixth day when they gather enough for two days, including the Sabbath. If they try to keep the manna for the next day (except the Sabbath), it becomes wormy and rotten. The Israelites learned not to take more than their share of resources available to them. They learned not to hoard or be greedy. The idea of use-value rather than exchange value was instilled, as there was no reason or any way to buy and sell manna. It could not become a commodity. It was simply food to be shared and eaten.

In the story of feeding the multitudes, Jesus has been talking about the kindom of God and has healed those who need to be cured. At Luke 9:12, the apostles urge Jesus to

> Dismiss the crowd so they can go to surrounding villages and farms and find lodging and provisions; for we are in a deserted place here.

A reasonable, practical request. No doubt the apostles were also hungry and tired.

Jesus says, "Give them food yourselves." How preposterous that must have seemed. There must have been at least fifteen thousand people, when women and children are counted as well as the five thousand men of the scripture. How could the apostles get food for all those people in a deserted place? And why would Jesus tell them to? Like the apostles, we ask God to find food and shelter for those in need—homeless and refugees around the world. Jesus's response is clear: the responsibility is on you and me.

The apostles respond,

> Five loaves and two fish are all we have, unless we ourselves go and buy food for all these people.

Again, the apostles are practical, as they ask, essentially, "Do you want us to travel to a local village and buy food?" They are solidly in the practical world of the commodity: food is bought and sold.

But Jesus replies, "Have them sit in groups of fifty." Jesus solves the problem outside the commodity society. He has the people sit in organized groups, the beginning of community. Then he models by sharing all that he and his friends have. Sitting in small groups, everyone brings out what little they have, and everyone is satisfied. Once started, generosity grows, and food that is blessed and shared tastes better than food bought or eaten alone. The problem of feeding people is solved without political leaders and without money. It is solved by cooperation among all the people. The wisdom of the consumer world insists that sharing doesn't work. Conventional wisdom tells us that we need to hold on to what we can get, and then we need advanced weapons and a strong military so that no one else takes what we have. Saint Francis of Assisi understood the potential problem well when he said, "If we had any possessions, we would need weapons and laws to defend them." Generosity is seldom tried, but we are still responsible for each other, according to the passages in Luke.

If we don't share, we participate in theft, because the world's resources don't belong to us. They are our Creator's. To have more than our share and give it away is not charity but simple justice. We have to ask ourselves why we have so much and others so little. Year after year, the figures remain: forty-five thousand children die each day from hunger and hunger-related diseases, and each year our first priority as a nation is military spending. The image always in my mind is of the mother who is holding her dying child in her arms. What do I say to her? I see the Trident missiles, the Aegis destroyers, the chart of our federal spending. This woman loves her child like I love my children. Unless we see every mother's child as precious as our own children, we will continue to choose military solutions instead of solving our problems by generosity and sharing.

If we take the time to reflect, the voice of conscience speaks to us. Anyone reflecting on the Aegis destroyer, the mother holding her child, and the Gospel stories would want to share what they have with those in need. But we shouldn't think it any big deal to share what we stole from others to begin with. Saint John Chrysostom suggested, "Not to enable the poor to share in our goods is to steal from them and deprive them of life. The goods we possess are not ours, but theirs." Today, many of the resources we use have been robbed at gunpoint from other nations so that we can maintain our standard of living. Many of the commodities we use in our everyday lives have been manufactured in sweatshops by people, including children, who make pennies an hour and are treated poorly.

In the scripture account, with God's help, with human cooperation, everyone's needs are met. What do we have to do to receive God's help? Listen and have faith. Listen and be organized. Listen and be in community.

Each of us has a story of a time a person has met us with hostility and we were able to respond with generosity. The whole situation changes. Hostility and fear leave and the possibilities of friendship open. We don't want to have hearts of stone. The people who gathered to listen to Jesus wanted to eat and yearned to share, but their fear was that there wasn't enough. The practice of generosity helps us to overcome the fear that is in and around us, and indeed, there will be enough.

The Great Commandments

by Steven Baggarly

When the Pharisees heard that Jesus had silenced the Sadducees, they gathered together and one of them, a scholar of the law, tested him by asking, "Teacher, which commandment in the law is the greatest?"

He said to them, "You shall love the Lord, your God, with all your heart, with all your soul, and with all your mind. This is the greatest and the first commandment. The second is like it: You shall love your neighbor as yourself. The whole law and the prophets depend on these two commandments."

Matthew 22:34-40

Religious authorities confront Jesus in the temple area at Matthew 22:15-40 with a series of questions. They approach to test the orthodoxy of his view of Mosaic law. His response is part of Judaism's great refrain:

Hear, O Israel! The Lord is our God, the Lord alone! Therefore, you shall love the Lord, your God, with all your heart, and with all your soul, and with all your strength.

Deuteronomy 6:4-5

A fine answer—certainly, loving God with one's whole being is the great commandment. Only Jesus doesn't stop there. He joins it to another line:

You shall love your neighbor as yourself.

Leviticus 19:9-18

The statement summarizes the passage at Leviticus 19:9-18, which commands, among other things, that landowners allow the poor access to crops in their fields and that they pay day laborers promptly, that they have respect for disabled people; show fairness in economic relations and judicial process; deal with honesty, forgiveness, and protection of the precarious lives of the poor. Jesus's answer equates loving God with pursuing justice for the poor.[1]

John further elucidates the relationship between God and neighbor:

If anyone says, "I love God," but hates their sister or brother, they are a liar; for whoever does not love a sister or brother whom they have seen cannot love God whom they have not seen. This is the commandment we have from God: whoever loves God must also love their sister and brother.

1 John 4:20-21

There is no love of God except in love of neighbor. Paul writes that

Love does no evil to the neighbor, hence, love fulfills the law.

Romans 13:10

Love won't allow others quietly to suffer injustice, poverty, or violence. The whole law and prophets, the entire history of God's relationship with humanity, points toward love that does justice for the poor and powerless neighbor. It is the true orthodoxy.

In Luke's version of the story, the questioner asks Jesus at 10:29, "Who is my neighbor?" In response, Jesus tells a parable about a man who is beaten, robbed, and left for dead. Two religious leaders ignore the man lying in the ditch until a passing Samaritan finally binds the man's wounds and sees to his care. Jesus implies that the identity of one's neighbor is so obvious that even an enemy Samaritan knows it. To love neighbor as self is to seek justice and do what is good for suffering, oppressed, and exploited people. Such a neighbor is another self.

Kim and I have been with communities of hospitality and resistance for more than ten years. Between the Saint Francis Inn in Philadelphia and the Los Angeles Catholic Worker, as well as the Norfolk Catholic Worker, our current home, we have tried to live while regarding the neighbor as another self, practicing corporal and spiritual works of mercy.

Four mornings a week in Norfolk, the Catholic Worker serves a meal on the street, just above downtown. There, we get to know people who live in abandoned buildings or cars, under bridges, and in shelters, bus stops, cemeteries, or even in self-storage containers or portable toilets on construction sites. A handful of these friends live with us at the hospitality house. Over the years, the house has been home to day laborers and the unemployed, parolees, mentally-handicapped folks, people with AIDS, those injured or recovering from an operation, substance abusers, refugees, senior citizens who are on the street, migrant workers, runaways, and single moms. People come from the downtown streets to use the phone, shower, do laundry, or spend the night on the couch. When money is tight, neighbors come by for food. The community also visits people in jail or in the hospital and claims the bodies of those with no family to give them a dignified burial rather than allowing the state to use them for medical experiments. Living in our hemisphere's most militarized zone, we remain constantly aware that works of war are the antithesis of works of mercy. War destroys crops and land, seizes food supplies, destroys homes, scatters families, contaminates water, imprisons dissenters, inflicts wounds, and burns and kills the living. War and its infrastructure are the primary causes of poverty, suffering, and pollution throughout the world. "Noncooperation with evil is as important as cooperation with good," Gandhi said. By opposing nuclear weapons and war making in the Norfolk area, we practice spiritual works of mercy. In addition to trying to serve impoverished brothers and sisters around us, we endeavor to be a voice for silenced people everywhere who are starved, threatened, and butchered by United States militarism. Through speaking, writing, vigiling, leafletting, staging rallies, and witnessing in civil resistance at nearby military sites, we publicly confront the planet's number one war makers: the United States government, its arms manufacturers, and their killing machines.

Like the sexism, racism, and poverty we see every day, weapons of war embody fear of neighbor and rebellion against God. Hammering on a nuclear-capable destroyer is part of our attempt to live sacramentally at the Norfolk Catholic Worker, an expression of our inward desire to convert whatever it is in ourselves and in the world that precludes love of neighbor and thus of God.

The Vine and the Branches

Mark Colville

I am the true vine, and my Parent is the vine dresser. Every branch in me that does not bear fruit, my Parent takes away; and every branch that bears fruit, my Parent prunes it so that it may bear more fruit.

You are already clean because of the word which I have spoken to you. Abide in me, and I in you. As the branch cannot bear fruit of itself unless it abides in the vine, so neither can you unless you abide in me.

I am the vine, you are the branches; those who abide in me and I in them, they bear much fruit, for apart from me you can do nothing. If anyone does not abide in me, they are thrown away as a branch and dry up; and they gather them, and cast them into the fire and they are burned.

If you abide in me, and my words abide in you, ask whatever you wish, and it will be done for you. My Parent is glorified by this, that you bear much fruit, and so prove to be my disciples. Just as the Parent has loved me, I have also loved you; abide in my love.

If you keep my commandments, you will abide in my love; just as I have kept my parent's commandments and abide in God's love. These things I have spoken to you so that my joy may be in you, and that your joy may be made full.

This is my commandment, that you love one another, just as I have loved you. Greater love has no one than this, that one lay down one's life for one's friends. You are my friends if you do what I command you.

*No longer do I call you slaves, for the slave does not know what the master
is doing; but I have called you friends, for all things that I have heard from
my Parent I have made known to you. You did not choose me but I chose you,
and appointed you that you would go and bear fruit, and that your fruit
would remain, so that whatever you ask of the Parent in my name may be
given to you.*
This I command you, that you love one another.

John 15:1-17

A young man—I'll call him Stevie—was recently released back to
the streets from our cell block after a two-month stay. Stevie, an
alcoholic with a mental illness that causes him frequent agitation,
is from Scotland. Like several prisoners here, Stevie doesn't belong
in jail or the streets. He belongs in a psychiatric facility. As fate would
have it, his last name happens to rhyme with "Armageddon," and
this seemed to be a contributing factor to his constant torment. Stevie
used to spend much of his time mumbling about the prophesies of
Nostradamus, and of his certainty that the world is going to end in
the year 2000.

Judging from the news, Stevie may be on to something. A frightening editorial in a recent newspaper reveals the dangerous folly
and unnecessary provocativeness of NATO's plans to expand right
to Russia's borders. The writer states that Russia's infrastructure is
crumbling and its military is starving, unpaid, and disgruntled. Even
more disturbing is that Russia's arsenal of nuclear weapons—thousands of atomic warheads—is not protected from sabotage, theft, or
unauthorized launch. The writer calls the decision to increase ten-
sions by bringing Poland, Hungary, and the Czech Republic into the
NATO Alliance a "fateful step," plunging the world farther "down a
one-way path to Armageddon."

It is easy to understand why so many Americans are of the belief
that current world events signal the rapid approach of the end times.
I was born a year before the Cuban Missile Crisis. My generation has
no experience of life apart from the constant threat of global annihilation. The effect on the subconscious is clearly difficult to esti-
mate, but its contribution to the cheapening of life and the widespread functional despair in our society is undeniable. Most of us
are mired in a lack of hope in the future. Many suspect that humanity cannot, or will not, change its catastrophic course.

This attitude permeates our religion, and with devastating effects.
A common element of contemporary religious belief is that the end
of the world will be an event controlled by God but initiated by
humanity with nuclear weapons. The Christian Right has always
theologized the virtue of United States weaponry, going so far as to

advocate first-strike nuclear war as the way to bring about the Second Coming of Christ. The sentiment was horrifically summed up by President Truman after the bombing of Hiroshima: "This is the greatest day on earth. Thank God that he has given us the bomb and may we use it in God's ways." Of course this kind of faith bears no resemblance to Christ's teachings, nor any other part of the Bible. It is simply religion at the service of empire, justifying its unbridled power by invoking the name of God.

Biblical faith is based upon God's intervention in human history in order to bring about justice for the poor, freedom for the oppressed, and the destruction of all systems of domination. Authentic Christianity finds the ultimate expression of this intervention in the cross of Christ. Theologian Jose Miranda insightfully explains the point:

> To believe that Jesus is the Messiah has a very concrete historical meaning which should be clear from reading the Old Testament and John. [It means] believing in a historical event. To believe that this man, Jesus of Nazareth, is the Messiah is to believe that with him the messianic kindom has arrived. It is to believe that in our age the kindom of God has arrived, an event which fulfills all hope.

Miranda goes on to point out that a fundamental element of biblical faith is "believing that our world is not past recovery." To believe in a salvation in the beyond, in another time and place, another world, is to embrace a faith other than that of the Hebrew scriptures and New Testament. To believe that this world cannot be healed, in other words, is to disbelieve the true message of the cross.

Only in believing that the reign of God is at hand, that today the scripture is fulfilled as suggested at Luke 4:21, can it be possible to do what Christ did, namely to stand against the forces of evil with the power of nonviolent love. This is, I believe, the essential message of the teaching on the vine and the branches at John 5:1-17. To remain in Christ is not a matter of spirituality or mystical union, but of deeds which "bear fruit." And in light of the previous footwashing scene at John 13:1-10, in which the disciples were commissioned to martyrdom, there can be no doubt with regard to what bearing fruit is all about. It is nothing less than actively accepting the cross by living according to the reign of God, which is here and now.

Two additional points strike me as important to note from the passage. First, the idea of a universal all-inclusive salvation is foreign to the Gospel of John. Branches that don't bear fruit are cut off, gathered up and burned. If our comfortable sensibilities as first-world

Christians are offended by this, we must remember that the Gospels speak from the perspective of oppressed and persecuted communities—those whom the Beatitudes call blessed at Matthew 5:1-12. For them, the imperatives of doing justice and actively participating in the reign of God are inescapable, as are the consequences of failing to do so. Second, even the branches that do bear fruit are pruned, indicating that we must be prepared for suffering as we oppose the domination system in defense of the poor.

As the world seems to move closer to the brink of destruction, the temptation to embrace a non-biblical faith in an other-worldly salvation does intensify. Yet at the same time the way of the cross becomes clearer: we must learn to live in active, creative hope for a just and nonviolent world, and we must be willing to purchase this hope with our lives. To embrace such hope is to remain in Christ, the true vine. The fruit to be borne is nothing less than the salvation of the world, the reversal of this course of destruction we appear to be on. The words of the Jesuit priest, Pierre Teilhard de Chardin, capture well the challenge facing all of us in the nuclear age:

> I wonder if [human] kind is not really at the point of being divided between those who believe and those who do not believe in the future of the universe. And I feel more determined than ever to join the former in the conquest of the world.

Light of the World

by Mark Colville

Jesus spoke to them again, saying, "I am the light of the world. Whoever follows me will not walk in darkness, but will have the light of life."

John 8:12

Some of the most profound sayings of Christ can appear on the surface to be the most abstract, prone to great trivialization and most appropriate for holy cards. Sometimes, to find meaning, we need the example of a life lived.

Franz Jaegersteatter was an Austrian peasant farmer, the father of three small children when the Nazis occupied his country in the early stages of World War II. Franz was a rather frivolous and wild young man. However, following his marriage to a devout Catholic woman, he went through a remarkable conversion. By his early thirties, Franz had put aside his childish ways and become an adult. Indeed, he had decided to commit the rest of his life to following Christ, a commitment that was soon tested when the Nazis demanded that he swear an oath to Hitler and agree to serve in the military.

Franz Jaegersteatter's church had made its peace with the Nazis. The Austrian Catholic hierarchy recognized the invading army's "legitimate authority" and subsequently encouraged Austrian men to sign the oath and to submit to military service. Franz's extended family offered no resistance to Nazi edicts. Moreover, all of the people he lived and worked among, as well as public officials, acquiesced to Hitler's outrageous demands. When this ordinary man decided that oaths and service to the Third Reich were a denial of Christ, he stood quite literally alone.

Imprisoned and threatened with execution, Franz stood firm. "Christ, too, demands a public confession of our faith," said Jaegersteatter, "just as the Führer, Adolf Hitler, does from his followers."

Scolded by his bishop and offered a noncombatant role in the army, Franz replied, "I cannot and may not take an oath in favor of a government that is fighting an unjust war." On August 9, 1943, Franz Jaegersteatter was beheaded by the Nazis he defied for principles that few of his friends or family seemed to understand. He died in near total obscurity, and those who were aware of his resistance thought it absurd, wrong-headed, and irresponsible. Jaegersteatter's sacrifice, by all accounts, became an utterly insignificant piece of non-history.

With no hope of vindication in this life, and with no support, the man clung to the truth. Where does one find such courage?

John's Gospel is filled with images of light and darkness, but the definitive one is Jesus's public proclamation at the temple celebration of Tabernacles: "I am the light of the world." To put the words in perspective and context, consider that the entire temple area would have been illuminated with torches for the culminating celebration of the feast. The torches ceremony was an expression of the Jewish eschatological hope that, at the end of time, all "people of light" would be gathered together by Yahweh at the Jerusalem Temple. Of course, for the original readers of John's Gospel, the hope had been dashed, because the temple itself had been destroyed by Rome around 70 C.E. Jesus's words, therefore, are to be understood as a bold statement of renewed, indestructible hope. Christ is the new temple, full of light. By his resurrection, he has conquered the forces of the Roman Empire and all forces of domination and darkness.

But the light also has a clearly-stated purpose, and that is to illuminate our walking: "Whoever follows me will not walk in darkness but will have the light of life." According to Jesus, there is no standing still. Human life is a journey, and we are either walking in darkness or light. In the real world, as Franz Jaegersteatter knew, that means we are either walking in resistance to evil or in complicity with it, and our very identity as children of God hangs in the balance. For that reason, alone, Jaegersteatter resisted.

Certainly he could have no inkling that his death would even be remembered by future generations, much less achieve any discernible effect.

The light shines in the darkness, and darkness has not overcome it.

John 1:5

Twenty years after Jaegersteatter's death, Gordon Zahn, a sociologist, stumbled across Jaegersteatter's story while researching the life of an Austrian priest. Zahn later wrote *In Solitary Witness*, which inspired Daniel Ellsberg, a Pentagon analyst and Marine veteran, to risk his career and even his life to make public top-secret papers on the United States government's involvement in the Vietnam War. Ellsberg released the papers to the *New York Times*, an act that enraged President Richard M. Nixon and other Washington hawks. Knowing the risks he was taking, Ellsberg called on the courage of Franz Jaegersteatter to guide and strengthen his own witness for peace. There can be no doubt that Ellsberg's act of resistance was instrumental in ending our government's genocidal war in Southeast Asia.

To walk in the light of life today is to refuse to allow the threat of persecution to purchase our silence before the crimes of empire. It is to make a public confession of hope, to place our bodies between the victims and the victimizers, to refuse to let the poor die defenseless or our dissent be filtered through "proper channels." In a society where everyone has a price, resistance is nothing more than the simple, consistent refusal to be bought.

The source of hope by which we can walk the path are the many men and women, some well-known and some who died in obscurity, who have challenged injustice and paid dearly for their resistance. Their lives illuminate our journey, and as we share their stories, especially in prison, we find our own burdens more easily borne. They call us forward to reconfirm our public stand with the nonviolent Christ, to be clear about our witness, uncompromising, and to endure courageously the consequences the empire imposes.

Franz Jaegersteatter and many others are, with Christ, the light of the world.

The Unity of all Life

... So that they may be one, as we are one, I in them and you in me, that they may be brought to perfection as one, that the world may know that you sent me.

John 17:22,23

"In the darkness of anything external to me, I find without recognizing it as such, an interior or psychic life that is my own," said the psychologist, Carl Jung. And, said Walking Buffalo, a Canadian Stoney Indian,

Did you know that trees talk? Well, they do. They talk to each other and they'll talk to you if you listen. Trouble is, white people don't listen to the Indian, so I don't suppose they'll listen to other voices in nature. But I have learned a lot from trees: sometimes about the weather, sometimes about animals, sometimes about the Great Spirit.

Christ sums up his mission and life in the teaching on unity in the Last Supper Discourses. Science increasingly reveals a startling unity in Creation. Discipleship includes embodying oneness with God, with humanity and with Creation.

Everything Jesus says and does at the Last Supper discloses his love for us and points to the unity of all life. Accordingly:

Jesus washes the disciples' feet at John 13:2-17 to prepare them for martyrdom, just as Mary had prepared him. Love of God, neighbor and Creation will alone bring about unity, a unity that begins in us and ends with us.

No one has greater love than this—to lay down one's life for one's friends.

John 15:13

Jesus gives a new commandment at John 13:34. The fourth Gospel depicts the new Creation, the new person, the new food eucharist, the new temple, the new worship, and the new commandment,

Love one another as I have loved you.

John 15:12

The new Creation and new person depend on obedience to the new commandment.

Jesus predicts that his followers' "belief" will cause "greater works" than his own at John 14:12. Faith and love will bring us from death to life. Life will be unified with God, neighbor, and the universe.

Jesus gives his peace to the disciples at John 14:27. Peace is the dominant theme of the New Testament, framing his passion and death, before and after. After the Resurrection, he will link peace to the wounds of his passion. Peace is identical with unity, peace founded on justice. Unity is the restoration of God's justice to the world.

Jesus describes himself as the vine and us the branches at John 15:5. Paul depicts us as members of a body, but Jesus uses the metaphor of the vine and branches. And he tells us flatly

Without me, you can do nothing.

John 15:5

That is to say, without him we can do nothing constructive, life-giving, loving, or just—only everything divisive, destructive, deadly.

At John 16:13, Jesus promises the Holy Spirit who will recall to mind everything Jesus taught them; even more, the spirit of God will guide them into "all truth." The Spirit of God will confirm Jesus's work in the world, ultimately returning to God a family unified in truth and revering Creation.

Jesus prays

that they may be one, as we are one, I in them and you in me, that they may be brought to perfection as one, that the world may know that you sent me.

John 17: 22, 23

On the cross Jesus unifies all things in himself, draws all things to himself. We need only give our fiat and live it.

Christ accomplished, once and for all, unity of the human family with God, and within itself. He overcame sin, law and death, putting them to death in his flesh on the cross. So unity became final and the redemption of the universe finally done, but not yet. The "not yet" has to do with us and our freedom of choice. The chaotic condition of humankind and the world testifies that people are not yet mature enough to make this sublime work of God's our own.

Perhaps we should see the liability of regarding Creation separately, as the "environment" or "ecology," as though to hold ourselves apart and remote. People are of the earth, are of the universe,—our bodies of the same atoms and molecules, our persons in constant exchange with the interiority of matter. So it behooves us to know something of our mother earth, "where we come from," our womb or nest which our ignorance and violence denies and punishes.

Imperial culture with its economic and military oppression gives the kiss of death to nature. Automatically, imperialism means control, making nature an enemy, against which one declares war. Consequently, Americans ravage and pollute the whole world while being primed to blow up everything in defense of our little contaminated paradise. With most people unaware, a hellish race goes on, stampeding us in one direction or another. Will we kill ourselves by nuclear war or by lethal toxins in air, soil and water?

We have punished nature. Nature will punish us. We have already begun to quail under an outraged nature—ozone depletion, global warming from prodigious consumption of fossil fuels, glaciers melting, oceans rising, acid rain, trees dying, terrible tornadoes and hurricanes. Our rejection of the divine revelation in Jesus is cut from the same bolt of cloth as our rejection of God's word in nature.

Like us, the ancients worshipped the elements of nature, granting the elements an ultimacy they do not possess. Clement of Alexandria wrote of philosophers who "worshipped matter" ignoring "the great original, the maker of all things, the Creator of the First Principles, God without beginning." Elements are the building blocks of any substance or entity, the very conditions of life. They had existence before our advent on earth, they transcend us, and live after our death. We cooperate with them, having a nonviolent relationship with them, or they resist us, "judging" our conduct.

Most of us are oblivious of the fact that we permeate the elements with our spirit, projecting into them our idolatry, fear, hatred, unrest. We have brought to subatomic matter our own darkness, finding there precisely what we have brought. The classic example of this is the Manhattan Project, in which scientists split the atom for war. What they brought to their work and the elements was a lust for unthinkable power—power over all lives on earth. Now the atom retaliates, beginning to take its revenge, like Frankenstein turning against its Creators. The scientific community and most Americans know nothing of nonviolence. The scientific community failed to see the connection between the two elementary questions: What can I know? How shall I live?

As a matter of survival, we must transform our view of the world, of others, ourselves and creatures. How did Martin Luther King, Jr., put it? "Nonviolence or nonexistence?" Nonviolence not only regards others as equal sisters and brothers, it also realizes that matter has a soul, a mind, being part of a living, pulsing, unified interdependent web of existence that we call the universe. Reality resembles a hologram in which an organism in some manner represents the universe, and each portion of the universe represents in some manner the organisms within it. Reality like truth is one. And we are one with God, with one another, with a unified universe.

In Psalm 148, the heavens, creatures and plants join in praise of God. Finally, we join the vast chorus of praise, for it is incomplete without us. God has fitted a body to us, just as to God's son in the Incarnation. About the meaning of the Incarnation, Oetinger says: "... corporeality is the ultimate end of all God's ways."

> The angels keep their ancient places
> Turn but a stone and start a wing!
> 'Tis ye, 'tis your estranged faces
> That mess the many splendored thing.
>
> Francis Thompson

Beatitudes

by Steven Baggarly

Blessed are the poor in spirit,
*   for theirs is the kindom of heaven.*
Blessed are they who mourn,
*   for they will be comforted.*
Blessed are the meek,
*   for they will inherit the land.*
Blessed are they who hunger and thirst for righteousness,
*   for they will be satisfied.*
Blessed are the merciful,
*   for they will be shown mercy.*
Blessed are the clean of heart,
*   for they will see God.*
Blessed are the peacemakers,
*   for they will be called the children of God.*
Blessed are they who are persecuted for the sake of righteousness,
*   for theirs is the kindom of heaven.*

Blessed are you when they insult you and persecute you and utter every kind of evil against you because of me. Rejoice and be glad, for your reward will be great in heaven. Thus they persecuted the prophets who were before you.

Matthew 5:3-12

The Beatitudes offer a synopsis of both the life of Christ and the life of discipleship. They are a definition of righteousness and right relationship rooted in the compassion and justice of Hebrew creation stories. The first two chapters of Genesis teach that all people are made in the image and likeness of God and share common parentage. Humankind is revealed as one family of profound dignity, all sisters and brothers loved by God. Indeed, all of creation—the heavens, the earth, and everything in it—God declares very good at Genesis 1:31. The "blessed ones" of the Beatitudes invoke the original goodness, suggesting that it isn't merely restricted to the Garden of Eden but is among us now and can be the future. To care for creation and work for the sisterhood and brotherhood of human-kind are what Jesus demonstrates and are precisely what fulfills us as human beings.

Implicit in the Beatitudes is the centrality given to the oppressed, impoverished, and suffering people by Jesus and the community of discipleship. The condition of the widow and the orphan best attest to just how far the world stands from the loving sisterhood and brotherhood God intended it to be. To understand the upside down world of the Beatitudes, we need to hone in on the still small voices that God hears, the voices of people whom society declares expendable. The experiences of starved, bombed, violated, and terrorized people underline the urgency for disciples to live Christianity's core values of service, voluntary poverty, nonviolence, resistance, and community.

The first Beatitude undergirds those that follow. Poverty of spirit means dependence on God. John the Baptist exemplifies the quality in his reference to Jesus at John 3:30:

He must increase; I must decrease.

Such poverty puts ego in its place.

The earth is God's and all it holds, the world and all those who live there.
Psalm 24

To be spiritually poor in the exemplary way of John the Baptist is to live knowing that everything belongs only to God, including our very selves. I witness such holy dependency regularly on our soup line when we run out of food. Those who have received our meager fare will share what little they have with latecomers who have nothing. I believe Kim and I have become more aware than ever of our spiritual poverty while preparing for the Prince of Peace Plowshares action. Amid much criticism and knowing that my particpation could mean long years in jail, we learned to entrust each other, our child, our community, our life's work, our families, our friends, and our future to God in order to liberate us to do what we feel is right.

Poverty of spirit counters the ethos of empire. It unravels myths spun by Wall Street, the Pentagon, and Madison Avenue which would have us believe that greed serves the common good, that might makes right, and that we are what we own. Rather than brutally pursuing United States global economic, military, cultural, and political hegemony, poverty of spirit seeks the end of all domination. Along with the rest of the Sermon on the Mount, which Dorothy Day called the "Christian Manifesto," the Beatitudes provide a blueprint for both the nonviolent toppling of empire and the framework for a world based on compassion and justice.

The subsequent Beatitudes flow from the first. The fourth, hungering and thirsting, emphasizes the centrality of restoring right relationships with God, neighbor, self, and creation. All point to the seventh as the way to "be" with such attitudes:

Blessed are the peacemakers, for they will be called children of God.

Active nonviolent peacemaking is the mission of the disciple in the world. Never has it been clearer than at the turn of the twenty-first century. Since 1900, more than 110 million people have been killed in wars, more than in the preceding five thousand years combined.[1] Untold hundreds of millions more have been maimed, raped, orphaned, tortured, or driven mad by war's furies. War continues to be the prime generator of famine and refugee populations and a breeder of disease. One of every twenty young men in the world is in the military. All told, humans may have killed as many as a billion other humans this century.[2] And since the dawn of the atomic age, the very life of our planet has hung in the balance, slowly poisoned by and at the mercy of a handful of men and women controlling nuclear weapons. There is nothing as crucial to the future of all creation as the making of peace.

Isaiah 2:4 assures us that the time of the messiah will be characterized by peacemaking, that all the world will

beat their swords into plowshares and their spears into pruning hooks; one nation shall not raise the sword against another, nor shall they train for war again.

God's instruction to people in all times and places is to dismantle weapons of war and remake them into tools that can help feed a starving world. In hopes of witnessing to the advent of God's messiah, the Prince of Peace, the six of us took hammers to a nuclear-capable Aegis destroyer at Bath Iron Works, beginning the conversion of its missile hatches and instruments on the bridge. One day the retooling of all armaments will be the norm, and no corporation, army, or court will be able to stand in the way.

The promise of peacemaking is the reestablishment of right relationships, "they will be called children of God." Making peace gives us a glimpse of who we are created to be—children of God, sisters and brothers, stewards of creation. Yet disarming our hearts and world exacts a price. The resurrected Jesus visits the disciples at John 20 and shows them his hands and sides, the marks of crucifixion that they will also bear. The persecution of the last two Beatitudes befalls those who venture to make peace, to stop war and killing. The use of force is the natural reaction of the state, to those who would impede its works.

On the cross, Jesus becomes the compassion of God, who brings about the salvation of the world. So are we all called to live compassion and justice, to be God's hands and feet in building the kindom, and to join the empire's scapegoats and victims on the cross. The cross captures the essence of the Beatitudes, and somehow amid the horror, there is redemption.

Finally, the Beatitudes assure that it is enough to know that when we suffer in our efforts to reconcile the human family, we are united with a rich lineage of those who did so before us, and we help to light the path for those yet to come.

> Resistance is the secret of Joy!
>
> Alice Walker

Sleeping and Watching

by Philip Berrigan

> *May he not come suddenly and find you sleeping? What I say to you, I say to all: "Watch!"*
>
> Mark 13:36

I am pondering the passage at Mark 13:36, and my thoughts return to the winter of 1943, to a nineteen-year-old draftee at Camp Gordon (now Fort Gordon), Georgia. The old Springfield rifle is heavy, the Georgia winters are damp and cold and dark and—Lord, Gawd!—I've gotta walk guard for four hours.

And do I ever watch! I watch for the officer of the guard. If he hears a weak challenge ("Halt! Who goes there?") or finds me forgetful of the password (Geronimo) or hiding or smoking, it's weekend KP for a month. The minutes and hours drag agonizingly by. I'm cold to the bone. Do I ever watch for six in the morning and the dawn?

So, in this way, the military forced "watching" on me. I didn't choose it. But "watching" should be voluntary, should be a nonviolent way of life. Scripture is full of it:

> *Yes, like the eyes of a servant on the hand of one's master. Like the eyes of a maid on the hand of her mistress. So our eyes are on the Lord our God till we are shown favor.*
>
> Psalm 123:2

> *My soul looks for the Lord more than sentinels for daybreak. More than sentinels for daybreak let Israel look for the Lord.*
>
> Psalm 130:6

Therefore, stay awake! For you do not know on which day your Lord will come.

Matthew 24:42

Be sure of this: if the master of the house had known the hour when the thief was coming, he would not have let his house be broken into.

Luke 12:39

Jesus warns us against "sleeping," against being out of it while the world lurches on in its mindless, violent way. Jesus summons us to regard the world as Gethsemane, to watch and stay awake. Three times he had to awaken Peter, James, and John in the garden as he suffered their abandonment when they slept and later their abandonment of him in his time of greatest need.

Psychological studies reveal that Americans live in less than forty percent awareness, as though our minds and spirits cringe before the banality and ugliness of national life. Such studies imply an enormous waste of potential lost to trivial pursuits—game-playing, fantasizing, daydreaming, television, self pity, brooding, boredom, gluttony in food or drink. Lost is the prospect of personal and social renewal: reading, study, meditation, prayer, teaching, service of the poor, nonviolent resistance to power-mongering government and corporations, justice and peacemaking. The scripture likens such crippled attentiveness to death—death before one dies.

Yes, Jesus commands us to wake and watch. Watch for who or what? Watch for the holy spirit of God who teaches us the life of Jesus Christ. The holy spirit continues the ministry and sacrifice of Jesus, consecrating people unto them:

She will teach you everything and remind you of all that I told you.

John 14:26

Upon request, the holy spirit will shower us with gifts that help us to become like Christ: wisdom, understanding, knowledge, counsel, piety, fear of God, fortitude. Upon request, the holy spirit will give us faith necessary to control our fear. "I believe, God; help my unbelief." Upon request, the holy spirit will speak the word of God to our hearts, the word of truth and life.

Watch the words of others, since God often speaks to us through sisters and brothers. Watch for conformity between words and deeds, and when the two are the same, watch only their deeds. Watch for heroic women and men who give their lives to tending victims—the bombed, starved, raped, tortured—and to exposing the victimizers from within prison and without. Watch the hope that they give you by the speech of their lives, and then dare to extend hope to others.

Watch the world through nonviolence and become a student of systemic evil. Watch nuclearism and the blind, venal paranoia of the nuclear club. Watch tens upon tens of wars going on worldwide and the arms sales of the United States, Russia, and Britain feeding those wars. Watch refugees in Yugoslavia, central Africa, Cambodia, and Bosnia. Watch the transnational money system that undergirds corporations. Watch corporations themselves as they declare themselves "stateless," as they automate, downsize, fire workers, pay less and less taxes, and punish the ecology.

Yes, watch corporations and their accountability to one thing: a financial system rightly called a global gambling casino. Watch them as they boast about "statelessness" while investing vast sums in lobbyists and "buyable" politicians. Watch how the biggest and the best—General Motors, Lockheed/Martin, Boeing/McDonnell Douglas, General Dynamics, Raytheon, and Hughes Aircraft—combine military and economic oppression. Watch the corporations as they scorn government after having obtained everything they need: the collapse of Communism, tariff, and trade agreements, deregulation, lower taxes, less trouble from unions, lower wages, police and military protection.

Only one weapon remains against such massive organizations of greed, luxury, and exploitation: direct action/civil resistance. When official deceit and betrayal become intolerable, when national life becomes more ugly and despairing, perhaps Americans will regain their faith in God and will again say "No!" to the political charlatans, nuclear warriors, and corporate parasites. Their "NO!" will take them to the streets and the official hell holes to expose and withstand the legality of terrorism and tyranny.

Watch, learn, act—the formula for a faithful and sane life.

Tying up the Strong Man

by Philip Berrigan

No one can enter a strong man's house and plunder his goods unless the strong man is first bound; then indeed his house may be plundered.

Mark 3:27

What do we think of Christ as one who acts like a thief by breaking and entering? What do we think about Christ adopting the common practices of thieves everywhere? What do we think about Christ redeeming the world in the manner of a thief? But that is precisely what Christ did. The whole Gospel of Mark is encapsulated in the tiny parable of the strong man in the third chapter. The strong man is Satan, or read the domination system, and the strong one is Christ Jesus come to tie up Satan once and for all. In the process, Jesus will teach us how to tie up Satan, so that, with him, we could plunder Satan's house, the world, restoring all the loot to God.

How did Satan acquire the world to become the world's evil principle? Walter Wink has pointed out that Satan is benign or evil depending on our spirit and conduct. In other words, Satan dominates the world because we have made the world a madhouse, full of rebellion, greed, hate, and savagery. Luke has this to say about Christ's temptation and ours to political power:

> Then he took him up and showed him all the kingdoms of the world in a single instant. The devil said to him: "I shall give to you all this power and their glory; for it has been handed over to me, and I may give it to whomever I wish. All this will be yours, if you worship me."
>
> Luke 4:5-7

What is the domination system? It is a coalition of "power" bureaucracies—government, transnational corporations, banks, the military, education, media, church, and synagogues—that personifies and institutionalizes the spirit of Satan, typically by lying and murdering. The domination system lusts to overlord people, to keep them stupid and malleable, to make of them drones, consumers, "good" citizens, patriots, taxpayers, and slaves instantly responsive to the will of politicians and those in power. The domination system is Satan insofar as it enacts the spirit of Satan. Paul would call it principalities and powers:

> For our struggle is not with flesh and blood, but with Principalities and Powers, with the world rulers of this present darkness.
>
> Ephesians. 6:12

So Christians have a breaking and entry Lord to follow and to live by—breaking into the world's stronghold to tie up and immobilize the domination system and to seize its booty for God and people. The tool for this is the nonviolent cross expressing itself in civil resistance. By teaching, feeding, healing, and breaking the law, Jesus subdued and penetrated the strong man's house. Then, on the cross, he tied him up and looted his house, killing the weapons of the strong man—sin, law, and death—in his own flesh.

The cross is still foolishness, a stumbling block and a scandal, just as in Paul's time. To the pragmatic American mind, the cross makes "no sense." But that's a foolish judgment on what is, in reality, the wisdom of God. For in actuality, the cross is faith, truth, love, justice, health, liberation, and salvation. The cross requires denial of the false self that tyrannizes us internally, so that we may confront the system that tyrannizes us externally. The cross is the nonviolence of God. It breaks our chains and restores our humanity, allowing us to become daughters and sons of God.

The cross is the struggle for justice, a struggle that singles out individuals and institutions responsible for injustice, where conniving, betrayal, and war are plotted—the White House, Pentagon, Congress, war plants and military bases, World Bank, Lockheed-Martin, International Monetary Fund, Nevada Test Site, Lawrence Livermore Laboratories. Other weapons dealers, money brokers, and power mongers.

It is important to note that Christ trusted the truth. He himself was the truth. He employed it as an offensive weapon. He went to the functionaries and hell holes of his day, not waiting for them to come to him. He took the truth of his person, his teaching, and action to the hell holes to expose them, to drag them into the light, where they could no longer destroy in darkness and secrecy. In the light, they would have some hope of recognition, of repentance and atonement.

The cross is the symbol of God's ineffable, limitless love. And when we bring the cross to the hell holes, using civil resistance to call them to accountability, we indict and expose their misinformation, secrecy, manipulation, oppression and complicity in murder. Evil cannot endure such a manifestation of overwhelming love.

We ought to beware that the cross of Christ

be not emptied of its meaning.

1 Corinthians 1:17

There are two aspects to preserving the "meaning" of the cross—transforming ourselves by obedience to it, and transforming the hell holes by applying it. Paul speaks of being crucified to the strong man's house, the world, and having it crucified to him at Galatians 6:14. Our liberation is accomplished in a rhythm—we come from the hell holes evaluating our nonviolence or justice, and we return to them for another witness with what we've learned.

Governments and corporations legalize killing, and so-called "left" Christians tend to resist the government because it legalizes killing in war, on death row, in the womb. Killing is the cardinal offense against the Creator, because God made us in God's image. It is also the cardinal offense against our neighbors, who are essentially sisters or brothers, also made in the image of God. Until we stop killing, no social change or uplift is possible.

That is not to say the government is the only villain, nor to ignore the corporations and their rapacity. For from twenty to thirty years at the end of the twentieth century, including the Reagan era, corporations used propaganda and the media to deflect public attention from themselves, their greed, and ruthlessness to the government itself. The transnational corporations and banks have had enormous success in sanitizing themselves, while making the government a whipping boy.

Despite hostility to some segments of the American people, the government may be influenced, even vulnerable to public opinion and action. In fact, it can be as responsive to public need as we want to make it. Not so the corporations and banks, however, who enjoy largely full police and military protection, and who are immunized from public scrutiny. Antitrust activity has virtually ceased, monopoly is seldom mentioned, billion dollar mergers are greeted with applause.

The following realities sum up corporate performances:

The world's 360 billionaires have a net worth equal to that of forty-five percent of the world's people, some three billion individuals.

More than one-fifth of American children grow up poor, the majority malnourished, some starving.

On an average, American CEO's income is 150 times greater than that of the American worker.

Nearly one-fifth of American workers work full time for poverty-level wages.

Fifty percent of African American babies are born to families whose incomes are under the poverty line.

And where is the strong man who causes these inequities? He is living in the national headquarters of Lockheed-Martin, Chase Manhattan, Boeing / McDonnell-Douglas, Raytheon, General Dynamics, and General Motors. How long will it be before the American people wake up, regain their faith, and rebuild a peace and justice movement? Until they do wake up, the strong man is on the loose in the United States.

The Primacy of the Childlike

by Philip Berrigan

I give praise to you Parent, Lord of heaven and earth, for although you have hidden these things from the wise and learned, you have revealed them to the childlike . . . No one knows the son except the parent, and no one knows the parent except the son and anyone to whom the son wishes to reveal God.

Matthew 11:25-27

This passage from scripture is a commentary on faith. Why has God hidden these things from the scholars and opened them to the childlike? The "things" of course, are the mighty deeds of Jesus, which the childlike see as God's seal upon God's son, worthy to understand and to "follow."

Does God hide these things from the wise and learned, does God hide the knowledge of Jesus Christ from them? Hardly. The wise and learned hide the knowledge of Jesus Christ from themselves. The wise and learned usually perform their singular role within the domination pyramid. And the injustice of that role suppresses the truth, as Paul makes clear in Romans 1:18. The wise and learned are interpreters for power in the patriarchal pyramid. Theirs is a tradeoff, comfort and recognition for mollifying the crimes of power to the people. The wise and learned, the intellectuals of the apparatus—academics, clergy, professionals of media, business and military—are creatures of the status quo, conformists who preach conformity. Faithful disciples of Faust and his bargain.

The wise and learned are invariably ignorant of the poor and consequently could care less. Jeremiah indicts them:

Your father did what was right and just, and it went well with him. Because he dispensed justice to the poor and weak, it went well with him. Is this not true knowledge of me, says The Lord.

Jeremiah 22:16

And Paul continues in the same vein:

Rather, God chose the foolish of the world to shame the wise, and God chose the weak of the world to shame the strong, and God chose the lowly and despised of the world, those who count for nothing, to reduce to nothing those who are something.

1 Corinthians 1:27, 28

The suppression of truth breeds a species of blindness. In the early 70s, during the first Nixon regime, an Eastern Airlines flight crashed near Dulles airport during a rainstorm, knocking out power to a hitherto secret alternative site of government, hollowed out of Mount Weather, Virginia. The crash blew Mount Weather's cover and the government reacted positively, allowing reporters into the facility.

173

One told of complete accommodations for executive, legislative and judicial branches, even a lake for water skiing. Then the press circulated an "essential and non-interruptable" list of high officialdom cleared for Mount Weather in case of nuclear war.

Hubert Humphrey, who had been vice-president under President Lyndon B. Johnson, and who was defeated for the presidency in 1968, discovered that he had been dropped from the "essential and non-interruptable" list. This outraged him, and he issued a statement to the effect that "if the American people heard that I was not protected during nuclear war, they would rise en masse in protest."

Mount Weather and the "essential and non-interruptable" list received media attention, with an article in *Parade Magazine*, for one. There is no record of anyone rising in protest.

The church has expressed a "preferential option" for the poor, but does that go far enough? The Gospel portrays Christ as becoming a Samaritan, becoming the blind and crippled that he healed, becoming the sheep or lamb and dying for them, becoming the dead Lazarus that he raised.

> *Amen I say to you, whatever you did for these least sisters and brothers of mine, you did for me.*
>
> Matthew 25:40

There is a saying in nonviolent resistance circles—only when we're in prison do we become truly one with the poor.

Do we desire numbering among the "childlike" who know God? who know Jesus Christ? Then certainly, let us serve our "least sisters and brothers"—the victims of famine and war, those with terminal cancer and AIDS. But equally, and in the interests of justice, let us ferret out what causes their misery—the greed, arrogance and war which cause the poor, which multiply the homeless, which sow the planet with rubbish and poison.

Let us resist the moguls of injustice and their systems of exploitation and death.

Biblical Muckraking

by Philip Berrigan

> *And this is the verdict, that the light came into the world, but people preferred darkness to light because their works were evil. For everyone who does wicked things hates the light and does not come toward the light, so that her/his works might not be exposed. But whoever lives the truth comes to the light, so that her/his works may be clearly seen as done in God.*
>
> John 3:19-21

For you were once darkness, but now you are light in the Lord, live as children of light. For light produces every kind of goodness, righteousness and truth. Try to learn what is pleasing to the Lord. Take no part in the fruitless works of darkness; rather expose them. For it is shameful even to mention the things done by them in secret, but everything exposed by the light becomes visible, for everything that becomes visible is light. Therefore it says, "Awake, oh sleeper, and arise from the dead, and Christ will give you light."

Ephesians. 5:8-14

I hate to stifle the reader with two long texts at the outset of this little commentary. My excuse is simply this—the word of God speaks of our reality more truthfully than I, or any human, can. Furthermore, I consider it a profound duty to open the scriptures for others, even as Christ opened them for the disciples on the road to Emmaus at Luke 24:32. Even as they have been opened for me.

The wealth of truth in these passages constantly astonishes me. They reveal the human tendency to hide evil conduct whether individual or bureaucratic (governmental); they comment on security clearances; they deal with "judgment" as understood in the New Testament; they provide a rationale for civil resistance.

But let's review the text and its comprehensive grasp of reality, then and today. Why does the government classify both material and people? For two main reasons: so that "top secret" information won't fall into "enemy" hands and secondly, so the public won't know about it. Disclosure to the enemy would allow them undue advantage, whereas revelation to the public might, in the worst case, terminate the practice of so much secrecy. Meanwhile, the enemy does precisely the same thing to us, reinforcing the spiral of violence and keeping it intact.

For it is shameful to mention the things done by them in secret.

Ephesians 5:12

As for security clearances for personnel—some are so ridiculously sensitive that those holding them cannot reveal their classification level. For high officialdom and intelligence gumshoes the domination system classifies them like so much paper, withholding their work from the concern of family, or from the scrutiny of media and public.

Governments are precisely like people in this respect, hiding dark deeds behind a legal, punitive cloak of secrecy, lest an exposé reveal official violence and deadly conduct.

A good question for the oligarchs and their classification of documents and humans is—what are you afraid of? And also—are you hiding something because you're ashamed of it?

Next, what is "judgment" in the Bible? Does God actively judge us at the end of our sojourn on earth? What of Christ's assertion that he came not to judge the world but to save it? A closer reading of the Gospel reveals that Christ's life judges us in the sense that our life must conform to His, our cross to His, our works to His. His conduct will measure ours, and find us worthy or unworthy.

Lastly, I've often regarded Paul's passage from Ephesians as a companion text to John 3:19. Both are unequivocal in viewing civil resistance as necessary. The aims of civil resistance are several, deeply aligned with one another. One intends therefore, to keep a higher law (you shall not kill) by breaking a law legalizing a gross crime (the American war game). Civil resistance, when creatively and nonviolently done is always iconoclastic. It subverts entrenched social idols like the state and its law and is worship of the true God.

Once again, the enactment of the true law must be, at the same time, an exposé of the hell hole itself, an unmasking of the dark criminality performed at the war department housed in the Pentagon, the White House, Andrews Air Force Base, Electric Boat Company, Williams International, Offutt Air Force Base—to name a few of the hell holes. One employs graphics, leaflets, chants, song, to translate the exposé to a public illiterate in symbols.

I've done civil resistance scores of times because it's the only way to subvert a criminal and nonrepresentative state, which is one with its law, the same reality as its law. Less importantly, civil resistance liberates me from the tyranny of the law, which legalizes me into complicity unless I break it.

Through the years, I've come to attach deeper significance to civil resistance, and to revere ever more deeply the example of Christ, who broke the laws of his day repeatedly, who was, as Gandhi termed him, "The greatest nonviolent revolutionary in history." Why did he break Sabbath laws, dietary laws, why cleanse the temple, why rise from the dead illegally? Because he was undercutting and destroying the scapegoating mechanism—that system of violent victimizing which cemented together the society of his day.

Increasingly, thoughtful people perceive American life as demented, a kind of national booby hatch—its leadership opaque and feral, its addiction to war, its enthronement of the rich, its abandonment of the poor, its contamination of the global environment. Take the cold war for example and its scapegoating of Communists. It kept this society cohesive for five decades, creating a spurious national purpose, manipulating all major institutions into a conspiracy of silence, justifying trillions in military spending, creating an imperial religion (nuclearism). Scapegoating the Soviets accomplished this, and the Soviets did the same to us.

Or take the transnational corporations and banks, and their role under GATT and North American Free Trade Agreement. They scapegoat outrageously, victimizing the public as well as workers at home and abroad, destroying jobs and small businesses, undermining the middle class, contaminating the environment, transcending governments and national laws, becoming in fact, "economic tyrannies." They mean to maximize production and consumption (profits), homogenize people globally, reduce them to an indistinguishable common denominator, make economic clones of them.

To sum up, in their adoption of violence as a necessary order, human communities create scapegoats and discharge their violence upon them. This prevents reconciliation, social cohesion, and a reinvestment of energy. In his trial and execution, Jesus—the sinless one—exposes the violent bankruptcy of the scapegoat mechanism for all to see. The present society, with its penchant for lying and murderousness, can't survive exposure of the scapegoating mechanism, which shatters the myth that only violence can overcome violence. Whenever the Gospel is truly heard and lived, the scapegoating mechanism is enervated, subverted and slowly destroyed.

"Follow Me"

Mark Colville

When they had finished breakfast, Jesus said to Simon Peter, "Simon, son of John, do you love me more than these?"

He said to him, "Yes, Lord, you know that I love you."

He said to him, "Feed my lambs." He then said to him a second time, "Simon, son of John, do you love me?"

He said to him, "Yes, Lord, you know that I love you."

He said to him, "Tend my sheep." He said to him the third time, "Simon, son of John, do you love me?"

Peter was distressed that he had said to him a third time, "Do you love me?" and he said to him, "Lord, you know everything. You know that I love you."

Jesus said to him, "Feed my sheep. Amen, amen, I say to you, when you were younger, you used to dress yourself and go where you wanted; but when you grow old, you will stretch out your hands, and someone else will dress you and lead you where you do not want to go." He said this signifying by what kind of death he would glorify God. And when he had said this, he said to him, "Follow me."

> Peter turned and saw the disciple following whom Jesus loved, the one who
> had also reclined upon his chest during the supper and had said, "Master,
> who is the one who will betray you?" When Peter saw him, he said to Jesus,
> "Lord, what about him?"
>
> Jesus said to him, "What if I want him to remain until I come? What
> concern is it of yours? You follow me." So the word spread among the brothers
> that that disciple would not die. But Jesus had not told him he would not die,
> just "What if I want him to remain until I come?"
>
> John 21:15-23

In January, 1991, the United States military began a wholesale slaughter in Iraq, leaving three hundred thousand children, women, and men dead by March. As the spectacle was cheered by the public, misrepresented by the media and lied about by the government, I, for the most part, lived in silent rage. I was recently married, had a two-month-old daughter, and worked full time with disabled adults in a group home. My sphere of commitment proved inadequate to incorporate any substantive action in defense of those my nation had condemned as enemies.

I screamed at the television news and put a bumper sticker on my car that read, "Desert Shame: Not in My Name." One night I even raced from work to a demonstration at an army recruiting station but arrived just as it was breaking up. Afterward, the realization hit hard that there was blood on my hands, and I couldn't wash it off. Just as my country's lust for violence had been laid bare, so too was I exposed. My life had taken a certain direction, in many ways a good one, but it was not to be interrupted by the high-tech mass murder in which my tax dollars and silence now rendered me complicit. I could bury myself in family responsibilities and meaningful work, but the cross remained; and I was refusing it.

The Gospel of John comes to a close with a fascinating conversation between Jesus and Peter some days after the resurrection. Jesus repeats the call to discipleship to Peter, an imperfect, struggling human being whose preparedness to take up the cross and shepherd the community of believers seems ever in question. "Do you love me?" Jesus asks Peter three times. We remember his three denials in the palace courtyard on the day of Christ's crucifixion. Now Jesus offers Peter an opportunity for reparation and atonement, and Peter eagerly accepts.

But there is more here than what appears at first glance. The English translation of the conversation fails to capture its subtle nuances. In Greek there are four different words for "love", each with a distinct meaning, and two of them are employed here. "Agape" is unconditional, self-sacrificing love, purer than the other forms, and this is the word Jesus uses the first two times he asks the question. Peter's response, however, is with "philia", or fraternal, brotherly or sisterly love. It seems that Christ is asking for a higher form of devotion than Peter is ready to profess, and perhaps this is largely the reason why Peter is distressed at the repetition of the question. Philia will not be enough, in the long run, to sustain a community in nonviolent resistance to empire, and Peter is about to assume a leadership role in such a community. "I will lay down my life for you," he had said on the night of his master's arrest, and then proceeded to disavow his identity as a disciple. Perhaps Peter is yet unsure of himself, and afraid to repeat the mistake.

And so, Jesus relents; the third time around he asks for philia. But before we conclude that Peter is being let off the hook, Jesus goes on to say that Peter is, in fact, destined to achieve the height of self-sacrificing love. He will lay down his life in martyrdom at 18. This is an affirmation of Jesus's confidence in Peter, despite his shortcomings, and it leads to an uncompromising demand: "Follow me."

Christians in the United States, and I'm including myself, seem to have perfected the art of deflecting, deferring, and denying this simple call to take up the cross. To apply the Gospel ethic in this society, it is necessary to go into nonviolent resistance, but most of the time we manage to keep busy with other things. Personal attachments to ego, reputation, possessions and bloodlines were clearly exposed by Jesus as the great inhibitors to following the cross, and these factors are no less evident today.

The cultural obstacles to Christian resistance are also legion, and quite effective, beginning with what I call "the socialization toward isolation." We are trained to think of freedom in terms of the imaginary notions of personal independence, self-sufficiency, and financial security. We are organized into nuclear family units, each one pursuing this false notion of freedom apart from and in competition with others. We obviously have common needs—housing, food, meaningful work, transportation—but because we struggle alone to acquire them, our lives become centered on self and immediate family. Instead of pooling resources and sharing burdens, we go into lifelong debt with mortgages, car payments, student loans and credit cards. The result is a lifestyle which leaves the cross behind.

The solution to these problems begins with community living. When Christ called and gathered the disciples he showed us that the building of community is the first step toward the cross, and the first step away from the values of the dominant culture. There is no better way to understand the sisterhood and brotherhood of all humanity than the daily practice of Christian community. Over time, this kind of lifestyle can begin to deprogram our individualism and consumerism. And it provides the freedom to focus our lives on the transformation of the world through nonviolent direct action. Community living is the first act of resistance.

Whatever our state of life may be, each of us has at least two things in common. We are all called to follow Jesus to the cross and, like Peter, none of us is totally prepared. Our following, then, depends on the clarity with which we allow the Gospel to judge our selves and our world, and the courage with which we move from where we are to where we ought to be.

Chapter 8

Peace without Words: An Artist's Interpretation of Isaiah 2:4

by Tom Lewis-Borbely

For the first time, I am showing the entire series of woodcuts I did the summer of 1971, imprisoned at Lewisburg Penitentiary while the war in Vietnam raged on. It was the last year of my three year sentence for burning draft records as a member of the Catonsville 9. As I write this I am again in jail, the first member of the Prince of Peace Plowshares to be returned to jail for not paying the United States Navy restitution of $4,703.89 to cover my portion of the damage done when we hammered the control panels of the Aegis Destroyer and spilled our blood over the ship from baby bottles, a symbolic and nonviolent disarming of a weapon of mass destruction. Currently the United States wages war in Kosovo with its massive killing power and weapons of mass destruction. Both sides in the war are creating a flood of refugees that parallels the Nazi Holocaust of the Second World War—people homeless, terrorized, and shell-shocked, literally, psychologically, spiritually. The United States showcases its technological superiority to the world with precise weapons ready to market for future arms sale. Meanwhile, the Pentagon refuses to stop bombing.

Today, I find it extremely difficult to create serious art work in prison. In the Cumberland County Jail I work on pencil portraits for prisoners to mail home to loved ones. I make two, keeping one for myself and giving the other away. Prisoners here are basically silent about the war in Kosovo. Most are supportive when they learn I am one of Plowshares members who protested at the Bath Iron Works in Maine. They all want to know if my family, my wife and daughter, agree with what I did. I share with them that my wife Andrea and I met at the Pentagon protesting war and weapons ten years ago. It was when I received no jail sentence after the first Plowshares protest at Bath Iron Works in 1991 that Andrea and I chose to have Nora, our daughter.

So why am I now showing work completed almost thirty years ago? I could say that art is as timeless as war. I could draw the parallel out, saying that most members of the Prince of Peace Plowshares also passed through or spent time in Lewisburg Penitentiary, jailed for war protests. But more simply, for me personally, artistically, and spiritually, it is now the proper time to show this woodcut series in its entirety.

The sunflower is the first block I cut. Cutting into the wood was a way for me to hope in something alive and beautiful. The summer of 1971, while I was in Lewisburg, my first marriage ended. With no

way out, I had no where to go but inside myself. The woodcuts became a life line to hold onto as I worked my way through darkness into beauty and hope. For me as an artist, the woodcuts were a visualized journey starting with beauty in nature, falling into emptiness and searching that space within myself to find a way out—literally cutting my way out of the void onto discarded pieces of wood found around the prison farm camp.

My last visit with Stasia was in the visiting room inside the wall where they pulled me from the farm for visits. I was taken through two check points with a complete strip search each way. The visiting room was large. We were allowed body contact once at the start of the visit and once at the end. We sat at a small table. On this visit, Anastasia would tell me that she was defining herself as a lesbian. The woman of her commitment and deepening love was waiting for her in the car outside the wall. She said she no longer loved me, but she respected me. At a rational level, this was not a shock to me. We had discussed her relationship and growing love at other visits. But emotionally I was thrown and fell into a pit, seeing my heart breaking as I fell inside myself.

As a prisoner, in most external ways you are powerless. As I listened to Anastasia, and loved her, and accepted her truth at that last visit, I was learning in a deeper

way what it meant to be powerless. I knew there was no help within the prison system; in fact, prison was a threat to healing. When a prisoner displayed psychological problems, he was isolated and then became involved in a process over which he had little or no control. When I first entered Lewisburg and was cleaning hallways above the receiving and orientating room, I saw a vision from hell—the "psycho ward" as it was called by prisoners. A large white room, white furniture, bright lights, men wandering aimlessly, at times pressing their faces against the thick glass of the heavy metal door. This was an unspoken but universal threat to all prisoners who began to act strangely or create serious problems within the system. Suddenly for me, this threat became real, looming over everything. Could my behavior become uncontrolled, uncontrollable, that summer of 1971?

Because the farm was minimum security, sharp instruments such as woodcutting tools were available in the arts and craft work space shared by the prisoners. I found scraps of wood around the farm. I imagine I was a curious sight to other inmates as I examined the wood in the evenings after working at the dairy. I often proofed a fresh, uncut board to study its grain, to see and hear what the piece of wood from prison had to teach me.

The two small self-portraits followed the sunflower. I think of these as a check-in with myself—how I saw myself coming into prison, young, vulnerable, hopeful, and how I saw myself at the present, hurting and searching. The woodcuts were a path taking me on this search, and I had no idea where the journey would go.

The next two woodcuts were on front and reverse sides of an old drawing board, twenty-three inches by thirty-one inches, given to me by an inmate who admired my work. The fractured space I created on the right side of that board took on the surreal quality of a nightmare. War in Vietnam with the American dressed to kill in the jungle. A president before the halls of Congress, looking like a ghost, saying "bomb them back to the stone age." American products, the fruits of war, surrounded by blackness. On the left side, a surreal madness. Children with kites, running with fear rather than joy as the kites become predatory birds. A young woman who fails to reach the flower. A fierce hopscotch game with a bizarre "home." The therapeutic power of art comes with the wellspring of images from the unconscious that can be searched, examined in the visual realm as they take shape.

The woodcuts had become my life line as long I could cut through my own pain. But that summer there was a threat to my art beyond my own frail creativity. The mafia controlled the art room because it was a good place to meet and talk, more private and less obvious than the crowded dormitory. It was also a good place for them to receive a brown paper bag of wine and Italian spaghetti which was stashed in a false-bottomed window well. The hole was covered with a board painted brown, dirt and foliage glued over that. If this was discovered, the arts and craft room would be closed down. So we coexisted in that space, myself a war protester, they pro-war. Our only bridge was my art work, admired but not understood.

The next work is the tree, cut on the reverse side of the surreal war images. I call it my favorite tree in prison. There was a large crab apple tree next to the milking barn at the dairy where I worked as a clerk and part-time milker. At times when my work was complete I would go outside and sit against the concrete block milking barn. I sat alone, my back against the wall, thinking, always praying. I lived with that crab apple tree changing seasons eight times. My favorite was the spring. The "our Father" was my prayer. For the woodcut that summer I cut the tree in winter, stripped of most leaves. The sky is as dark as the black sun. The earth to the left is disturbed by

threatening images, more dangerous because of their lack of clear form.

The next woodcuts that I completed are perhaps my favorites. Each print was made of two pine boards; side by side there are four

related images. The first is clearly about falling into a dark pit. Male and female images fall without knowing what waits. In the second of the paired woodcuts, the chaos of the falling images resolves into a more balanced configuration, almost a dance as the images reach up and out, searching. The last image is simply a "yes" to something new; faith in what has come from the search even as it is unknown, not fully realized yet. This particular set of works is for me the spiri-

tual heart of the entire series, falling and rising, moving from darkness into hope. In their abstraction, they invite you to enter into this mystery.

Most of the woodcuts I did at Lewisburg Penitentiary examine different aspects of pain. I began these works by meditating on the

oles, marks left when the living tree was damaged, dimin-
d. Rather than avoiding these imperfections, I enhanced them,
soaking the wood in water or brushing up its surface. The wood
from nature, found in prison, was marked with a life of its own. I
put my faith in its pattern and tried to follow it as I cut. These knots
became the starting point for the images.

The last woodcut in the series is the largest, made from four ply-
wood boards left over from a building project at the prison. This was
the largest woodcut I had ever done, twenty-seven and one-half
inches by fifty-nine inches. I cut fiercely, using a large razor knife
and my tools. Human figures reaching up and out, praying and
searching, dominate the work. Hands reach toward an image of a
cross of resurrection emerging from the wood but not yet realized.
The wheat symbolizes hope and eucharist. A dark sun breaks into
light.

Although I have shared my own pain out of which these works
were created, I trust they go beyond the personal to create a journey
that everyone can enter through their own experience of pain—a
journey out of darkness into hope and vision.

Footnotes

From "The Good Shepherd" by Susan Crane
[1] Patricia Treece, *A Man For Others: Maximilian Kolbe Saint of Auschwitz in the words of Those Who Knew Him,* p. 75

From "God and Mammon" by Steven Baggarly
[1] *The Other Side* (The Other Side, Philadelphia), May-June 1995, p. 12

[2] Jeff Gates, "Opening the (Bin) Gates of Wealth to All Americans," *The Virginian-Pilot* (Norfolk, VA), October 25, 1998, pp. 51-53

[3] *United Nations Human Development Report,* 1998

[4] Ruth Leger Sivard, *World Military and Social Expenditures 1996,* (World Priorities, Inc., Washington, DC), 1996, p. 30

[5] Michael Campbell-Johnston, "A Civilization of Poverty," *The Tablet,* July 12, 1997, pp. 888-890

From "The Widow's Mite" by Steven Baggarly
[1] Sivard, *Women: A World Survey* (World Priorities, Inc., Washington, DC), 1995, p. 17

[2] *United Nations Report 1989*

[3] Sivard, *World Military and Social Expenditures 1996* (World Priorities, Inc. Washington, DC), 1996, pp. 4, 36, 31, 34

[4] *Ibid.,* p. 30

[5] Russ Ervin Funk, *Stopping Rape: A Challenge for Men* (New Society Publishers, Philadelphia), 1993, p. 7

[6] *Ibid,* p. 50

From "Shalom" by Steven Baggarly
[1] Sivard, *World Military and Social Expenditures 1996* (World Priorities, Inc., Washington, DC), 1996, p. 12

[2] William Arkin, "What's New?" *Bulletin of the Atomic Scientists,* November-December, 1997, pp. 22-27

[3] "Civilian Nuclear Plant Will Produce Tritium for Weapons," Associated Press, *The Virginian-Pilot* (Norfolk, Virginia), December 23, 1998

[4] "US-Russia Relations: Avoiding a New Cold War," *The Defense Monitor,* Volume 27, Issue 5, 1998, p. 4

[5]Louis Vitale OFM, "US, India, and Pakistan: Stop Testing!", *Desert Voices, The Newsletter of Nevada Desert Experience,* Summer 1998

From "Condemned" by Steven Baggarly
[1]Sivard, *World Military and Social Expenditures* (World Priorities, Inc., Washington, DC), 1996, p. 26

[2]Arkin, Robert Norris, and Joshua Handler, *Nuclear Weapons Data Book,* National Resources Defense Council, 1998

[3]*The Bulletin of Atomic Scientists,* September-October 1998

[4]Richard Thaxton, "Nuclear War by Computer Chip," *The Progressive,* 1980, quoted in Christopher Grammis, Arthur J. Laffin, and Elin Schade, "The Risk of the Cross," Seabury Press, New York, 1981, pp. 64-68

[5]Joseph Gerson, "Nuclear Extortion after the Cold War," *The Nonviolent Activist,* May-June 1988, p. 8

[6]*The Nuclear Almanac: Confronting the Atom in War and Peace,* compiled and edited by the MIT faculty, Addison-Wesley Publishing Co., 1984, pp. 283-300

[7]Shaun Gregory, *The Hidden Cost of Deterrence: Nuclear Weapons Accidents,* Brassey's, 1950, pp. 147-184

[8]Rosalie Bertell, "No Immediate Danger," The Women's Press, Toronto, 1985

[9]Andrew and Leslie Cockburn, *One Point Safe,* Doubleday, New York, 1997

[10]"Lebed Claims Russia Has 'Mislaid' 100 Nuclear Bombs," *The Times of London,* September 6, 1997

[11]"Check, please!" *The Bulletin of the Atomic Scientists,* September-October 1998, pp. 34-43

From "Worship in God and Spirit" by Mark Colville
[1]Wes Howard-Brook, *Becoming Children of God,* Orbis, Maryknoll, NY, 1994, p. 107

From "Faith Equals Love" by Steven Baggarly
[1]used with permission of *Fellowship Magazine,* Box 271, Nyack, NY, 19/60, July 1980